CHANTERELLE DREAMS,
AMANITA NIGHTMARES

CHANTERELLE DREAMS, AMANITA NIGHTMARES

The Love, Lore, and Mystique of Mushrooms

GREG A. MARLEY

CHELSEA GREEN PUBLISHING
WHITE RIVER JUNCTION, VERMONT

Project Manager: Patricia Stone
Developmental Editor: Brianne Goodspeed
Copy Editor: Helen Walden
Proofreader: Ellen Brownstein
Indexer: Lee Lawton
Designer: Peter Holm, Sterling Hill Productions

Printed in the United States of America
First printing August, 2010
10 9 8 7 6 5 4 3 2   10 11 12 13 14

Our Commitment to Green Publishing

Chelsea Green sees publishing as a tool for cultural change and ecological stewardship. We strive to align our book manufacturing practices with our editorial mission and to reduce the impact of our business enterprise in the environment. We print our books and catalogs on chlorine-free recycled paper, using vegetable-based inks whenever possible. This book may cost slightly more because we use recycled paper, and we hope you'll agree that it's worth it. Chelsea Green is a member of the Green Press Initiative (www.greenpressinitiative.org), a nonprofit coalition of publishers, manufacturers, and authors working to protect the world's endangered forests and conserve natural resources. *Chanterelle Dreams, Amanita Nightmares* was printed on Natures Book Natural, a 30-percent postconsumer recycled paper supplied by Thomson-Shore.

Library of Congress Cataloging-in-Publication Data
Marley, Greg A., 1955-
  Chanterelle dreams, amanita nightmares : the love, lore, and mystique of
mushrooms / Greg A. Marley.
       p. cm.
  Includes bibliographical references and index.
  ISBN 978-1-60358-214-8
  1. Mushrooms. 2. Mushrooms–Identification. 3. Cookery (Mushrooms) I.
Title.

  QK617.M397 2010
  579.6'16–dc22

                                              2010021496

Chelsea Green Publishing Company
Post Office Box 428
White River Junction, VT 05001
(802) 295-6300
www.chelseagreen.com

DEDICATION

This book is dedicated to the concept that we are all connected in our world. Just as mushrooms are intertwined in a web of relationships with plants, animals, and other fungi in the forest, my work has progressed within a web of connection and support. The keystone support in my life comes from my wife Valli and our son Dashiell. It is to them I dedicate my work—for helping me believe in myself, for helping create the time and space to focus, and for providing the most consistent (and valued) distraction from the lonely work of writing. Oh, and for making sure I don't get the big head.

CONTENTS

Acknowledgments, vii

Introduction: Tales from the Forest Floor, ix

Part I. Mushrooms and Culture
1. Passionate about Mushrooms: The Russian and Slavic Experience, 3
2. Overcoming Distrust: Mushrooming in America, 14

Part II. Mushrooms as Food
Introduction: Leading with Our Stomachs, 25
3. The Foolproof Four: Updated for a New Millennium, 31
4. Chanterelles, 60
5. *Boletus edulis*, 72
6. The *Agaricus* Brothers, 80

Part III. Dangerously Toxic, Deadly Interesting
Introduction: Poisonous Mushrooms: Not as Bad as You Fear, 91
7. Mushroom Poisoning: The Potential Risks and Ways to Avoid Them, 94
8. *Amanita* Nightmares: The Death Cap and Destroying Angel, 112
9. False Morels: The Finnish Fugu, 122
10. A Fallen Angel, 132
11. The Poison Pax: A Deadly Mystery, 136

Part IV. Mushrooms and the Mind: The Origin of Religion and the Pathway to Enlightenment
Introduction: Entheogens: A New Way to View Hallucinogenic Mushrooms, 143
12. *Amanita muscaria*: Soma, Religion, and Santa, 148
13. Psilocybin: Gateway to the Soul or Just a Good High?, 163

Part V. Mushrooms within Living Ecosystems
14. Honey Mushrooms: The Race for the World's Largest Fungus, 185
15. Fairy Rings and Fairy Tales, 192
16. Fungal Bioluminescence: Mushroom Nightlights, 200
17. Who's Eating the Truffles?, 207
18. Woodpeckers, Wood Decay Fungi, and Forest Health, 217

VI. Tools for a New World

19. Growing Mushrooms in the Garden: A How-to Story, 227

Appendix of Recommended and Supplemental Reading, 241
Endnotes, 247
Index, 257

ACKNOWLEDGMENTS

My goal in writing this book was to bring an appreciation for the pursuit of mushrooms and knowledge of them to a broader audience, including people for whom mushrooms remain a mysterious and suspect subject. The lore and stories of great mushrooms that constitute my vehicle are built upon the words and experiences of our mushroom-loving ancestors and living mushroomers around the world. My work rests upon the research and explorations of generations of naturalists and scientists and the knowledge base they have created. And, of course, I owe a debt of gratitude to the experiences, both good and bad, of the countless people who collect and eat wild mushrooms and have done so for many generations. How have people learned what can and should not be eaten, other than through trial and error?

On a more immediate basis, I am thankful for the mushrooming teachers in my life for sharing their information and passion for things fungal. The late Sam Ristich, the mushroom guru of Sligo Road, was ever generous with his knowledge and passion, and if I did not spend as much time as I wanted with him, I live with that loss. I am regularly grateful for the friendship and support of my friend Michaeline and her non-judgmental guidance and ready ear. I realize as I push the limits of the formal writing style of my biology education and my social work graduate education that I need to acknowledge David Arora and thank him for the refreshing combination of good science and irreverent whimsy with which he writes.

Finally, to the good folks at Chelsea Green, thanks. Thank you, Joni, for believing this material would become a dynamic book. I also appreciate the gentle and dogged determination with which Brianne worked to keep my language clean and my sentences in the active tense.

Introduction

TALES FROM THE FOREST FLOOR

Nature alone is antique and the oldest art a mushroom.
THOMAS CARLYLE

*M*ushrooms—in their many colors, shapes, and sizes and with their complex life histories and growing habitats—are a fascination to everyone who possesses a love of nature. The deeper secrets and the tales of their lives offer an intriguing glimpse into a hidden world of complex relationships, powerful chemistry, mind-expanding potentials, and deep religious and magical associations. On a practical level, people are most interested in questions of edibility, toxicity, and health promotion, and in these areas, mushrooms touch our lives on a regular basis. When you expand the sphere of mushrooms to include all members of the kingdom Fungi, then their beneficial, neutral, or malignant influence touches us many times each day. As we eat our morning yeast-leavened bagel, lunch on blue cheese or Brie, take an antibiotic or antifungal for an infection, or unwind with a glass of wine or beer, fungi are an often unseen and underappreciated part of the picture. Fungi, and the mushrooms that represent a tiny but visible portion of this kingdom, are loved, worshipped, feared, and reviled, but most of all, they are ignored as they intersect our busy lives. Our relationship with the world of fungi is defined by a vast gulf of ignorance and lack of awareness. We don't see what lies before us, and we know little about what we do see.

Who knows, for example, that as we walk on the needles and leaves carpeting the forest floor, that with each step we tread upon many miles of fungal hyphae, the microscopically thin threads that comprise the vegetative body of mushrooms? Collectively these hyphal threads combine to form an unimaginably vast network of mycelium growing just beneath the surface of the ground and connecting to the roots of the majority of green plants. This network of interconnected fungal mycelium and plant roots carries nutrients, water, and chemical messages throughout the forest ecosystem. Paul Stamets, author of *Mycelium Running*, refers to this system as "Earth's natural Internet."[1]

We know so little about fungi, and yet within our collective sphere of knowledge lies an ever-growing number of fascinating tales about mushrooms and their role in our lives and in our world. As I edge closer to my fortieth year of an ongoing love affair with the world of mushrooms, it is my intention to share a few of the many compelling stories I have learned. My goal is to help each reader take another step in transforming our culture from mycophobic (mushroom fearing) to mycophilic (mushroom loving). This can happen only when we gain a better understanding and appreciation of the mushrooms around us. The steps toward embracing mushrooms are built upon growing awareness of, and intimacy with, the lives of the fungi intertwined in our world.

The terms "mycophilic" and "mycophobic" were coined in 1957 by an international banker and famed amateur mycologist, R. Gordon Wasson, to describe differences between ethnic groups with regard to their attitudes, beliefs, and use of wild mushrooms. Wasson first realized these differences in 1927, while he was on honeymoon in the Catskills with his new bride, Russian-born pediatrician Valentina Pavlovna. Many years later the well-known ethnomycologist would recall the initial experience that started him down the path from mycophobe to mycophile.

> We had been married less than a year and we were off on our first holiday, at Big Indian in the Catskills. On that first day, as the sun was declining in the west, we set out on a stroll, the forest on our left and a clearing on the right. Though we had known each other for years we had never discussed mushrooms together. All of a sudden she darted from my side, with cries of ecstasy she flew to the forest glade, where she had discovered mushrooms of various kinds carpeting the ground. Since Russia she had seen nothing like it. Left planted on a mountain trail, I called to her to take care, to come back. They were toadstools she was gathering, poisonous, putrid, disgusting. She only laughed the more: I can hear her now. She knelt in poses of adoration. She spoke to them with endearing Russian diminutives.[2]

For a mycophile like Valentina, each mushroom species had a personality and a spirit, and it made little difference whether they were eminently edible or dangerously poisonous. She knew and loved each for what it was and for the story it held in her world. Wasson refused to touch them. He had been raised to ignore and distrust all mushrooms. "I, of Anglo-Saxon origin, had known nothing of mushrooms. By inheritance, I ignored them all; I rejected those repugnant fungal growths, expressions of parasitism and decay. Before my marriage, I had not once fixed my gaze on a mushroom; not once looked at a mushroom with a discriminating eye."[3] The recognition of the impact of their polar-opposite cultural attitudes and fount of knowledge regarding mushrooms was striking for the Wassons. Over the next several years, they devoted their spare time to exploring multiple aspects of mushrooming in different cultures around the world. They identified and labeled mushroom-loving and mushroom-fearing cultures and more closely examined how attitudes, beliefs, and practices related to mushrooms were woven into people's lives in mushroom-loving cultures. Their studies took them across Europe and into Asia and finally to Mexico and Central America, where their pursuit of reports on the use of mind-altering mushrooms in rituals led to the discovery of the ceremonial use of hallucinogenic mushrooms. Wasson's participation in a ceremony where he ate "magic mushrooms" was described in a famous 1957 article in *Life*. "Seeking the Magic Mushrooms" introduced hallucinogenic mushrooms to the western world for the first time. In the end, the Wassons coined the terms mycophilia and mycophobia to describe the cultural rift regarding mushrooms, and their work continues to strongly influence the study of mushrooms in culture today.

Strongly mycophilic cultures exist in Russia, Siberia, the Czech Republic, and many other Eastern European, Scandinavian, and Baltic countries. Mushrooms are also interwoven into the fabric of daily life as food, medicine, fable, and folklore in China, Japan, and Korea. Wasson described these regions and their cultures using, perhaps, overly optimistic language. According to Wasson, "These are the areas where mushrooms are considered friends, where children gather them for fun before they can read and write, where no adult feels the need for a mushroom manual" and described these lands as places where mushroom-poisoning "accidents are unknown." We know that a lot of people are poisoned by mushrooms in mushroom-loving lands (see Chapter 1), but Wasson had a point to make. He summed it up by saying that in a mycophilic land, "all the references are friendly, favorable, and wholesome."[4]

By contrast, in America wild mushrooms are widely looked upon with distrust and disfavor. Coming from dominant cultural roots entwined in Anglo-

Saxon norms, Americans mistrust and fear the mushrooms springing up in the lawn, garden, and forest following a rain. If it does not come cooked on a pizza or aseptically wrapped in a clear layer of plastic from the store, a mushroom is not to be trusted. When I ask participants in talks I give on wild mushrooms what their parents told them about mushrooms as they were growing up, they say: "Don't touch that. It's a toadstool. It could kill you! Quick, go wash your hands!" For the most part, Americans' questions about the mushrooms grow-ing on our lawns are not about beauty, but about ugliness; not about poten-tial edibility, but about the risk of toxicity and how to make them go away, permanently. Our beliefs have deep roots in British culture. In the words of British mycologist William Delisle Hay in his 1887 book *British Fungi*, "The individual who desires to engage in the study [of wild mushrooms] must face a good deal of scorn. He is laughed at for his strange taste among the better classes, and is actually regarded as a sort of idiot among the lower orders. No fad or hobby is esteemed so contemptible as that of the 'fungus-hunter' or 'toadstool-eater.'" In referring to British culture, Hay went on to state, "This popular sentiment, which we may coin the word 'fungophobia' to express, is very curious. If it were human—that is, universal—one would be inclined to set it down as instinct and to reverence it accordingly. But it is not human—it is merely British."[5] No culture has colored our American viewpoint on mush-rooms more than the British.

My family was as typical as the one next door. As a child growing up in New Mexico, we ate no mushrooms, at least not in any recognizable form. This was true in spite of the fact that my mother and her French and German parents collected and ate several wild mushrooms from around their ranch in Montana when she was a child. My fourth-generation Anglo-Saxon Irish father was able to thwart any of my mother's dangerous tendencies toward mushroom experi-mentation. His beliefs and attitudes were perfectly in line with the norm for his background and generation (i.e., one does not eat those damp putrid evil fruits of the earth). Raised as a second-generation Irish Catholic living off the ranch in the town of Bozeman, Montana, his parents and grandparents had no family history of using wild mushrooms. He then raised his family in a city at a time when American food production was becoming increasingly mecha-nized, processed, and corporate. I grew up with Velveeta cheese, Swanson TV dinners, Wonder Bread, and tuna noodle casserole. The closest we came to anything resembling a mushroom was using Campbell's cream of mushroom soup in the casserole. The very idea of collecting the puffballs off our lawn (which I did as an adolescent) and transforming them into sauce for the egg noodles or elbow macaroni was as foreign and suspect as eating tofu became to many older adults in the next generation.

Yet many Americans have ancestral roots in rural agrarian Europe and Asia, where collecting and eating wild mushrooms was a seasonal, much-loved, and relied-upon part of the diet. In every mushroom class I teach, in every talk or walk I offer, there invariably is someone who offers the reason for attending as an effort to recapture the connection to mushrooms present in his or her childhood. They talk fondly of collecting mushrooms with an aunt, uncle, grandparent, or some other beloved person. The elders retained the connection with mushrooms from "the old country" and shared their passion with the children in their lives. The students tell of the mysterious, unshakable certainty with which their guides would distinguish edible from non-edible mushrooms. They recall the pleasurable experience of collecting in damp woods and wet fields, the transformation from basket to pan, and the shared pleasure of eating their mushroom treasure. Invariably they speak emotionally of their regret over the loss of knowledge about mushrooms, the loss of the tradition of mushrooming in their families. Then they talk about their desire to reconnect to the mushrooms in their world, to reconnect with a deep, nurturing set of family and archetypal roots symbolized in the generational relationship with mushrooms. They seek a return to their roots of mycophilia.

Why did the elders not bless the following generations with the gift of mushrooms? Did they drop the ball or did the emerging generations, flung hell-bent into the race to make their mark in America, turn their backs on their forest roots and family traditions? It may be a blend of both. Immigrants to America over the past 150 years have entered a process called acculturation by which they are immersed into the values and norms of the dominant culture and, over time, become integrated. This process often has involved a sense of isolation from ethnic roots coupled with a devaluation of traditional practices of the homeland and an idealization of the new culture of the melting pot. In late nineteenth and early twentieth century America it also often included general movement from a European rural agrarian life to one that was urban and industrial. Many new immigrants settled first in the cities. New foods, unfamiliar land and forest, and a new language probably furthered their movement away from integrating local mushrooms and other wild foods into their diets. The accommodation of diet and food was rapidly accelerated in the 1950s and 1960s with the increase in processed foods and the idealization of "instant" food, pushing people further away from their own rich dietary traditions. As immigrant families turned away from historic roots related to food and lifestyle, America as a whole was turning away from our farm-based food roots. The mass exodus from farms and ranches into towns and cities was accompanied by a vocational shift to factory and office work and a trend toward buying food rather than growing, foraging, or raising it. "Mushroom" began to refer to one species of bland, pale, supermarket origin most often seen canned or as a minor ingredient in the ubiquitous casserole. Or, as in my middle-class suburban family during the 1960s and 1970s, generally not seen at all.

Times change. America slowly came awake to a curiosity about, and an appreciation for, more diverse and traditional foods including the world of wild or "exotic" mushrooms. The decades following the 1960s were a time when many Americans recognized that the homogenization of the melting pot came with the devastating loss of individual and cultural identity. Many sought to reconnect with their ethnic roots before cultural memory was lost forever. One of the most visible, enduring, and endearing aspects of culture is culinary and revolves around the dining table—that bastion of conveyed love, social connection, and nurturing. Though not everyone has family dining traditions they're looking to brag about, almost all will tell you that the memories of dinnertime traditions are enduring and powerful. Rediscovered food roots have resulted in the rapid proliferation of ethnic restaurants, cookbooks, and cooking classes. Once we began to expand our food horizons to include traditional ethnic dishes, we needed the proper ethnic ingredients. Many European and Asian dishes included the use of "exotic" mushrooms far removed from our pale supermarket variety, and adventurous chefs and family cooks required a source for wild and exotic mushrooms. This need could be filled by importing, but what about the wild mushrooms surrounding us in forest, field, and garden? In the 1970s America began to turn away from Wonder Bread and to look toward nature as source of healthy and natural food we had almost left behind.

The movement to rediscover our ethnic roots through diet also coincided with a period when many people were re-evaluating their overall relationship with nature and the environment. The term "environment" took on entirely new meaning through the 1970s as we struggled to address the effects of 100 years of industrialization upon it. The "back to the land" movement was born of the 1960s urban and suburban disillusionment and a search for deeper meaning and reconnection with the natural world. For some, myself included, the appreciation of nature included, in late adolescence, a growing interest in wild foods and foraging (thank Euell Gibbons). My growing fascination with wild mushrooms was further fueled by the possibility of filling a basket and cooking pot with great edibles. The two streams, connecting to ethnic heritage and recommitting to a connection with nature, are embodied in the vision of the Slow Food movement, which emerged out of France and Italy in the 1990s. The Slow Food movement celebrates regional and ethnic traditions related to food production and preparation, and a strong desire to support regional and sustainable food practices. The movement has further energized people to integrate the use of local foods, including mushrooms. More Americans are rediscovering a family history of wild mushrooming or creating their own traditions of incorporating mushrooms into their lives as a way to develop a relationship with nature and as a source of interesting, healthy, and desirable food. No mushroom in America embodies this better than the morel.

The morel has become the most widely collected and consumed wild mushroom in America, and because it draws such broad appeal from people in all walks of life, it may represent a change agent, a harbinger of a broader acceptance of wild mushrooms in the United States. Morels are not just a "blue state" food consumed in the glittering urban kitchens of the educated, sophisticated, and elite. No way. They are found and collected in abundance in the Midwest and mountainous Southeast by rural and country folk who might bring their mushroom bags into the woods along with their turkey call and shotgun.

Everyone who collects mushrooms for the table is responsible for learning the skills needed for accurate identification in order to avoid the risk of poisoning. Those skills are vital as you sift through 2,000–3,000 species in search of the great edibles. For me, however, learning the more intimate stories of mushrooms and their impact on us and the forest environment broadened my appreciation and deepened my relationship with them. When I first started mushrooming, my interest was drawn to understanding their diversity, but my curiosity quickly focused on the interrelationships of fungi in their environment as I studied botany and ecology in college during the 1970s. My gastronomic interests also drove me to focus on the edible mushrooms, to learn about cooking with them, and then to direct my interest toward growing exotic mushrooms at home. Over the past ten years my fascination with the medicinal and health-affirming potential of mushrooms became a passion and then a business.

The web of interconnectedness between mushrooms and the rest of nature seems limitless. Consider, for example, an obscure dark gray finger of a mushroom known as the goldenthread cordyceps, *Cordyceps ophioglossoides*. It is a parasite with a yellowish stem and yellow root-like mycelia that connect it to its host, a type of false truffle called *Elaphomyces* that is buried in the soil. The false truffle lives in a complex symbiotic relationship with the roots of the hemlock tree, and those roots also may be connected symbiotically with several other species of fungi, which can include the porcini, *Boletus edulis*, and the destroying angel, *Amanita bisporigera*.

The interrelationships don't end there, however. The northern flying squirrel is a rarely seen nocturnal rodent prone to spending the day in tree cavity nests. It is attracted to the strong scent of the false truffle as the truffle begins to mature and digs up the nut-like fruit in the night. Along with other fungi, truffles make up a dominant part of the squirrel's diet for much of the year. The spores of the false truffle are unusually thick-walled, enabling them to pass unscathed through the digestive tract of the squirrels. The well-nourished rodent then deposits the spores in its feces, where the spores are more likely to find a new host tree than if they were dependent on the truffle alone for dispersal. In short, a common squirrel that we rarely see due to its nocturnal lifestyle feeds primarily on truffles and other underground fungi that we also almost never see unless we spot the elusive parasitic cordyceps easing its obscure head above the forest floor. The truffles rely on animals to unearth and consume their fruit as the only way to distribute their spores, and the forest trees require root associations with fungi like the truffles in order to obtain vital nutrients for growth.

The interrelationships don't end there, either. As the hemlock declines, it becomes prey to fungi that attack and decay the heartwood of the trunk. The rot-softened wood provides an opening to woodpeckers for feeding and nest cavity excavation. Who else, beside the woodpeckers, do you suppose uses these cavities as homes? The shy nocturnal flying squirrel.

This kind of story—and the natural connections it illustrates—brings mushrooms to life for me. Stories make the abstract real, build familiarity, and transform understanding from a vague recognition of separate elements seen on the forest floor to an inkling of the dynamic and intricate web of relationships that move in choreographed dance steps in a natural world we rarely glimpse. These are the kinds of mushroom stories you will find on the pages ahead.

As America travels the path toward embracing mushrooms, toward mycophilia, we will need to develop (or recall) a language and stories about mushrooms as we invite them more deeply into our lives. There are signs that this is already under way. Our growing fondness for morels is one sign. Where forty years ago there were few mushroom field guides available, there are now many that cover specific regions of the country and some that represent the entire United States. Web sites celebrating and offering education about mushrooms are springing up like, well, like mushrooms. Another sign of movement to embrace mushrooms, though not as uplifting, is the increase in the number of mushroom-related poisonings reported in this country. Mycophilic cultures have far more people poisoned by mushrooms each year largely due to the fact they have so many more people eating wild mushrooms. An inevitable, though unfortunate, result of America's growing interest in wild edible mushrooms will be the increase in these poisoning cases.

All of these signs of interest will grow as we develop our relationship with the world of mushrooms. For the moment, I invite you to share in a few of the stories about those denizens of the forest floor.

PART I

MUSHROOMS AND CULTURE

PASSIONATE ABOUT MUSHROOMS
The Russian and Slavic Experience

If you think you are a mushroom, jump into the basket.
RUSSIAN PROVERB

*J*uly wafts in with warm winds, sultry days, cool nights, and the gentle, persistent rain the Russian people refer to as mushroom rain. On the evening train back to the city, someone alert to the mood of the forest sits with a basket of mushrooms in his lap, the top covered carefully with cheesecloth to protect the precious cargo from debris, drying breezes, and, of course, prying eyes. Anyone able to get a glimpse into the basket might see the colorful mushroom caps of *syroezhkas* (*Russula*), some *gruzd* (milk-caps, *Lactarius*) and, if the hunter was lucky or skilled, perhaps an early *beliy grib* (white mushroom, *Boletus edulis*), the most prized of the Russian mushrooms. Although the hunter is fatigued from a long-day's tramp in the forest, his eyes have a gleam of triumph, the satisfaction of a hunt long awaited, carefully executed, and successful. The mushrooms are here!

Word quickly spreads through neighborhoods, bars, workplaces, and the street. Workers of all backgrounds, education, and professions wait impatiently for the day they can throw off the shackles of the job and head to the forest with their families, boots, pails, and baskets. In smaller towns, businesses are shuttered and local officials close the municipal offices. Older couples and babushkas look to spend as many days as possible in the forest; this is a chance to earn extra income needed to supplement meager or nonexistent pensions. It is the season of *za gribami*—looking for mushrooms—and Russians of every stripe heed the call of *razh*—mushroom passion—to troop through the woods in an annual ritual of seeking, collecting, eating, and preserving the year's fungal bounty.

Eager mushroomers, clad in layers of clothing and stout footwear to protect their bodies from branches, bugs, and weather, arise before dawn to catch a train or a bus to the forest. They've learned to get into the forest ahead of the crowd or else there may be little left as the hordes move through. Family members arrive at a favored area, often where they have gathered annually their whole lives and perhaps where their parents and grandparents gathered before them. Families quickly separate into smaller groups and individuals to scour pine and aspen glades efficiently for their favorite mushrooms. Children, sharp of eye and low to the ground, learn at the knees of parents and grandparents to recognize the desired mushrooms and the ones to avoid. They fill their own baskets under the watchful eye of the family expert, usually the matriarch, who holds the knowledge about which species to keep and which to discard.

There is a bumper sticker sometimes seen along the coast of California, "The worst day of surfing is still better than the best day at work." For Slavic people, including expatriates, change the surfing to mushrooming and you'd have a good start on a regional slogan. The Slavs go mushrooming like Americans go to malls—compulsively, often, and with gusto.

A gifted Russian painter of mushrooms and passionate mushroomer, Alexander (Sasha) Viazmensky, wrote about mushroom hunting in Russia on the occasion of his first visit to the U.S. "The feeling I experience towards woods and towards mushrooms is nothing else but love. And if there is love, there is jealousy around, directed to everyone who also loves the object of your love. When mushroom hunters run into each other in the woods they silently curse at each other, although exchanging pleasantries out loud."[1] Tempers flare, and the territorial imperative can fuel violence when these otherwise unmarked boundaries are crossed and treasured territory invaded. During the height of the season, thousands of people will flock to the forests and, by the weekend's close, it will be as if a broom has swept all the edible species from the forest. Again according to Viazmensky, "In Russia, mushroom hunting is the favorite activity of enormous numbers of people. Many more people are mushroom picking than, for example, fishing. Children, men and women of all ages are indulging in mushroom hunting. American Mushroomers! What happy people you are because you are so few."[2]

Mushrooms are deeply woven into the culture and traditions of this region of the world. Russia, Ukraine, Poland, the Czech Republic, Slovakia, Latvia, Rumania, Belarus—all have a strong cultural and historical connection to the forest and mushrooms. These traditions inform the habits and skills that people need to seek mushrooms, but the passion runs deeper. Cabins and homes for rent in the countryside almost invariably mention mushroom hunting as a local draw, and even on Internet dating sites people include mushroom hunting as a hobby and something they seek in a potential mate.

Mushrooms are an inseparable part of the Slavic diet, and few meals are without their complement when mushrooms are available. Pickled mushrooms dominate salads and dried or brined mushrooms are used in cooking soups and a variety of other dishes. Many regional cuisines include a traditional Christmas Eve mushroom soup, and each year, dried forest mushrooms are set aside carefully so there will be enough for the holiday soup in a lean mushroom season. These traditions, like many, were carried over to America by families of emigrating Slavs. A quick Internet search yields many mentions of and recipes for Christmas Eve mushroom soup coming from Polish, Slovakian, and other Slavic heritages. A Slovak woman from Ohio named Jane included this comment with her recipe: "This was passed down from generation to generation. I don't have a recipe for this soup, but I will try to estimate the portions." She went on to explain some of the history of the soup in her family. "My grandmother used to use mushrooms my grandfather and dad would pick up in the woods. I believe they called them sheephead. We can't find the mushrooms for sale and are afraid to go and look for them in the woods. We don't know the good from the bad."[3]

Her comments echo those of many second- and third-generation immigrants who work to hold onto mushroom-related traditions but have lost access to the knowledge and the confidence to collect wild mushrooms even where they are available. Removed from a regular use of mushrooms and in a new country, they seek to retain the tradition, especially during those special holidays and at family gatherings.

The importance of mushrooms in the lives of Slavic people isn't seen only in the cuisine, however. Many ancient Slavic folk tales feature mushrooms and forest mushroom characters in the story line. In lands where traditional life was forest-based, the Taiga, that great northern belt of forest, became the setting of many folk and fairytales. Perhaps the best-known folk tales in Russia involve Baba Yaga, the ancient crone who guards the gate between this world and the underworld, between mortals and fairies. In some stories she is a benign, though frightening, force and in others she is malevolent, known to eat the unwary and to decorate her forest home with the bones of her victims.

As a child, I learned numbers and the ABCs through songs, stories, and games. I used many of the same stories with my son. In Russia, toddlers learn the names and characters of mushrooms through stories, poetry, and songs. One well-known nursery rhyme involves the mushroom king, Borovik, calling his mushroom troops into battle. The story exists in many variations, but they all serve as a way to teach children.

The Mushrooms Go to War

Borovik, mushroom white,
Colonel of the mushroom might,
Sitting under a large oak
Looking at his mushroom folk
Summoned them, ordered them
To go to war.

We can't go, said the ink-caps,
Our foot's too small for the steps.
We don't have to go to war.

We can't go, said the belianki,
We are noble white dvorianki.
We don't have to go to war.

We can't go, said the toadstools,
We are brigands, we are crooks.
We don't have to go to war.

I can't go, said the morel.
I am too old and not too well.
I don't have to go to war.

Said the russet ryzhiki,
We are simple muzhiki.
We don't have to go to war.

We'll go, cried the groozd,
We are brave and willing.
We shall go to war
And make a great killing.[4]

Many Russian tales feature food and drinks that are given or exchanged and that are sometimes magical or intended for the dead. Mushrooms often are possessed with such magic, and illustrations for the fairy tales often show Baba Yaga amid the bright red fly agaric and other mushrooms. The tales often are populated with a mixture of woodland creatures and children. In one, Baba Yaga captures and intends to eat a hedgehog sitting atop a mushroom and eating another mushroom. The hedgehog convinces Baba Yaga that he can be more useful in other ways, and changes into a small boy who leads the hag to a magical sunflower.[5] According to one Slavic researcher, "In another legend, Baba-Yaga puts the hero in touch with magic creatures (spirits), Lesovik and Borovik, who live under a mushroom and provide the hero with magical gifts which show him the way to reach his goal."[6] Whether depicted as benign or malevolent, Baba Yaga often appeared with mushrooms.

Mushrooms also are featured in the writings of a number of Slavic authors, both contemporary and classic. Pushkin, Tolstoy, and Nabokov all created characters who were mushroom hunters. In his memoir, *Speak Memory*, V. I. Nabokov reminisces about his mother's infatuation with mushroom picking. "One of her greatest pleasures in summer was the very Russian sport of *hodit' po griby* (looking for mushrooms). Fried in butter and thickened with sour cream, her delicious finds appeared regularly on the dinner table. Not that the gustatory moment mattered much. Her main delight was in the quest, and this quest had its rules."[7] The Russian author Sergei T. Aksakov referred to mushrooming as the "third hunt" to describe the qualities of experience as perceived by the hunter. "Although it cannot be compared with the more lively forms of hunting for the obvious reason that these are concerned with living creatures . . . here is an element of the unknown, of the accidental, there is success or failure, and all these things together arouse the hunting instinct in man and constitute its particular interest."[8]

Indeed, as any mushroom hunter readily knows, there is a strong primitive element of the hunt to any mushroom outing. The decision of where to hunt for mushrooms is based on past experience of the quarry's preferred habitat, knowledge of current and recent weather conditions, awareness of the patterns of other mushroom hunters, and a healthy dose of intuition, which all combine to shape the hunt and predict the outcome. In the forest, no hunters will share the locations of their spots or even divulge optimism regarding the possibility of finding any mushrooms at all. This primitive, instinctual behavior of the hunt is as true in Russia and all Slavic lands as it is in our own backyards. In fact, people become so intent on the collection that, at times, they throw caution to the wind.

In 2000, a great wet mushroom year across northern Europe, citizens in the far north Russian town of Krasnoselkup risked life and limb to gather mushrooms. The local airfield was known as the best mushroom site in this region with a very short season, and mushroom gatherers were so intent on their harvest that they placed themselves in the path of incoming air traffic, causing several aborted landings. Concerned local officials established a fine, equivalent to $1,000 (equal to three months' average wages) for anyone caught mushrooming on airport property. One air traffic controller acknowledged that only the threat of fines was effective in ending the high-risk mushrooming practice.[9]

Though popularly referred to as the "quiet hunt," mushrooming in Eastern Europe is often a social gathering as whole families or groups of friends head out into their favored territory. At the end of the day, or the end of the weekend for those lucky to have a dacha in the country in which to stay the night, the weary mushroom hunters head back toward the city. They troop onto trains packed with other mushroom hunters wet from dew or rain, speckled with soil, leaf, and needle from the forest, and deliriously happy if their hunt has gone well.

Once the mushrooms are transported safely back home and into the kitchen, the work of preserving the harvest begins, though it may wait until after a meal of fresh mushrooms. The mushroom most esteemed by Russians is *beliy grib*, the white mushroom or *Boletus edulis*. In years when they are plentiful, this mushroom fills the baskets and they are eaten fresh, as are the *lisichki* or chanterelle, *Cantharellus cibarius*, either boiled or boiled and fried. These and many other species also are preserved for winter use by drying or perhaps by boiling followed by marinating, pickling, or salting. Some species in the genera of *Russula* and *Lactarius* (milk-caps) are soaked in water or boiled to rid them of their acrid peppery taste before final cooking or preservation in brine. These species would make people sick without such preparation.

Because much of the mushroom harvest coincides with the farm harvest, historically mushrooming has been an activity for the very old, the very young, and women. For this reason, and perhaps others, it is common for the family mushroom expertise to rest in the capable hands of a grandmother who passes it down to a daughter or granddaughter.

There may be many historic factors combining to nurture the current national-istic passion for mushrooming that ignites Slavic people. A recent poll in Russia estimated that 60 percent of adults go mushroom hunting each year and only 18 percent report having never collected wild mushrooms. In the neighboring Czech Republic and Slovakia, mushroom hunting is seen as a national pastime. There, up to 80 percent of the Czechs and Slovaks spend at least one day per year searching for mushrooms, according to Slavic scholar Craig Cravens. He reports that the activity began during times of famine, especially during the devastating Thirty Years War and the two world wars.[10] Families foraged the fungi as an emergency food supply. Now it has become a national hobby.

For all these northern peoples, mushrooms, with their relatively high protein content and vitamins, are a good source of food. Russians began referring to them as "Lenten Meat" when the Tsarist-era Russian Orthodox Church required believers to fast more than 175 days per year.[11] This meant no meat or meat fats were to be consumed on fast days. (It makes the meatless Fridays of my own Catholic youth seem mild.) And the church's prohibition against the use of meat fats during fasting may be a basis for the Slavic practice of boiling many of the mushrooms as a method of cooking.

With the breakdown of the Soviet Union, the food production and distri-bution system in place during Soviet times was seriously disrupted. In many areas of the former USSR, food shortages became common and food prices rose sharply as subsidies ended and the fear of famine emerged. For many people during the 1990s, this meant shortages of food, and often, a disruption in income as government workers and pensioners went unpaid. Access to wild mushrooms again became vital for many as a no-cost, basic subsistence food. Many rural Russians also used wild mushrooms as a source of income, collect-ing them in the forest and selling them in towns and cities.

This re-emergent reliance on mushrooms as a staple food source came at a time when some people, especially those in cities, had not collected mush-rooms on a regular basis for years, and the knowledge they had as youths had begun to fade. Unfortunately, there was no diminishment in self-confidence and, as a result, during the 1990s and into the new millennium, the incidence of serious mushroom poisoning increased throughout the former USSR. Many medical providers and public health officials have attributed this increase to the lack of familiarity that many city dwellers have in distinguishing between edible and toxic species.

Many regional mushroom guides are available for Russians and other Slavs who are interested in consulting a formal resource, but unfortunately, many Slavic people don't use them for identification even when they are easily available. They learn their mushrooms as children and rely on family and other informal teachers for assistance. More than one resource I consulted mentioned that many collectors resent the implication that they might not know enough to avoid poisonous species and will resist offers for help in confirming the edibility of their collections. Those who have a history of collecting edibles from a specific location may rely more on their past success at that location than on knowledge of the mushrooms themselves. When they get sick, people may attribute toxicity to environmental contamination, mushrooms taken from the wrong location, or edible mushrooms that somehow had mutated into poisonous ones.[12] Health officials in the southern Russian city of Voronezh have collected and tested suspect mushrooms and found that they generally contained toxins typical of known poisonous mushrooms and none were determined to have mutated. Voronezh, a city of about one million, made headlines several times over the past decade as an area with one of the highest incidences of mushroom poisonings in Russia. It is located in the part of Russia and Ukraine known as the Black Soil region, known as a fine mushrooming area. Mikhail Zubirko, MD, of the local sanitary and epidemiological department, reported on some of the people he sees sickened by mushrooms, "These are city people who do not know their mushrooms very well: 74 of the patients being treated for poisoning did not know what mushroom they had eaten."[13] This sense of confidence not supported by adequate knowledge is perhaps the shadow side of a strongly mycophilic culture. It is particularly problematic when city dwellers revisit their mushrooming roots without the support of the family matriarchs to go through the collection basket and discard the bad mushrooms.

Each year a large number of people are poisoned by mushrooms in Russia, Ukraine, and other Slavic countries. It is difficult to gather accurate numbers, but in 2000, a particularly good year for mushrooms and a bad year for mushroom poisonings, there were an estimated 200 deaths attributed to mushroom poisoning in Russia and Ukraine alone. (In contrast, an average of one or two people are killed by poisonous mushrooms each year in the United States.) In both regions, deaths are overwhelmingly attributed to consumption of *Amanita phalloides* (see Chapter 8 for more information). Health authorities in Russia became so alarmed about the sharp rise in serious poisonings that, in the middle of the 2000 season, they closed off broad areas of the country to mushroom picking and had police patrolling the local markets and forest edges to encourage caution or enforce the ban on sales of wild mushrooms. Several large regional hospitals, including the one in Voronezh, reported being overwhelmed with severe poisonings and having to transfer mild cases to other hospitals for treatment. Apparently, even medical personnel are not immune from mushroom poisoning. Two doctors from the regional hospital in Voronezh were hospitalized for mushroom poisoning in 2005, sickened by mushrooms they collected and ate on their days off.[14]

In Ukraine, the regional medical center in Kiev reports dealing with so many mushroom poisonings during the short season that it has prompted a team of doctors to look upon their work with mushroom poisoning victims in terms of disaster response.[15] The director of the medical center reported that their Ukrainian Center of Emergency and Disaster Medicine might have as many as twenty victims of amatoxin poisoning simultaneously and treat up to 1,000 mushroom-poisoned patients per year. They cared for 196 victims of *Amanita phalloides* poisoning in 2000 alone!

In mainstream America and other mycophobic cultures, the twin myths— that most wild mushrooms are poisonous and if you eat one you will likely die—keep most people from experimenting with eating mushrooms unless they are absolutely certain of the identity and safety. These myths and the assumption of the generally malign nature of mushrooms act as a barrier to people who might otherwise look to them as a potential food source. These same myths also act as a protective shield, however, ensuring that few people will foolishly experiment with eating wild mushrooms and end up poisoned. In Slavic culture, the assumption is that mushrooms are good and the gods placed them on earth for people to collect, eat, and enjoy. Children learn 100 common mushrooms in school as adolescents. Collecting and eating mush-rooms is considered normal and most of the time is safely done, otherwise the number of people poisoned would be far higher. But for the small percent-age of Slavic citizens who possess inadequate knowledge to distinguish edible from toxic species and do not realize it, these assumptions combine to place them at high risk for being seriously sickened. This is the dark side of a region passionate about mushrooms. I also have little doubt that, as the number of Americans collecting and eating wild mushrooms increases, there will be a corresponding increase in the incidence of poisoning here.

Russian Mushroom Names and Terms

Beliy grib	White mushroom	*Boletus edulis*
Blednaya poganka	Pagan mushroom	*Amanita phalloides*
Borovik	Pine mushroom	*Boletus pinophilus*
Dojdevik	Puffball	*Lycoperdon* spp.
Gribnič	Mushroom lover	
Gruzd	Milk mushroom	*Lactarius* spp.
Hodit po griby	Mushroom picking	
Opyata	Honey mushroom	*Armillaria* mellea
Lisichki	Little fox mushroom, chanterelle	*Cantharellus cibarius*
Maslyata	Yellow bolete	*Suillus luteus*
Maslyonok	Buttery mushroom	*Suillus luteus*
Mukhomar or muktor	Fly killer, fly mushroom, or fly agaric	*Amanita muscaria*
Podberyozovik	Rough bolete	*Leccinum*
Podosinovik	Aspen mushroom	*Leccinum aurantiacum*
Ryzhik	Orange milk mushroom	*Lactarius deliciosus*
Razh	Mushroom passion	
Smorchok	Morel, the wrinkled one	*Morchella*
Sobirat griby	Mushroom picking	
Syroezhka	Russula	*Russula* spp. "27 kinds"
Veshenka	Oyster mushroom	*Pleurotus ostreatus*
Za gribami	Looking for mushrooms	

The light side of Slavic mushrooming outshines the dark by far. The new mushroomer in Eastern Europe will find himself surrounded by a broad encouraging support system. The number of role models out collecting on a regular basis and the extensive history of mushrooming all combine to ease the path to learning and building confidence. Now if our novice mushroomer can get anyone to show him where they find *beliy gribs*, he will be all set.

OVERCOMING DISTRUST
Mushrooming in America

If only one could tell true love from false love as one can tell mushrooms from toadstools. With mushrooms it is so simple—you salt
them well, put them aside and have patience.

KATHERINE MANSFIELD, 1917[1]

The individual who desires to engage in the study [of wild mush-
rooms] must face a good deal of scorn. He is laughed at for his
strange taste among the better classes, and is actually regarded as a
sort of idiot among the lower orders. No fad or hobby is esteemed so
contemptible as that of the "fungus-hunter" or "toadstool-eater."

W. D. HAY, *British Fungi*, 1887[2]

I discovered the world of wild mushrooms as a teenager. It was June of 1971
when, at age fifteen, I climbed onto a Greyhound bus in Albuquerque,
New Mexico, and traveled the 2,000 miles to Rhinebeck, New York, in order
to spend two months at Camp Rising Sun. Before that I hadn't been further
east than El Paso, Texas. I left behind a climate of high desert with an average
annual rainfall of less than 9 inches and spent the summer in the woods of
the mid-Hudson River valley, in the foothills of the Catskill Mountains. New
York State averages almost five times the annual precipitation of New Mexico.
I knew I was in a different world when, early on the third morning of the
bus trip, I opened my eyes to the green hillsides of western Pennsylvania and
sleepily wondered who watered all those trees. The dense vegetation obscur-
ing the ground was a new and fascinating universe to someone accustomed to
walking dry hills with little but dust to impede the view of distant mountains
and mesas. Though the lush landscape initially captured me, over time the
subtle beauty of mushrooms perched on moss or festooning a moist log is what
held my attention. I spent five summers in New York State between 1971
and 1980. During the second year I bought my first mushroom field guide, a

Dover reprint of Louis Krieger's 1936 *The Mushroom Handbook*, and began in earnest to untangle the stories of these fascinating and mysterious forest dwellers. More than thirty-five years later, I find several lifetimes of untangling still ahead.

Following my initial summer in the Northeast, I spent hours back in New Mexico foraging in the woods and mesas with my Euell Gibbons guide, *Stalking the Wild Asparagus*, looking for anything that seemed remotely edible. It comes as no surprise then that my initial interest in the beauty and mystery of wild mushrooms broadened into their potential as food. In the mid-1970s, I lacked mentors who could guide me and, being a cautious adventurer, I slowly began to learn the common groups of mushrooms, both edible and poisonous. The first mushroom I ate was a puffball (*Calvatia* sp.) that I found growing under the apple trees in my parents' yard in Albuquerque. I consulted my one field guide, and followed Krieger's wisdom about the genus *Calvatia*. "The beginner is advised to start with these puffballs in risking his life in the cause of mycophagy. But there is no risk, for they are all both safe and good to eat so long as the flesh is white, dry and compact."[3]

I wish I could say I had the confidence and support of my family as I sliced the firm white globes into rounds and fried them in margarine with salt and pepper. My own eager confidence was part adolescent bluff as I ignored the whispered doubts in my head regarding my identification skills. In spite of my fears, it tasted good and no one got sick. The low casualty rate was assured, as only I was willing to indulge in the small feast.

The following year I added the meadow mushroom (*Agaricus campestris*; see #4 in the color insert) to my list of edibles, first collecting these from the sprinkler-watered, manure-enriched ball fields at the University of New Mexico (UNM) campus. In 1977, I took my first organized class in mycology at UNM, and that autumn found a massive flush of shaggy manes (*Coprinus comatus*, #4) fruiting from the dead buried roots of a massive cottonwood tree that had been removed on campus several years earlier. For three successive years I collected large quantities of the young firm buttons of the shaggy mane and learned just how delicate and tasty they are sautéed in butter or as the main ingredient in a simple cream soup. The incredible abundance of this particular site also motivated me to learn how to cook and freeze mushrooms for use through the winter.

Looking back to those days, it's easy, in hindsight, to appreciate the slow process of adding new mushrooms to my list of edibles. In the late 1970s, New Mexico did not have an organized mushrooming club. I was not aware of anyone else out collecting mushrooms for food and fun, so my practice developed slowly, in a vacuum. Only after moving to Maine in 1981 did I begin to connect with other mushroom hunters to compare notes and share information and excitement. Though I was comfortable learning from field guides, nothing can boost confidence better than seeing a mushroom in the hands of a knowledgeable person.

In America, the eager newcomer setting out to learn mushrooms is both at an advantage and a terrible disadvantage. The advantage lies in the number of good field guides available to assist the tenderfoot hunter in learning the hobby. The typical mushroom field guide is organized by family groups, spore color, or other easily followed themes and always includes background material to help develop identification skills. It's a bit like going to a grocery store in another country and finding, to your relief, that although the labels are in a foreign language, the pictures show what everything is, and all the similar foods are grouped together in easily navigable aisles. If, in this foreign market, you could find a knowledgeable local guide familiar with the foods and the layout of the store, your anxiety would be markedly reduced. That's where experienced mushroomers come in. They can give novices the confirmation that they know what they're doing—or the opposite, if they need to develop more competence to balance misplaced confidence. And therein lies the disadvantage for the novice mushroomer in the United States: It's often hard to find a knowledgeable guide. Although many people learn to identify mushrooms with a good field guide, the confidence needed to trust eating the first few mushrooms is not easily acquired from a book.

Some people are attracted to wild mushrooms by an appreciation of their beauty, the mystery of their appearance in the wild, or as a way to better understand their inter-relatedness within the web of natural history. In the mushroom walks, talks, and classes I give, although such folks are present, they are a small group compared to the people driven by their desire to learn the edible mushrooms and, of course, where to find them. Mycophagy (the eating of mushrooms), at least wild mushroom mycophagy, is still a relatively unusual pursuit in America. Those enthusiasts who seek and consume wild mushrooms often are viewed as eccentrics or risk-seekers. Yet a growing number of Americans seek the knowledge they need to begin eating the mushrooms they find growing in the fields and woods. If you are considering mushrooming as a foraging pastime, be prepared to meet resistance from others in your life. I know spouses who are unwilling to eat the mushrooms collected by partners and neighbors who smile and nod when they accept a basket of surplus mushrooms only to slip them into the compost bucket once the generous collector has departed.

In our mycophobic society, most people assume that, in the absence of other information to the contrary, a wild mushroom is poisonous and that, further, it has the potential to kill or seriously sicken people foolish enough to allow it to pass their lips. Here is a portion of an announcement for a mushroom walk in rural Ireland, another mycophobic country. It exemplifies the local beliefs about mushrooms in many anglophile cultures:

> THE IRISH WILDLIFE TRUST, SLIEVE FELIM BRANCH ARE HOLDING A "FUNGI FORAY" NEXT SUNDAY 16TH OCTOBER AT GLENSTAL WOODS. Mushroom-hunting is ranked as one of the most dangerous pastimes in the world. Knowing which are the edible mushrooms is the hardest part of the hunt. They have bizarre names like the Sickener, Death Cap, Angel of Death and Panther—so it's not surprising that 99 per cent of Irish people avoid some of the country's 3,000 varieties of wild mushrooms, only about 120 varieties of which are edible. There are several Irish species that can kill you, even in quite small quantities, and there is little that medical science can do once you've eaten them. Others merely make you violently sick or give you hallucinations. This concentrates your mind when you're using field guides to identify species.
>
> Bearing in mind the dangers, it is always recommended that mushroom hunting is only undertaken with the assistance of an experienced guide.[4]

The announcement reveals a set of beliefs commonly held by the mushroom-fearing public:

- There is little to distinguish between an edible and a toxic mushroom species.
- Few wild mushrooms are edible, and most are poisonous.

- Once sickened by a dangerously toxic species, little can be done to save a life.
- Mushroom hunting is one of the world's most dangerous pastimes.

Even mycologists are not immune to the hysteria. In a recently published guide to mushrooms, Charles Fergus opined, "It is not known how many people

A Few Facts about Edible and Poisonous Mushrooms

- There are more edible mushrooms in our woods than poisonous ones, and more still that are non-edible but not poisonous or with an unknown edibility.
- Handling a toxic mushroom will not make you sick. Mushroom toxins have not been shown to be absorbed through the skin, except for a few very rare cases of mushrooms causing rashes.
- Very few of the wild mushrooms you see are dangerously toxic. The vast majority of toxic species cause symptoms that are, while unpleasant, not life threatening to a healthy individual. There are only about two dozen potentially deadly mushrooms in the United States.
- Mushroom toxins are grouped by their modes of action in the body. The majority of mushroom poisoning cases involve gastrointestinal distress from which the victim recovers within 24 hours. Very few have lasting effects.
- Over a thirty-year period, based upon reports to the North American Mycological Association (NAMA) Mushroom Poisoning Case Registry, on average, one or two people die of mushroom poisoning in the United States every year.[5] Hardly the most life threatening of pastimes. The trend, however, is toward an increased incidence of mushroom poisoning in the United States as more people collect and eat wild mushrooms. Across Europe and Asia, where far more people collect and eat mushrooms, there are many hundreds of poisoning cases each year and a number of deaths. Accurate records are difficult to come by, but in a bad year it would not be unrealistic to say a few hundred people might die. This mortality level is over a region where millions of citizens annually collect and eat wild mushrooms.

die from mushroom poisoning each year, but probably scores in America and hundreds in Europe."[6] The real number of deaths in America average two per year, though in a bad year, well in excess of 100 might die across Europe.

For many Americans, there is no clear distinction between the edible mushroom and the poisonous "toadstool." A review of several dictionary definitions indicates the same confusion regarding whether a toadstool can be edible or if the term covers only those mushrooms considered non-edible or poisonous. Toadstool is a term coined by the British to refer to those mushrooms considered poisonous or otherwise unsavory. In 1609, the French cleric St. Francis de Sales summed up the attitude that prevails in mycophobic regions today, "I have the same opinion of dances that physicians have of mushrooms; the best of them are good for nothing. Because mushrooms are spongy and porous, they easily attract all the poison around them. If they are close to serpents, they receive their venom."[7] Those of us fond of both dances and mushrooms are twice damned.

It is widely reported that about 5 to10 percent of the species of mushrooms worldwide are toxic and about 10 to 20 percent are edible. Estimates vary, in part because of the way we define poisonous and the limits of our knowledge. *The Dictionary of Edible Mushrooms* reports that there are almost 700 known and named edible mushrooms in use in various countries of the world. In a 2004 report on the uses and importance of edible wild fungi worldwide, researcher Eric Boa, working with the international Food and Agricultural Organization, reported on the edibility of 1,154 species from eighty-five countries through the use of regional sources and guides.[8] The desirability of a specific mushroom is based on taste, texture, ease of preparation, and other associations, including how many toxic mushrooms resemble the edible one. The desirability of a particular species is difficult to quantify and varies greatly from culture to culture. A mushroom prized in one country may be ignored in another and even considered toxic in a third.

How does someone start gathering mushrooms for food? It varies depending on your family background, the availability of supportive mentors or organized mushrooming groups, and certainly on your own personality. America has been slow to embrace wild mushrooms as food, but the wave has begun. Thousands of people are joining the hunts for morels across the Midwest and southern mountain states and mushrooming groups abound along the West Coast, but in most other regions, mushroom hunters are as rare as chanterelles

Russulas: Better Kicked than Picked?

There is a lot of variation in how different cultures perceive the edibility of mushrooms, and one of the most striking examples is seen in the genus *Russula*, a very common group in most temperate forests. Russula is both the genus and the most often used common name for this group, though a few authors in recent years have suggested the name brittlegills, referring to a trait of having very brittle flesh that easily breaks and crumbles. Field guides published in Europe, especially in those countries outside Great Britain, list many species of this group as edible and may report *Russula* as a generally safe genus to eat as any species will, at worst, only cause mild gastrointestinal problems. In his report of how mushrooms are viewed in countries around the world, Eric Boa noted that the genus was not recommended as food in the United States, yet over 100 species were listed as edible in Ukraine[8].

A comparison of *Russula* edibility, as presented in several North American field guides, along with French, German, and British guides, clearly showed that European and European-trained mushroomers are more positively disposed toward considering *Russulas* edible. Though the information about edibility isn't as black and white as Boa depicted, the European guides clearly reflect *Russulas* as safer to eat than the North American guides do. It's worth noting that of the North American guides, the one that includes the most species and the most edibles is Roger Phillip's *Mushrooms and Other Fungi of North America*. Phillips is an Englishman and the author of an earlier popular guide to European and British mushrooms. American field guides commonly list more species of this genus as non-edible and often caution the reader regarding eating any members of the *Russula* group. There has been a history of some severe gastrointestinal problems in a few people who have eaten some of the black-staining *Russulas* and even a couple of reported deaths in Japan.

Due to the great difficulty in identifying many members of this genus to species using field characteristics (those not requiring either chemical tests or the use of microscopic examination of spores), many American amateur mycologists lump these colorful summer mushrooms into the slanderous "JAR," which stands for "Just Another *Russula*." Others adhere to the philosophy "Better kicked than picked" as a guide to the genus. Many, with frustrated identification efforts behind them, merely note the genus along the forest trail and pass on in their search of more satisfying fungal prey.

Eastern Europeans, especially those of Slavic descent, prize many *Russulas* as an excellent candidate for the table. Even many of the peppery species of *Russula* and the related milk-cap *Lactarius* are collected, boiled, and pickled as a much-sought mushroom pickle. Some of these are mushrooms considered poisonous in the United States, and indeed, they would sicken a person who did not prepare them properly. A Lithuanian man recently took a mushrooming class I offered and was quite happy to find that we Yanks avoid the *Russulas*. His feeling, as he gleefully took possession of my mushrooms, was that there would be more for him.

in the deserts of New Mexico. They are around, but it takes a keen eye to spot them and a keener understanding of where to look. America contains a rich treasure of edible mushrooms generously scattered from Maine to Oregon and all states in between. Some are edible species you will be likely to find in most states, and others are more locally restricted. Sometimes a good edible species of mycorrhizal mushroom is associated with only one species or genus of tree or shrub and will be found fruiting only where their symbiotic host tree grows. Other species are restricted to a specific climate type. How do novices begin learning the mushrooms growing in their area? Follow the suggested guidelines for new mycophagists in Part II and have the patience to start slowly.

Mushrooming is an avocation that easily can span a lifetime, and it will take a full lifetime to begin to learn all that mushrooms have to teach. As long as you can walk, you can collect mushrooms for enjoyment and for the table, and when that time has passed, the young people you have mentored will bring you mushrooms seeking your knowledge and leaving you dinner. Because we live in an area of the world where wild mushrooms often are feared, many people you meet will view collecting and eating mushrooms from the wild as a suspect activity, but if you can resist the tendency to rush too quickly into eating, you have a much higher likelihood of having a positive experience and earning the support of family and friends in this hobby. Collecting and eating wild mushrooms has brought me pleasure for more than thirty years: the pleasure of the hunt, the challenge of learning new mushrooms (edible and toxic), and the great delight of cooking and eating the incomparable variety of available mushrooms. For me, however, the edibility pathway is closely bound with the toxic trail and I never discuss one without an adequate treatment of the other. My role as a wild mushroom guide and teacher challenges me to balance incompatible roles. I love to ignite interest and passion for wild mushrooms, as well as expose people to the potential for great meals. And, at the same time, I know it's critical to ensure that my students develop a good appreciation of the risks and temper their passion with prudent caution. I am not altogether at peace with the dual roles. Most Americans have so much inbred distrust of mushrooms that they're willing to forego the pleasure of wild mushrooms, pick up a pound of portabellas at the market, and call the resulting meal exotic. But there are also a few people willing to throw caution to the wind and who operate under the assumption that if it looks edible it must be—a personality type that scares me and provides juicy stories for the Darwin Awards. In the pages that follow, you will see and feel the dynamic interplay of my conflicted psyche.

PART II

MUSHROOMS AS FOOD

Introduction

LEADING WITH OUR STOMACHS

Ta femme, tes truffles et ton jardin,
garde-les bien de ton voisin.

Your wife, your truffles and your garden;
guard them well from your neighbor.
OLD FRENCH PROVERB

For more than twenty years, I've been teaching people about mushrooms and leading walks throughout Maine. Hundreds have joined me for beginner's walks and talks, and I regularly lead more in-depth classes on mushroom identification and the use of medicinal mushrooms. Easily, the most common question I get is: "What mushroom is this?", quickly followed by, "Can I eat it?" Sometimes the truly directed person will skip the first question.

These two questions are significant. The question of identity is in keeping with the roots of western culture or, perhaps, of human nature. We need to know where an object fits in our world, and the first step toward this understanding is a name. My son began to categorize construction vehicles by their appearance and function and, within the categories, into specific types at an astoundingly early age. Well before the age of two, he knew an articulated bucket loader from one not articulated and could differentiate a variety of similar dump trucks by name. He moved on from construction vehicles to horses and then into the even more complex and diverse taxonomy of dinosaurs. The need to know and to name was strong in his small psyche. The need to categorize things into groups and to further categorize the groups into distinct named entities seems fundamental for many people. Knowing the name of the mushroom, or anything else, gives it a place in our world and makes it ours.

That second question, "Can I eat it?", may relate to the deep-seated forager in most people, the connection to a hunter-gatherer heritage set in pre-agrarian times. The drive is primitive and survival-based, the need to exploit the knowledge of the natural world to feed and shelter self and kin. Mushrooms are one source of sustenance in the wild and come with a definite, predictable seasonality.

Though they cannot be counted on to provide massive calories, mushrooms do provide a source of protein and vitamins when other traditional food sources may be less available, for instance in a year when crops fail due to flooding or due to a cool wet summer in Northern regions. For people reliant on crops, mushrooms can be an emergency food in famine years and a supplemental food every year. Most Americans have ancestral roots intimately tied to foraging just a few short generations past.

Today, Americans generally forage for mushrooms along the aisles of the produce section of the supermarket, and the more adventurous at outdoor farmer's markets or specialty stores offering wild mushrooms. Mushrooms are primarily grown, purchased, and used as a food ingredient to supplement the taste, interest, and nutrition of meals rather than as a main course. However, they should never be discounted as a valuable addition to a healthy diet. Mushrooms are a fairly good source of protein. Depending on the species, they contain from 10 to 45 percent protein on a dry weight basis. This makes them equal or superior to almost all vegetable sources and below only milk, eggs, and meat. (It is important to acknowledge that mushrooms need to be cooked in order to break down the indigestible cell wall material and make the nutrients available.) Mushrooms are naturally low in fats and are a good source of several essential vitamins and minerals. Depending on the mushroom type, they contain varying amounts of B vitamins (niacin, riboflavin, and biotin), vitamin C, and consistently high concentrations of vitamin D-2, also known as ergosterol. The vitamin D-2 converts into vitamin D in the presence of sunlight or ultraviolet light. In addition to vitamins, mushrooms contain appreciable amounts of the minerals sodium, potassium, and phosphorus and lower concentrations of calcium and iron.

In some tropical and third world regions where carbohydrates are easily obtained, protein is often the limiting factor in rural diets. Mushrooms offer an easily grown or collected source of protein. The Food and Agricultural Organization of the United Nations (FAO) review of edible wild fungi underscores the use of wild mushrooms as a significant food source in certain countries in Africa, Asia, and the former USSR. In all, the review identified eighty-eight countries across the globe in which mushrooms are collected for food and where they also offer an alternate source of income.[1] In some developing countries, mushrooms remain an important basic food during times of the year when traditional root crops are not available. In other regions of low protein availability, farmers are being taught low-tech methods to cultivate edible mushrooms, such as varieties of oyster mushrooms, using agricultural waste. As the mushroom mycelium breaks down the plant waste, it produces protein that is then incorporated into the fruiting bodies. In this way, farmers can grow a crop high in needed protein for families and community while converting agricultural waste into a source of income.

In the United States, most people who collect wild mushrooms for food do it for the unique flavor and texture that mushrooms add to a skillfully prepared dish rather than as a survival source of nutrition. Reclaiming traditional foods from regional cuisines or exploring new fusions of taste gives us the opportunity to expand on the choice of mushrooms beyond the pale supermarket button. Wonderful dishes centered around regional wild mushrooms have been perfected over time in diverse cuisines worldwide. Generations of skilled cooks in Italy have passed on classic dishes that show off the specific taste and texture of fresh porcini (*Boletus edulis*). Other dishes harness the deep flavor of dried porcini to infuse a meal with rich earthy fungal essence. If chanterelles (*Cantharellus cibarius*) are fruiting, an experienced mycophagist and cook would never dream of using the same methods and recipes that make porcini shine. The subtle aroma and flavor of chanterelles call for totally different pairings—eggs or chicken, cream sauce, and simple butter sautés are in order. The same experienced cook would never consider drying a chanterelle as a method for preservation, as that would destroy the texture, aroma, and flavor that define this midsummer golden beauty.

The best, time-tested mushroom meals require few complex cooking techniques and even fewer special ingredients beyond the right kinds of mushrooms. The first step is to familiarize yourself with different types of mushrooms and the menu possibilities. Then assemble the ingredients and have fun with them. The following pages will introduce you to some of the best wild mushrooms in the world and some of the most common and easily identifiable mushrooms you are likely to find in your region. Some of the best edibles are also among the more easily identified, and are fairly common across much of the United States. So head out and learn a few good local mushrooms or find

Guidelines for the New Mycophagist

I developed this set of guidelines for anyone who is considering hunting for and eating wild mushrooms. Although the guidelines may seem extensive and cautionary, it's important to consider them all. Additional resources such as books, Web sites, and mushrooming organizations are listed in the Appendix.

Before Collecting Any Mushrooms for Food:
Learn as much as you can about mushrooms. Spend as much time and effort learning the poisonous mushrooms as you do learning the edible ones. Become familiar with the toxic mushrooms that resemble the good ones you intend to eat. Safe eating requires knowing both. Here are some resources to help you learn, with details in the Appendix:

1. **Buy and use one or more good mushroom field guides** that cover your region of the country.
2. **Become familiar with the best mushroom identification and information sites on the Internet.**
3. **Take part in mushroom classes or public walks.**
4. **Join a mushroom club or mycological association.** Though they might sound high-brow, mycological associations are actually a friendly mixture of experts, hobbyists, and beginners united by an interest in mushrooming. (See the Appendix for options).
5. **Befriend an experienced local mushroom guide.** Home-baked cookies are a powerful inducement.

When Collecting Mushrooms:
1. **Start slow and stay safe. Be conservative** about the groups of mushrooms you collect for eating. Begin your mycophagy with the common well-known edible species in your region, such as the "Foolproof Four."
2. **Avoid collecting mushrooms from potentially contaminated sites.** Some mushrooms can concentrate heavy metals and other contaminants. Avoid busy roadsides, landfills, golf

courses, power lines, railroad beds, or other industrialized or potentially polluted land.

3. **Take only young or prime specimens,** leaving old ones to drop their spores. Old mushrooms are perfect breeding grounds for bacteria. They are 85 to 95 percent water and loaded with up to 45 percent protein.

4. **Collect a number of specimens in various stages of growth** in order to gain a good understanding of what changes occur to the mushroom as it ages. There are often remarkable differences between the appearance of the button and mature stages of a mushroom.

5. **Collect all parts of the mushroom,** above and below the ground.

6. **Do a spore print** to confirm spore color as an aid to identification.

After Collecting Mushrooms:

1. **Do not eat a new mushroom prior to having collected it several times.** Each time, confirm identification (including taking a spore print for color). This is increasingly necessary as you collect and eat more obscure species.

2. **Never eat a mushroom unless you are 100 percent certain of the identification and its edibility. When in doubt, toss it out!** This is vitally important!

3. **Avoid eating mushrooms that closely resemble or are related to toxic species.** Why bother, when there are so many great edible, easily distinguished mushrooms?

When you are certain that you have correctly identified and weighed the risks of the mushrooms you intend to eat:

4. **Keep some uncooked specimens for comparison,** just in case of mistaken identification.

5. When you are trying a new mushroom, **cook up a small amount and try a few bites.** This first meal of a new species is never shared with family or friends.

6. **Always cook your mushrooms well.** Some mushrooms are toxic when raw, and all are more easily digested following cooking.

7. **Be cautious with new friends who dine at your table**. If they are not familiar with wild mushrooms, let them know what they are eating so they can make the decision for themselves. It's not unheard of for a case of "mushroom poisoning" to crop up as a result of someone's anxiety about the meal they've just eaten. There is a strong body–mind connection, and the stomach is firmly wired into that pathway.

Anyone who approaches mushrooming with open eyes and is prepared to follow these guidelines will be well protected from getting sick. Remember: Eating wild mushrooms need not be an extreme sport or a competition for developing the longest list of species eaten. Many devoted lifelong mushroom hunters have learned two or three species they know and love that provide them with an opportunity to be out in nature and to collect an ample supply of edible mushrooms for the entire year. Always keep your hunger for knowledge ahead of your hunger for mushrooms.

a local source to purchase wild mushrooms and enjoy the process and the prospect of great eating.

You can give a woman a basket of wild mushrooms and feed a family for a day, but if you teach her to identify and use a few species of great wild mushrooms, she can provide a family with great mushrooms for life. Trite, yet true.

∽ 3 ℃

THE FOOLPROOF FOUR
Updated for a New Millennium

Strange that mankind should ever have used the mushroom.
All the various species of this substance are of a leathery consistence,
and contain but little nutriment.
The condiments or seasonings which are added are what are chiefly
prized.
Without these, we should almost as soon eat saw dust as mushrooms.
> WILLIAM ANDRUS ALCOTT, *The Young House-keeper* (1846)

*A*s I make my way through the world as a teacher and a guide for people who want to learn about mushrooming, I frequently am asked about which mushrooms are my favorites, which are the best, and which mushrooms are safe to start out eating. True of many endeavors—the initial bike ride, the first kiss, the first bungee jump—the first step in picking and eating a wild mushroom is the hardest and requires forethought, planning, and, inevitably, a leap of faith. (Of course, there are always people who leap blindly, without prior thought, a personality type I'll address in the chapter on mushroom poisoning.) For the virgin mycophagist, the first mushroom collected, identified, and successfully transferred from the forest floor to the basket, from the basket to the pan, from the pan to plate, and finally from the plate to stomach, is an experience fraught with a mix of anxiety, anticipation, and excitement. For me it was that puffball in New Mexico. For someone in the Midwest, it would most likely be a morel; in New England it could be a chanterelle, a meadow mushroom, or a hen of the woods. The overwhelming majority of Americans never begin eating wild mushrooms. What if someone could make the initial leap less daunting? Many mycologists—both amateur and professional—have done just that by easing fears, teaching skills, and normalizing the idea of eating wild edible mushrooms. My work rests on the cushion of their leadership and guidance.

In 1943, an American mycologist named Clyde M. Christensen (1905–1993) created the concept "Foolproof Four" to describe four edible mushrooms that were common, easily identified, and very unlikely to be confused with any poisonous species. His book, *Common Edible Mushrooms*, was one of the early American mushroom field guides that sought to bring the much feared and maligned world of mushrooms into people's parlors and kitchens.[1] Christensen, a professor of mycology at The University of Minnesota, challenged the pervasive American belief that all wild mushrooms are suspect, fit only to be mowed over and removed from the lawn or the garden at first sight. "All too often these evanescent plants are looked upon as strange unearthly things, to be feared and avoided, if not trodden upon and destroyed." With the support of the depression-era Work Projects Administration staff for preparation of the colored plates, Christensen wrote his small guide. He used clear, direct language to describe mushrooms and supportive words to encourage folks to gather, learn about, and make meals from the common mushrooms in their lawns, fields, and woods. He made no effort to cover all common species and avoided the tendency to overwhelm his audience with too much information. At the end of his book, he even added a series of recipes made with common wild mushrooms, written and contributed by well-known cooks and mycologists across America. Christensen sought to bring the enjoyment of mushrooming to a mycophobic America more than twenty years before Gordon Wasson used the terms mycophobic and mycophilic. In doing so, he coined a phrase and a short list of edibles that would endure for decades to follow.

Clyde Christensen's Foolproof Four include the sponge mushrooms (morels), puffballs (the sulphur mushroom or sulphur polypore), and the shaggy mane, or shaggymanes, as he referred to them. He included all morels in the genus *Morchella* without differentiating among species and referred

Clyde Christensen's Foolproof Four include:

- Morels (or sponge mushrooms), genus *Morchella* without species named
- Puffballs (all puffballs growing above ground and with white interiors) including *Calvatia* and *Lycoperdon* species
- Sulphur mushroom or sulphur polypore, *Polyporus sulphureus*
- Shaggy mane, *Coprinus comatus*

to them as sponge mushrooms, one of the common names for this group. Christensen also did not separate out the species of puffballs, but included all puffballs that grow above ground and have a pure white interior, including all *Calvatia* and *Lycoperdon* species. In choosing the sulphur mushroom (*Polyporus sulphureus*), Dr. Christensen recognized one species from a very large genus, a species that is now included in the genus *Laetiporus*. The last of the four is the shaggy mane mushroom (*Coprinus commatus*), a single distinct species within a very large group of mushrooms, the inky caps.

During the six decades following publication of *Common Edible Mushrooms*, a lot has changed. The understanding of mushroom toxicology and genetics has expanded rapidly, and our ability to track mushroom poisoning and the species and toxins involved has improved immensely. Many of the older taxonomic groups have been divided into new genera and additional species to reflect what's been discovered about their relatedness. This expanding knowledge affects our understanding of morels, puffballs, the sulphur shelf, and shaggy manes no less than it affects our understanding of other mushrooms. What has become of the reputations of the Foolproof Four and our understanding of them as distinct species and good safe edibles?

MORELS, AKA SPONGE MUSHROOMS
Genus: *Morchella*
Species: **M. esculenta**, **M. elata**, and **M. crassipes**, etc.

No single wild mushroom has captured the hearts, imagination, and stomachs of the American public like the morel. There are numerous morel cookbooks, and any decent gourmet shop will be stocked with a variety of morel products (read kitsch). The taste of morels seems to defy rational description; most people resort to poetic analogies referring to ambrosia, heavenly sauce, or a bit of nirvana. In his book, *Morel Tales*, Gary Fine quotes one morel hunter as saying that, until he ate a morel, nobody had ever been able to describe to him what they tasted like. "People just say they are 'wonderful' or 'like nothing else' while smiling knowingly as older girls do when asked by younger girls about love. But now that I have had my first taste, I can say that morels are tender and they are sweet. . . . As a matter of fact, they are 'wonderful' and taste 'like nothing else.' Just like they were described to me."[2]

I recall one late spring fifteen years ago when I removed a tarp covering a lawn mower outside the home my wife and I rented in Thomaston, Maine, and discovered two perfect, young, 2–3-inch yellow morels, *Morchella esculenta*, fruiting in the old leaf litter and wood mulch beside the rear wheels. Since they were next to the house and protected from discovery by another hungry mushroom hunter, I decided to allow one mushroom time to grow larger and mature further before it met its final destiny in a sauté pan. Because morels grow slowly, it was another eleven days before I cut the now 7-inch morel and sliced it into thin rings. Simply sautéed in butter with salt and pepper and then added to a lightly cheesed omelet, it transformed a perfectly good omelet into a slice of heaven. The flavor of morels improves as they age, and the extra eleven days of growth deepened the rich morel taste. What began as an omelet became an archetypal experience in dining worthy of the finest restaurant.

There is a morel mystique that further adds to the sense of reverence with which enthusiasts speak about the coming of this rather odd and unappetizingly drab-looking ground-dweller. Unless you are blessed with living in the mid- to northern Midwest, morels are difficult to find in any numbers with any consistency during most years. I live in eastern Maine and, because I love the taste of morels, I have spent countless hours searching from mid-May to mid-June over the past twenty-five years. As someone who has embraced New England's parsimony, I am embarrassed to estimate a number of morels-per-hour-searched value to my hunt, but suffice to say, the number would be less than one, and if you did not count the past five years, far less than one. The combined wisdom of age, time spent in study and pursuit of morels, and the act of sharing stories of success and failure with other area mycophiles have brought me to the lofty position of successfully finding morels along the coast every year. Thus, I feel worthy to share some of that wisdom.

TAXONOMY

When Clyde Christensen added morels to his Foolproof Four list, he didn't differentiate among species within the genus *Morchella*, noting, "There are several species, but they are all enough alike to be described as one." At the time, Christensen was living in an America that recognized perhaps three common species of morels: the morel, half-free morel, and black morel. In addition, there were a significant number of named species that closely resembled the common morels. Like many mushroomers, Christensen referred to the group as the sponge mushrooms due to the honeycomb appearance of the cap.

Morels, as we understand them today, are even more confusing than when Clyde Christensen was writing. (Thankfully, all the species in the genus *Morchella* are edible, though a few in related genera can cause sickening.) Morels belong primarily to the genus *Morchella* and there is a very active debate regarding the true number of species included in the group. According to the author Michael Kuo in his 2005 book *Morels*[3] and on his Web site, www.mushroomexpert.com,[4] North American *Morchella* can be divided into four morphologically distinct species groups. In New England, we primarily see *Morchella esculenta*, the yellow morel, and *M. elata*, the black morel. The yellow morel has several forms that are 'at times' split into separate species but are similar enough to be lumped together for this discussion. Black morels also are divided into additional dark-formed species of similar characteristics. Morel taxonomy is under active revision in this age of molecular and genetic analysis, and though all agree that the process is not complete, it seems clear that the U.S. morels will be grouped into related clans or clades of yellow morels, black morels, and a few others that don't fit into either group. The morels represent a very small portion of the division of fungi known as Ascomycetes or sac fungi. These fungi form and mature their microscopic spores in sac-like mother cells called asci from which they are forcibly discharged upon maturity. The asci in morels line the surface of the honeycomb pits on the cap.

DESCRIPTION
(The following description is for the yellow morel, *Morchella esculenta*.) Fruiting bodies are 3–6 inches tall (with occasional late-season varieties growing 12 or more inches) and 1–3 inches wide, with a generally conical sponge-like cap fused at the base to a pale central stalk (see #2 in the color insert). The stalk and cap are completely hollow with somewhat brittle flesh. The surface of the cap is composed of a honeycomb of pits that are vertically elongated at maturity and not arranged in rows. The color is variable, ranging from almost white-gray when the mushroom is young to pale yellow tan and at times light brown in older specimens (#1). The pits are generally darker than the intervening ridges. Stalks are narrower than the cap, pale yellow-tan, minutely roughened, and broadening at the base. The flesh is thin, brittle, and has a

rich earthy odor that becomes more pronounced with age. The spore print is
ochre-yellow.

Look-Alikes
The early morel, *Verpa bohemica*, is sometimes found in midspring. This is a
small-capped morel with a longer stem and more infolded cap surface rather
than the true pits of most morels. It is widely eaten in the western United
States and in Europe but causes gastrointestinal distress in some individuals.
It is not known whether this toxic reaction is due to inadequate cooking or
idiosyncratic reactions, but beware of eating this mushroom, especially for the
first time.

Known as the half-free morel or, in the Midwest, peckerheads, *Morchella
semilibera* generally fruits early in the morel season and, in most years, it is
rare in New England. I have found it under poplars and birch in moist rocky
terrain. This mushroom generally resembles a small-capped morel with an
elongated stalk that is watery and fragile. When cut longitudinally the cap
clearly shows itself to be "half free" of the stalk. This species is edible with a
similar flavor to other morels, though less pronounced.

In spite of the specific name esculenta (meaning succulent), *Gyromitra
esculenta* and related species of false morels (#13) are mushrooms to leave
in the basket or on the ground—anywhere but the cooking pot. The various
species of false morels can be very toxic and are responsible for a number of
deaths in Europe and serious poisonings in America. (See Chapter 9 for a full
discussion.) My advice: Never eat this group! Our common false morel fruits
earlier than most yellow *Morchella* and is commonly found in association with
pines or in mixed woods. Unlike the true morels, *Gyromitra* caps do not show
the typical pitted structure of the true morel. Rather, they show brain-like folds
and convolutions. In addition, where morels are generally conical in shape,
the false morels are more rounded or irregularly shaped.

Caveats
Cook your morels! Morels contain a heat-labile toxin that is neutralized
by cooking. For those adventurous cooks and those who like their vegeta-
bles cooked only lightly, this can pose an unexpected problem. In his book
Mushrooms: Poisons and Panaceas, the pathologist and amateur mycologist
Dennis Benjamin describes a 1992 banquet in Vancouver, British Columbia,

whose guests included a number of city leaders, among them the head of the Department of Health. The chef for the evening made a festive salad to which he added a liberal number of chopped raw morels. Though likely thinking that the morels would add a touch of class, the result was 77 (out of 483) poisoned guests, many of whom required medical attention for severe gastric distress.[5]

As this book moved into the final stages of editing, a new study was being published detailing the results of analysis of a number morels collected in old commercial apple orchards from New Jersey to Vermont, along with analysis of soil samples from each site. The study, carried out by Eleanor and Efrat Shavit, was prompted by the arsenic poisoning of a long-time member of the New Jersey Mycological Society and an admitted morel maniac who reportedly collected thousands of morels from old apple orchards across New Jersey each spring since the 1970s. Following a long illness of increasing severity, the victim was diagnosed with acute arsenic poisoning in 2007 and, after ruling out alternate sources of contamination, attention focused on his morel-rich diet as the potential source of his problem. He was treated with intensive chelation therapy for nine months and regained his health.

From 1900 to 1980, an estimated 49 million pounds of lead arsenate and an additional 18 million pounds of calcium arsenate were applied to crops across the United States.[6] Both lead and arsenic tend to be quite stable in inorganic form in the soil and it is recognized that much of the pesticide residue remains in the topsoil of fields and orchards where it was applied. The pesticide was the main one used in commercial orchards for more than fifty years, and an estimated 200 pounds per acre might have been applied on average. Following early indications that morels are able to accumulate metals from their environment, the Shavits, working with a small group of committed volunteers, arranged for soil and morels to be carefully collected in twenty-nine locations of apple orchards that were active between the mid-1800s and mid-1900s. The analysis revealed that morels are able to accumulate high levels of arsenic and lead from the soil and, although they do not reach the level of an acute poisoning risk, eating morels from these contaminated sites in large amounts over time can easily lead to toxic levels of these metals.[7] It certainly warrants a much more cautious approach to collection and eating morels from old commercial apple orchards. If in doubt, consider testing the soil from sites where you regularly collect morels. I would avoid feeding orchard morels to children.

Each year, as I track the reports of mushroom poisonings across the country, there are a few cases where morels have caused gastric distress. There is no clearly discernable pattern to the victims, but a few common themes emerge. People who get sick often had alcohol with their meal of morels. In some cases the mushrooms may not have been fully cooked or were eaten raw. At other times it seems that an individual's unique make-up is such that they are unable to tolerate this species. People who develop GI distress after they eat represent an incredibly small percent of the people who eat morels. To be sure you enjoy these delectable finds comfortably, eat only a small quantity the first time and be sure to fully cook your gourmet repast.

ECOLOGY, HABITAT, AND OCCURRENCE

Morels are saprobes, using as their food source the leaf duff and wood in the soil. They also have been shown to form symbiotic, mycorrhizal associations with various tree species during parts of their life cycle. Their mycelia colonize broad areas, and often the fruiting body appears far from the original site of inoculation or obvious food source. The fruiting bodies can arise from over-wintered sclerotium produced the year before or can form directly from the mycelium. A sclerotium is a dense knot of compact hyphal tissue able to act as a form of battery, storing energy and tissue during periods of adverse weather and fueling rapid growth or fruit production when environmental conditions again become favorable. This energy-storing ability may be the primary reason that morels can fruit early in the year.

Now that we recognize that morels can form symbiotic mycorrhizal relationships with trees during portions of their life cycle, their growth and fruiting patterns make more sense. Recent studies suggest that morels living in symbiosis with trees are triggered to fruit heavily as the tree is nearing death or in the years immediately following its death. The food energy in the dead root tips plays into the surge of food energy needed to produce fruit as the mycorrhizal fungus switches to full saprobe on the dying or newly dead roots.[8] This helps explain why morels often are found in greatest abundance in the two years following a forest fire and as elm trees die from Dutch elm disease. Trees stressed by infection or insect infestation also can trigger greater fruiting of morels, as can a mechanical injury to the trees or tree roots. A close Maine mushrooming friend of mine told me that she saw heavy fruitings around a young elm and an apple tree in the year following a field being disked, fertil-

How Saprobes Feed

Saprobic fungi feed by growing their root-like hyphae into contact with their source of food, generally some form of dead plant tissue, and releasing powerful enzymes into the space surrounding their hyphal cells. These enzymes break apart large organic molecules or polymers of sugar such as cellulose, hemicellulose, and lignins into their component simple sugar–building blocks. The fungus is then able to transport some of these simple sugars into the cell for use as food. To put it simply, rather than ingestion of complex food followed by digestion into simple components (as happens in animals), fungi digest complex food outside of their "body" followed by ingestion into the cells. This same process occurs in the small patches of mold mycelium seen on bread left overlong in the breadbox. In a mycelial matrix composed of miles of hyphal strands, the degradation of organic matter into its component parts happens on a massive scale and results in a quantity of nutrients becoming available in a short period of time. Plant roots living in the same area benefit from the release of nutrients and their growth is enhanced. The lush growth along the leading edge of a fairy ring is caused by the fungal activity releasing nutrients previously bound up in dead plant tissue.

ized, and limed, and also around an apple tree following a driveway construction that disturbed the root system.

Morels occur singly or in small clusters. They often hide behind and amid sticks and vegetation. The edge of a boulder or log on the ground form common microclimates for fruiting. When you see one morel, stop, stay quiet lest you scare off its kinfolk, and scan the area around your find. By far, the best place to look for a morel is in an area where you have already found one. They blend well with their surroundings, and your first morel always will be the hardest to spot. Once you have the visual image burned into your brain, the next one is easier to pick out of the background litter.

In general, morels favor climates where there is a distinct winter followed by spring warmth; they don't grow as predictably in areas with milder winters or where there is a less distinct passage from winter cold to spring warmth.

Look for yellow or blond morels in your region when spring is in full glory with the explosion of newly emerging leaves taking center stage seemingly overnight after a week of warm weather accompanied by adequate rain. Here in northern New England look for shadbush in full bloom, the lawn almost ready for the initial mowing of the season, red oak leaves the size of squirrel ears, the apple blossom buds swelling into bloom, and the blackflies starting to bite. (#2) For Maine and the more northern Midwest, this generally means that the season begins in mid-May, but the timing varies due to weather patterns and your location in the state as well as the influence of altitude and slope aspect. The season generally lasts three or so weeks, longer in a cool wet spring. Black morels generally fruit two weeks earlier than yellows.

Morels grow in association with a range of tree species, most notably apples, elms, ash, and aspens in the Northeast. In the West, they grow with those same species, as well as with spruce, fir, and pines. In the Midwest and Southeast they are found associated with other trees such as the tulip magnolia and various nut trees. They tend to favor well-drained soils that are somewhat sweet or alkaline, and often can be found in areas of limestone bedrock or glacial gravelly soil, as well as in areas where there has been a recent fire.

Forest fire creates temporary conditions of sweet soil, and in the one to three years following a forest fire, morels can be found fruiting in large quantities. Historically, some European landowners would set fire to their land in hopes of increasing their morel yield! In the western United States, morel hunters use this knowledge of fire association to great advantage; commercial collectors from California to Alaska target areas where forest fires burned the previous year. Many enterprising commercial collectors travel with the seasonal mushroom wave as morel harvests peak from south to north, and a few make their livelihood in a time-honored tradition of the hunter-gatherer following their food sources through the seasons.[9] My friend Michaeline Mulvey recalls eager mushroomers finding hundreds of *M. elata* following a large forest fire in western Maine some years ago.

Look for limestone areas and/or rich woods that support a good number of sugar maples, white ash, and basswood, or tree species that grow in sweet soil in your region of the country. Search old untended or overgrown apple orchards under and between the trees, especially where a tree is dying or has recently died. My most consistently productive collection site is an unproductive apple orchard with sixty- to seventy-year-old trees and abundant grass between the trees. I find individual morels and clusters in the grass and in among raspberry canes and dead branches beneath the trees. Morels also can be found around dying or newly dead elms, especially where the elms are growing on limestone soil. It is also worthwhile to look in garden beds the year following the addition of masses of bark or wood mulch. I have seen large fruitings of morels in these sites, though generally only for one to two years.

The bottom line: Morels are where you find them. The bottom, bottom line: This is one mushroom well worth finding! If all else fails, plan a trip to Michigan in May.

Across America morels fruit from January (California) into July (Rocky Mountains of Montana and Canada) as spring marches north. The peak times are from late March and April in southeastern states, late April and May in the Midwest and West Coast, and May through mid-June in the northern Midwest, New England, and the mountainous regions of the western United States. In different regions they are associated with various species of endemic trees and microclimates from sandy beach areas in parts of California and along the Gulf Coast to forests of spruce and fir in the mountains of Montana and Alberta. If you are a motivated novice, you'd be well advised to connect with experienced morel hunters in your area to learn about local habitat types that produce morels. Don't bother asking about specific sites for collection. That type of brazen behavior is likely to elicit tall tales or outright deception as the morel collectors seek to protect their secret spots and have fun at your expense. I can state with some authority that experienced mushroom guides are not above the occasional well-baked bribe. At some point, inevitably, it will be up to the new hunters to take to the woods, scout their territory, and train their eyes to find this tasty, shy, elusive fungus.

For those who live in the Midwest and northern Midwest, many states hold annual morel festivals complete with competitions about the most morels found, the largest individual, and the most severe case of poison ivy. Michigan is home to the National Morel Mushroom Festival, which held its fiftieth annual gathering in May 2010 in Boyne City, as well as many other local festivals. Illinois, Iowa, Michigan, Indiana, Minnesota, Kentucky, Illinois, and Ohio all have annual morel celebrations in their rural towns and small cities. In 1984, the Minnesota state legislature named the morel as the official state mushroom, facing some ridicule in the process, as Minnesota was the first of only two states to have a state-designated mushroom. (The other is Oregon, whose mushroom is the Pacific golden chanterelle.) Knowing the bounty of midwestern morels, in May and early June as spring greens and apple blossoms bring on thoughts of morels in cream sauce, I sometimes wish I were a midwestern man.

In Tennessee, Kentucky, Arkansas, and the mountains of northern Georgia, the morel season begins in the early spring, and when they come up there's often a mountain man looking to bring 'em home. I recently got an email from a well-known chef who related meeting a local Virginian preparing to head into the woods from a Blue Ridge mountainside parking lot. The man, garbed in camouflage and equipped with a couple of five-gallon mud buckets, was headed up slope to gather "morls." When asked by the carload of food professionals how he liked to eat his morels, he said stewed with meats or simply pan fried, but that his favorite was to dip them (first cooked, I presume) in melted Cracker Barrel cheese. The morel cooking tips published and online reflect the diversity of tastes, from classic risottos and crepes to quiche and pasta sauces. On the more rustic level are morels coated with crushed corn flakes or potato chips and fried in butter, or the seasonally appropriate deep-fried wild turkey with fried morels.

In the heartland of America, morels have become a great unifier of people. In the words of one Tennessee turkey hunter: "It doesn't really matter how you cook either one, but I always try to eat my morels with a freshly harvested wild turkey. Most of the morel hunters in Tennessee find their shrooms while they are chasing gobblers through the woods. Here's my favorite recipe."

DEEP-FRIED WILD TURKEY AND SAUTÉED MORELS
Pluck your turkey (after scalding). Inject your turkey with Cajun butter (16 ounces) and rub Cajun seasoning salt over the whole turkey. Heat peanut oil to 375 degrees in a deep pot that will hold a turkey and 4 or 5 gallons of peanut oil. Fry about 3 minutes to the pound once oil has reached 375 degrees. Most wild turkeys will weigh between 10 and 15 pounds dressed and plucked. Keep your oil at a constant temperature. Sauté morels in butter and soy sauce. Add a dash of the Cajun turkey rub. (Courtesy of Keith S., Kingston Springs, Tennessee)

EDIBILITY, PREPARATION, AND PRESERVATION

Cut morels at ground level with a sharp knife. Leave any old, over-mature ones to continue to release spores for the future. In general, morels do not begin to release their spores until they are quite mature. When cleaning your catch and preparing them for cooking or preservation, it is a good idea to cut them longitudinally in order to expose any sluggy or buggy hitchhikers within the hollow confines of stem and cap. Brush off any soil or debris adhering to the mushroom or, if needed, rinse with water and towel dry.

Morels dry well, retaining their full flavor. Sliced in half, they dry readily in a food dehydrator or on screens in a warm oven. Store fully dried morels in a sealed freezer bag or canning jar and the flavor will last for years. Morels also can be sautéed and frozen in serving-sized containers. In the Midwest, some collectors clean the morels and lightly coat them with flour. They are then frozen either raw or partially fried in butter and can later be popped into the frying pan right out of the freezer.

The rich, full flavor of morels is well suited to many preparations. Sautéed in butter and added to scrambled eggs with the scant needed salt and pepper shows off the flavor and will make a breakfast you long remember. In a cream sauce they will grace simple egg noodles, a chicken dish, or even toast.

SIMPLY MORELS

½-1 pound fresh morels, sliced lengthwise
2 tablespoons butter or butter/olive oil mix
Salt and freshly ground pepper to taste
½ cup cream to finish (optional)

To really enjoy the flavor of your freshly collected morels, keep it simple. In a large shallow pan or iron skillet, melt 2 tablespoons butter for each ½ pound of morels (you also can use olive oil or a mix) and add the morels. Cook thoroughly over low heat for 5–10 minutes, adding salt and freshly ground pepper to taste. For a truly decadent finish, add cream and heat to just under boiling. Enjoy this dish right out of the pan, on rice, or over meat or chicken.

SIMPLE MORELS À LA THE HINTERLAND

1–2 pounds fresh morels, sliced lengthwise

2 or 3 eggs, beaten

2 cups crushed saltine (or other) crackers, flour, a corn meal and
   flour mixture, crushed corn flakes, or crushed potato chips

Lots of butter, olive oil, or bacon fat

Salt and pepper, or seasoned salt, garlic salt, Cajun seasonings, etc.

There are as many variations to this recipe as there are for homemade
mac and cheese, but the basic theme is consistent. Using fresh morels
cleaned and sliced lengthwise, dip the morels into the egg mixture
and then dredge them in a coating of whatever happens to be in the
pantry and complements the mushrooms. Season with salt, pepper,
and other spices. Each aficionado swears by his or her own special
coating, the simplest being just flour, salt, and pepper.

Once coated, pop them directly into your favorite cast iron skillet or wide sauté pan into which you have already added generous
quantities of butter. Fry them over medium heat for at least 4–5
minutes per side until they are fully cooked and browned. Enjoy
them hot as an appetizer, main dish, side dish, breakfast, lunch, or
snack. Whatever coating or fat you use, this is the most common
method for cooking wild morels across the hinterlands of America.
And it is good!

SAUTÉED MORELS IN A CREAM SAUCE

15–20 fresh morels or reconstituted dried, cut in half if large

1 large shallot, chopped fine

1 large clove garlic, minced

2 tablespoons butter

2 tablespoons olive oil

¾ cup chicken stock

¼ cup white wine

1 cup heavy cream

Salt and freshly ground pepper to taste

Put olive oil in heated pan over medium heat. Add garlic and shallots, stir and sauté until softened but not brown. Add butter until melted, then add morels. Stir and cook until mushrooms are soft, about 3–5 minutes. Add wine and chicken stock, salt and pepper, and cook for 5 minutes. Add cream and cook on low until thickened somewhat. Do not allow to boil. Additional ground pepper is nice here. Enjoy over egg noodles or fettuccini, or alongside rice or couscous.

This can be made easily with chicken. I use boneless thighs cut into generous bite-sized bits. Start by browning the chicken in olive oil over high heat. When well browned, remove chicken from the pan, set aside, and continue with the rest of the recipe, adding the chicken back in with the wine and chicken stock.

PUFFBALLS

Genus: *Calvatia* and *Lycoperdon*

Species: *C. gigantea, C. cyanthiformis, L. pyriforme,* etc.

As I walk through the woods or along the edge of a field (or even as I am driving in my car) and spot a desirable edible or medicinal mushroom, I get a zing of electricity that quickens my heartbeat and brings a grin to my face. The hunter, at last, has his chosen prey in sight. When I come upon a giant puffball, *Calvatia gigantea,* (#3), or a group of these fungal behemoths lounging in a field, that zing is instead a jolt as I see the immense bounty of mushrooms before me. Puffballs are many mushroomer's first edible.

Picture a balloon, generally spherical, straining at the confines of its envelope and packed with all the air it can hold. The puffball represents the most obvious fungal strategy for maximizing the number of spores an organism can make and distribute in a given area of space and volume. It is a round ball ranging in size from a marble to much larger than a basketball and, at maturity, is completely packed with spore dust. The entire interior mass of the puffball is composed of gleba—spores and the hyphae needed to support their growth—surrounded by a thin envelope of skin and, in some species, a base or column of sterile tissue to raise the spore mass above the surface of the ground.

TAXONOMY

Puffballs are categorized as gastromycetes ("stomach fungus") because they make spores in their "stomachs." This is a relatively large and diverse group of fungi with a number of genera. In the northeast United States the two most common genera are *Calvatia*, composed of medium to large puffballs more commonly found in open grassy areas, and the much smaller *Lycoperdon*. These small to medium puffballs usually are found in the woods and, when mature, release their spores through a small apical pore or operculum at the top of the fruiting body.

Puffballs tend to be found more commonly in drier regions of the world because producing spores within an enclosed sac reduces the risk of their drying out in desert air before maturing. For suburban or rural American kids, a mature puffball is great fun to kick or throw around since a cloud of an almost unbelievable number of spores will explode from it on impact. Studies carried out (no doubt by unpaid graduate students) have estimated that a 12-inch-diameter giant puffball matures somewhere in the neighborhood of 7–9,000,000,000,000 spores. Yes, that means 7–9 trillion! According to David Arora in *Mushrooms Demystified*, 7 trillion puffball spores lined up side to side would circle the Earth at the equator, and if each spore produced one mature puffball, they would reach to the Sun and back![10]

But it's the immature puffball that interests those of us who collect them for the table. A young puffball is firm and fairly dense. If, when it is sliced longitudinally from top to base, it is pure white inside, you have a mushroom worth eating, or at least trying. As a puffball ages, the tissue becomes soft and slimy, turning yellowish or greenish yellow or even purple in one group. At this stage it not only looks less appetizing, it becomes quite bitter. You wouldn't get sick from one yellowish puffball, but the bitterness is pronounced enough that one bad mushroom will spoil the pot. Eat only firm puffballs with pure white centers.

DESCRIPTION

Along the coast of New England, we commonly see five species of puffballs with good cooking potential, although others also occur. These same species and a number of similar and edible cousins are found regularly across much of the United States and Canada. West of the Mississippi River, in the prairie and mountain states, there are far more species of puffballs, quite a few with great edible potential; consult a regional field guide in your area for local species variations.

The **giant puffball**, *Calvatia gigantea* (#3), is a large to huge white-skinned puffball that normally grows to about 16 inches in diameter, not uncommonly up to 24 inches, and at times exceeds 3 feet. The body is a bit more broad than tall, resulting in an irregular globose shape. Its cream to white surface skin thinly covers the gleba with no sterile base. The gleba is initially pure white and firm, and slowly ages yellowish to olive green as the spores mature. When mature, the skin irregularly flakes off, exposing the olive-green to yellow spore mass to the elements for dispersal. *C. gigantea* is a saprobe that feeds on dead vegetation and generally is found in open fields, field edges, or occasionally in forested areas (including under a Norway maple in our area). It can fruit singly or in scattered groups and, rarely, in arcs or fairy rings.

The smaller **purple-spored puffball**, *Calvatia cyathiformis*, is also a denizen of fields and lawns and also can be found in roadside ditches and along grassy shoulders. The fruiting body is up to 8 inches across and of generally equal height. Initially round with a flattened top, the fruiting body develops into a somewhat pear-shape; picture a loaf of bread sliced in half or the shape of a skull. The purple-spored puffball develops the same shape in longitudinal cross section. Unlike *C. gigantea*, the purple-spored puffball has a thick layer of sterile tissue along its base that serves to elevate the spore mass above the soil surface. This persistent sterile cup often can be found well into the winter and spring, months after the spores have dispersed, as a shallow purple cup-shaped remnant. Like its larger cousin, *C. cyathiformis* has an interior that begins as firm pure white gleba and with age becomes purple and goopy as the mass of spores begin to mature, and finally a mass of purple powdery spores. Edible when young, firm, and pure white inside, it is considered by some to be choice and by others as a passable edible. Given its skull-like shape, it is ironic that I see it most frequently in graveyards in New England. The similar *C. craniformis* is known as the skull-shaped puffball and is equally edible.

If you spend much time in the woods in late summer and fall, the **gem-studded puffball**, *Lycoperdon perlatum*, is the most common species of puffball you're likely to see. Individuals, small groups, or occasionally, as I found recently in a spruce plantation, troops of hundreds of these 1–3-inch puffballs grow on leaf or needle duff and rarely, on well-rotted wood. The individual puffballs are somewhat pear-shaped, white to cream in color, and covered with a fine coating of small spines or scales, giving the appearance of studs. As the fruit ages, these spines generally wear off and leave faint circular outlines in their passing. The interior of the puffball starts firm and white and soon softens and changes to yellowish and then greenish. Though gem-studded puffballs are edible when they're young and white, by the time the color changes the taste becomes quite bitter. Instead of the general disintegration of the skin as in *Calvatia*, the *Lycoperdon* species develop a small opening called an operculum at the apex of the body through which the mature brownish spores are released by the action of raindrops and wind.

From a distance, the **pear-shaped puffball**, *Lycoperdon pyriforme*, closely resembles its gem-studded cousin. Both tend to be smaller than 2 inches in diameter, grow commonly in clusters, and are found primarily in late summer and fall in the woods. On closer examination, however, several differences emerge. *L. pyriforme* is found growing on well-rotted wood, especially stumps and logs lying on the ground and less often on rotting organic debris on the ground. The individual fruiting bodies are pear-shaped with a sterile base, as in *L. perlatum*, but tend to be more elongated and have only minute warts, almost granular in texture, across the surface. It is common to see thick white strands of mycelium called rhizomorphs trailing from the sterile base of this puffball when it is pulled from the ground. It is considered equally edible when collected in the young, firm, pure white stage and equally bitter if eaten when it's too mature.

There are a number of other less common puffballs. If you intend to expand your list of edible puffballs, identify the new type to species and, as with all new edibles, sample a small amount initially for desirability and safe eating.

POISONOUS LOOK-ALIKES

There is one group of easily distinguished puffballs that can cause problems if eaten. The genus *Scleroderma* ("hard-skinned") contains several common species that are quite distinctive in two ways. First, the outer skin of the fruiting body is thick and tough when fresh and leathery when dry, lending the common name "pigskin puffball" to at least one member of this group. The second is that the interior gleba of these puffballs is a dark gray to purple-black color from a very early (and firm) stage, making it unlikely that one would mistake it for the white flesh of an edible puffball. *Scleroderma* puffballs have been known to cause moderate to severe gastrointestinal distress.

Lycoperdon marginatum, sometimes called the peeling puffball due to its habit of sloughing off its studded skin in small sheets, is another species to avoid. Though generally reported as edible when young and firm, this species has been shown to contain hallucinogenic compounds and is reportedly used in Mexico as an intoxicant. There have been no complaints regarding people experiencing hallucinogenic episodes in the United States that I can find, though it has caused some incidences of gastrointestinal distress in the western states.

CAVEATS

It's important to pay attention to the interior of any puffball you intend to eat to ensure that the flesh is gleba and it's not an immature *Amanita* button. Amanita mushrooms start out as small rounded buttons at ground level, completely enclosed within a membrane skin called a universal veil. When they expand into the mature fruit, the veil ruptures, leaving behind remnants of a sac attached to the base of the mushroom or scars of the universal veil on the swollen stalk base and "warts" or patches of the veil tissue scattered across the cap. In the button stage, poisonous amanitas occasionally have been mistaken for puffballs. However, the longitudinal cross section of an amanita button will always show the outlines of the cap and stem, not the undifferentiated flesh of the puffball. Each year there are reports of unwary mycophiles eating immature amanitas mistaking them for puffballs, primarily in the western United States. Be aware and eat warily!

ECOLOGY, HABITAT, AND OCCURRENCE

Puffballs are primarily saprobes, feeding on partially rotted plant material from leaf and grass or on dead rotted wood. Some grow and fruit on disturbed, packed ground without an obvious food source. Most grow on well-rotted wood or in open grassy areas. At times, species such as *C. gigantea* form arcs or fairy rings of fruiting bodies.

EDIBILITY, PREPARATION, AND PRESERVATION

There is little consensus regarding the gastronomic merit of our gastromycetes. Gary Lincoff, in his *Audubon Guide to North American Mushrooms*, practically raves about puffballs, giving most a "Choice" rating.[11] Other mycophiles, including Michael Kuo, are lukewarm about eating puffballs, opining that they merely take on the flavor of the butter used for cooking.[12] After my initially excited stage of dining on puffballs as a young adult, I left them behind for most of twenty years as I expanded my repertoire of edible fungi to include more famous gems. I came to appreciate again the flavor of the giant puffball several years ago when I entered one in a public tasting of four common autumn mushrooms simply sautéed in olive oil with salt and pepper. When compared with the sulphur shelf, horse mushroom (*Agaricus arvensis*), and hen-of-the-woods (*Grifola frondosa*), the puffball stood proud. It brought home to me just how tasty puffballs can be. Butter flavor indeed!

~⊚∕∘

PUFFBALL PARMESAN

This is a variation on a recipe attributed to Hope Miller. This can be used with the giant puffball or with other medium-sized varieties.

1–2 pounds puffballs, sliced into ½-inch slices
2 eggs, beaten with 3 tablespoons milk
1 teaspoon salt
1–2 teaspoons freshly ground pepper
1 cup flour
¾ cup freshly grated Parmesan cheese (or mix of Parmesan and
   Romano)
¾ cup dry bread or good cracker crumbs
4–8 tablespoons butter or butter/olive oil mix

Use firm white puffballs. Clean the puffballs, cutting off the base and removing any soil. Some folks prefer to peel them; I don't. Slice into ½-inch rounds. Beat egg and milk in wide shallow bowl. Mix together flour, cheese, breadcrumbs, salt, and pepper in a second shallow bowl. Melt butter and add oil in a wide, shallow, thick-bottomed pan and heat until hot, but not smoking. Dip slices into egg mix and dredge in crumb/cheese mix. Fry puffball slices until well browned on both sides. Drain on paper towel and serve hot.

~⊚∕∘

SULPHUR SHELF OR CHICKEN MUSHROOM
Genus: *Laetiporus*

Species: *L. sulphureus*

Imagine walking through the woods in Maine in the early fall. Your senses are filled with the deep moistness and myriad shades of green and brown with gradations of reds, yellows, and light touches of blues and purples. In the midst of this palette, you come upon a large fruiting cluster of the sulphur shelf, or chicken mushroom. The brilliance of the bright orange and lemon yellow colors is visually over the top and can be seen from a great distance. (See #5 in the color insert.) There are few mushrooms able to compete with the sulphur shelf for sheer radiance and ebullience. With its large overlapping clusters gracing the side of a tree or on a downed log, it is eye-catching and pulse-quickening for those who know how tasty this mushroom can be.

Taxonomy

At one time, essentially all mushrooms having a leathery or woody texture and whose spores were generated from pore-like openings were classified in the genus *Polyporus*. As we learned more about mushroom taxonomy, various groups were split out of *Polyporus* and into separate genera and today there are scores of genera in the family *Polyporaceae*. The sulphur shelf was placed in the genus *Laetiporus*. Though Dr. Christensen treated the sulphur shelf as one entity, we now know that it consists of a complex of closely related species within the genus. The species in the sulfur shelf complex are found throughout North America and Europe and can grow on a wide range of tree hosts. In New England we find bright orange and yellow *L. sulphureus* growing on the wood of hardwood trees. *L. cincinnatus* is found growing in a rosette pattern on the ground at the base of hardwoods, usually oak. It has a whitish pore surface and a more pale orange-pink cap surface and is equally edible (some say superior) to the classic sulphur shelf.[13] *L. huroniensis* is a saprobe on overmature conifers, but this is somewhat rare in Maine and more common in southern New England and the northern Midwest. In the western United States, *L. conifericola* is generally found on conifer wood as the name implies. Finally, *L. gilbertsonii* generally is found growing on eucalyptus in the western United States.[14]

DESCRIPTION

The sulphur shelf is seen first emerging from the wood of a standing tree or downed log as a series of pale yellowish globules that develop orange tops with yellow edges and undersides over the following days. At this young stage the flesh is quite soft, tender, and juicy. It bruises easily and can exude copious amounts of a yellowish liquid. Over the course of several days to a week, the fruiting body develops into a set of overlapping shelf-like projections with thin and, at times wavy, margins. (#6) The top remains bright orange until faded by sunlight and age. The pore surface is sulfur yellow with 2–4 tiny pores per mm that become visible as the fruit matures. The spore color is white. On a large log or tree, clusters of fruiting shelves easily can total in excess of fifty pounds. As the fruit matures, it becomes increasingly tough and almost woody in texture, though the growing margins of the individual shelves often remain tender.

CAVEATS

An important note of caution! Over the years, there have been a few people who react to the sulphur shelf with moderate gastrointestinal distress, and occasional reports of numb lips and tingling tongues. When you eat this mushroom for the first time, eat a small portion and see how you tolerate it. I have seen an estimate that up to 10 percent of people cannot tolerate the sulphur shelf. This seems way too high a number when compared with my observations over the years and the documented reports in the literature. However, I personally know several people who are unable to tolerate it. The reason for the reactions has been discussed by many and is understood by few or none. Certainly, it should always be thoroughly cooked before eating, as sulphur shelf contains a toxin neutralized by cooking, and undercooked or raw mushrooms will sicken people. There are those who believe that those related species growing on conifers, such as L. *huroniensis* and L. *conifericola*, will cause GI distress and should be avoided. Others, especially on the West Coast, believe that the mushrooms fruiting on eucalyptus confer toxicity. Still others will place the blame on individuals eating specimens that are too old and tough. Perhaps as the mushroom-eating public develops a better understanding of the differences among species, the cause of sulphur shelf toxicity may become clearer. Until then, enjoy this mushroom in a young stage, collected off hardwood trees, cooked well, and, if it is your first time, try a small portion to confirm that it is a mushroom friendly to your chemistry.

Ecology, Habitat, and Occurrence

The sulphur shelf is a weak parasite on living trees and a vigorous saprobe on dead wood. Its mycelium colonizes the heartwood of a mature living tree through a wound and can live and fruit for many years without causing noticeably reduced vigor to its host. As it grows and colonizes the tree, the mycelia rot the heartwood, feeding on the cellulose of the wood and vastly weakening the main roots, the trunk, or both. Once a tree or branch dies and falls to the ground, the mushroom will continue to flourish, fruiting for a number of years on a large log and eventually reducing it to crumbling remains. I recently photographed a luminously beautiful cluster gracing the top of a red oak log. The mushroom has been fruiting on the same length of downed oak in June for more than twenty years, slowly fruiting further out from the butt end of the tree as the fungus consumed the nutrients in the wood.

The sulphur shelf is able to grow on a wide variety of trees, though in New England it is most common on oak, ash, and cherry. It can be found fruiting on living trees or dead wood and occasionally can be found fruiting on the ground where there is buried wood or roots (see *L. cincinnatus* above). This species will fruit throughout much of the summer and fall beginning in June and continuing through October with a tendency to peak in early autumn if the rain cooperates. Though the fruiting bodies will recur on the same tree for many years, it is unusual for fruit to be produced every year. In Maine I have observed that a sulphur shelf tree will fruit every two to three years on average, more often on oak and less often on ash.

Edibility, Preparation, and Preservation

With the combination of bright orange top and yellow pore surface, this fungus cannot easily be mistaken for another mushroom. It is considered to be a good edible and enjoyed by most mushroom hunters, including me. These are the two principal reasons Dr. Christensen had for including the sulphur shelf in his list of foolproof edibles. The firm flesh, bright colors, and good flavor make it an attractive staple in many mushroom dishes. The bright colors are not affected by cooking, so this fungus adds flavor and color to soups, omelets, stir-fries, and sauces. The texture of the chicken mushroom is firm and holds up well in simmered sauces, soups, and dishes.

~⊙∕○

CHICKEN MUSHROOM STIR-FRY

Because of its firm texture and beautiful color, this fungus lends itself to a stir-fry. The color remains with cooking and brightens any mixture of meat and veggies used. Though this is written as a vegetarian recipe, it can be adapted easily to chicken or another meat. If using meat, add it with the oil and ginger and quickly cook through. Remove before adding veggies and return it when the sauce is added.

Vegetables:
(Use these or be creative with your combination of fresh veggies.)
1–2 medium-size carrots, sliced ⅛ inch
1–2 cups baby bok choy or other Chinese cabbage chopped into
  bite-size pieces
1 red pepper, cut into bite-size pieces
2 cups chicken mushroom sliced into ¼-inch, bite-sized pieces
1 cup onions, cut into bite size (I like sweet onions for this dish.)
1 head broccoli, cut into florets
20–30 snow pea pods
1 thumb-size piece of ginger, julienne-sliced into matchstick-like
  pieces
3 tablespoons white wine (or stock) for stir-frying
1 tablespoon peanut oil for frying

Stir-fry sauce:
⅓ cup stock (vegetarian or chicken stock)
2 tablespoons fish sauce (or soy sauce)
1 tablespoon lime or lemon juice
6–8 cloves of garlic, minced
1 teaspoon honey (or brown sugar)
2 teaspoon cornstarch dissolved in 4 tablespoons water
1 teaspoon red chili flakes OR 1 teaspoon chili sauce OR
  ½ teaspoon cayenne pepper
1 teaspoon sesame oil (optional)

Start the sauce in a small, heavy saucepan by placing all ingredients except cornstarch and sesame oil over heat. Allow to boil gently for about 5 minutes and then reduce heat, add cornstarch, and stir till sauce thickens (should take 30–45 seconds at most).

For the stir-fry, make certain all your ingredients are prepped and ready before starting; things move swiftly. Make sure you are constantly in attendance to keep your ingredients moving in the pan.

Heat a wok or heavy, high-sided frying pan over medium-high heat and add peanut oil, ginger, and the carrots and cook for 2–3 minutes before adding mushrooms and allowing to cook for another minute.

Add a little wine as needed to keep the ingredients from drying out.

Add the rest of the veggies and ⅓ of the sauce and continue cooking for 2–3 minutes. (If using chicken or shrimp, add the mostly cooked meat back in at this point). Broccoli should be softened somewhat but still firm and bright green.

Add the rest of the sauce and correct for taste.

Serve over your favorite type of rice.

SHAGGY MANE, AKA LAWYER'S WIG
Genus: *Coprinus*
Species: *C. comatus*

The shaggy mane welcomes in the autumn weather in the same way that morels are a harbinger of spring. This bullet-headed mushroom is a common resident in suburban and rural landscapes and pops up from disturbed open ground around the time you start searching under the car seat for the window scraper the morning you greet that first heavy frost. (See #4 in the color insert.) It is a heartwarming sight to see a lawn or field with dozens of these benign whitish missiles protruding through the grass. The shaggy mane's reputation as an easily identified, safe edible without problematic look-alikes remains unsullied in the new millennium. Yet, in my experience, shaggy manes are the least frequently eaten of the Foolproof Four.

TAXONOMY

Taxonomists have not been as gentle with the organization of this group as mycophagists have been with their edibility. The genus *Coprinus* has undergone a complete overhaul following recent molecular analysis of the family of meadow mushroom fame. The shaggy mane, the originally described species of the genus, remains a species of *Coprinus* but with only three others. The remaining 160 or so species have been divided among three other genera based on molecular and morphological analysis. If you are interested in more details about *Coprinus* taxonomy, consider seeking out the work of Scott Redhead[15] or refer to the papers listed on Tom Volk's page on shaggy manes.[16]

DESCRIPTION

Shaggy manes have a distinctive cylindrical or bullet shape that stands out in the open areas where they occur. The bodies are typically 4 to 8 inches high (but occasionally much taller), and no more than 2 inches wide. The cap is white with a pale brown apex and covered with coarse brown-tipped scales, giving it its common name. When the mushroom is young, the cap almost completely covers the stalk that reaches down through the grass duff to anchor in the ground. With age, the pure white, hollow stalk, several inches longer than the cap, becomes more visible along with a fleshy movable annular ring that soon disappears.

The gills of the shaggy mane are completely covered by the young cap as it hugs the stalk. They are densely packed and initially pure white, though with age they begin to turn pink and then rapidly darken to black as, from bottom to top, they melt into an inky liquid mass of spores. This is known as deliquescing, a process in which the cells of the cap self-digest as a method of aiding spore release. The gills "melt" beginning at the base of the cap and, as the spores are released, the gill tissue turns into a watery mass and exposes the tissue above to the air for spore release. In the process, many of the spores become a part of the inky mess that gives this genus its common name, "inky caps." In days long past, this black mushroom spore goo was used as writing ink and proved to be quite durable.

ECOLOGY, HABITAT, AND OCCURRENCE

Shaggy manes are saprobes that grow on buried wood or in soil that is rich in partially decomposed vegetable matter. You will find them fruiting just before and after the first frosts of autumn. Occasionally they also fruit lightly in the spring but cannot be counted on. Look for them on recently disturbed or "made" ground where earth moving, landscaping, lawn creation, or logging has resulted in buried wood, dead roots, or other forms of buried organic matter. Shaggy manes can grow singly, but are more commonly found fruiting in trooping numbers clustered or scattered over open ground in lawns, fields, roadsides, or waste ground. At times they fruit in great profusion in a small area and the lucky passing mycophagist can leisurely pick only the cleanest young, firm fruit.

A few years ago, the owners of a large seaside estate that was, unfortunately, located close to a highway decided to redouble their privacy by building a 6-foot-high berm of earth that they then planted in rugosa roses and evergreen shrubs. The berm was made up of a mixture of soil transported in for the job mixed with soil pushed up from the land beyond, and was therefore a jumble of soil and plant material. A year later and for the two following seasons, shaggy manes appeared in huge clusters of scores of mushrooms as the fungus took advantage of the mass of easily available dead organic matter. In a manner typical of this species, the third year there were a few and this past year I saw none, as the task of breaking down the easily available duff was complete.

EDIBILITY, PREPARATION, AND PRESERVATION

Once you have found the bounty and picked the crop, all pretenses of leisure ends since you must cook or freeze your prize within a day or you will be left with an inky mess. Picking these mushrooms only seems to increase the speed of decay, and refrigeration does little to slow the breakdown process. Cooking stops the process of "inkinization" and sautéed mushrooms can be kept refrigerated for several days or frozen for later use.

Shaggy manes, like all edible inky caps, are best picked and eaten when they are young and firm. If they have begun to darken, the mature tissue can be cut off, but only the pure white caps and stems are fit to eat. I have, however, known people who actively encourage the breakdown and use the resulting ink to make a land-based "squid ink" pasta. Shaggys are best cooked lightly in butter or light olive oil and enjoyed simply with salt and pepper. They have a distinct, full, and pleasant flavor and are also a great addition to a cream soup. To preserve for future use, lightly sauté the caps and freeze them in individual portions in zip-lock bags or small containers. Do not even think of trying to dry these mushrooms unless you pick them quite young and can use a hot-air dryer!

~◎~

SHAGGY MANE POTATO LEEK SOUP

The first time I made this easy soup and served it to friends almost guaranteed I'd make it again. They haven't stopped asking for the next chance to enjoy it. This recipe also can be used with other mushrooms and adapts well to horse or meadow mushrooms.

1 pound fresh shaggy manes (more or less), cleaned and chopped coarsely

1 large leek or 2 smaller (use white and pale green portions), sliced into rings

3–5 medium potatoes

1 cup chicken stock

1 cup heavy cream

½ cup dry white wine

2 tablespoons butter or mixed with olive oil

Salt and freshly ground pepper to taste

2 cups water

Fresh dill for garnish (optional)

Peel (optional) and quarter potatoes. Add to soup pot and just cover with the water. Boil moderately until quite tender, 20–30 minutes.

Remove dark green leek leaves and roots. Slice lengthwise and rinse under cold water to remove all grit trapped between layers. Slice leeks crosswise into half rings. Heat medium pan over a medium flame. Add butter/oil and cook leeks gently for about 7–10 minutes, making sure they do not dry out. Add a few dashes of wine or stock at a time to keep moist.

When the leeks are nearly done, add the mushrooms and a generous grind of pepper and sauté for 5 minutes. Add wine and chicken stock and stir until blended.

When potatoes are tender, remove from heat and blend both potatoes and mushroom leek mixture in a food processor until smooth. Use as much of the potato water as needed to maintain a somewhat thickened consistency. Return to pot.

Simmer very gently, stirring occasionally to avoid scorching. When almost boiling, add cream and salt and pepper to taste. Heat gently but do not boil.

In a world that is constantly changing, the relative endurance of the Foolproof Four is heartening, but it is also telling because, of course, even they are not entirely foolproof. People often ask me questions designed to confirm their assumptions about the edibility of a mushroom. The typical question is, "Aren't all _____ mushrooms edible?" People who have known me for a long time recognize my frozen pause as I decide on the most appropriate way to burst the questioner's bubble. Making decisions on the edibility of a mushroom can be made only one species, even one mushroom, at a time, based on certainty of both the identification and edibility of the mushroom. Even in a list of four safe mushrooms—a list that has endured for more than sixty-five years—two of the mushrooms are known to occasionally disrupt the fragile gastrointestinal equilibrium of some people who eat them, and our understanding of all of them has undergone significant revisions since Christensen first presented the world with his list. Any list of foolproof mushrooms must carry with it a caveat and the reality of individual vulnerabilities and, therefore, is never completely foolproof.

I occasionally think about developing a Foolproof Four list for Maine, or a Triumphant Three, or Fantastic Five, or a Sumptuous Six. The mushrooms would be different, but the concept remains the same. There is value in shining a light on a select group of mushrooms, easily identified, commonly occurring, and safely edible. For the novice mushroomer, such a list is one part of a roadmap into the new territory of mycophagy, where the initial exploration always brings anxiety and perceived peril along with the excitement. In the following pages I describe a few great wild mushrooms that would be apt candidates for foolproof list in Maine, the Northeast, and many other temperate locales.

~) 4 C~

CHANTERELLES

Aurum et argentums facile est,
Lenamque tonamque mittere;
Boletos mittere difficile est.

It is possible to live without gold and silver,
and one can resist the temptations of seductive women,
but to abstain from eating mushrooms is difficult.
MARTIAL (43–104 AD)

There are certain diverse pleasures that mark summer in New England. The Fourth of July parade with sirens, banners, bands blaring, and sunburned toddlers scrambling for candy tossed from passing floats is, to some, a signal of the formal shift from late spring to full summer. For others, the first raking of Maine blueberries in early August ushers in the midpoint of the season when we no longer need to explore the depths of the freezer for berries to make a pie or cobbler. For those of a fungal bent, summer's true arrival cannot be acknowledged until the first chanterelles poke warm golden caps from beneath their leafy covers. Of course, being mushrooms, with all the predictability of a Siamese cat, the date on which summer arrives in the guise of my first chanterelle omelet can vary a fair bit from year to year, strongly dependent upon the vagaries of weather. Here on the coast of Maine we can generally count on the first harvest by the second week in July, after the strawberries and before the first blueberries.

There are undoubtedly many reasons why chanterelles are at the top of the mushroom heap in popularity, but chief among them is their great flavor. Other reasons are their relatively common occurrence in Maine's woods and the ease of identification. The combination of vase shape, bright golden coloration, and blunted ridges in place of knife-like gills make chanterelles distinctive and easily discerned. The bright color and their habit of growing in scattered clusters make them easy to spot on the forest floor. When I am walking through a forest looking for chanterelles, my eyes scan the woods in an arc of perhaps thirty yards, knowing that their bright coloration will shine out through the predominate greens and browns of the forest floor like stars in the black heavens. Once I spot the first mushroom, I slow my pace and examine the area around the first mushroom, carefully looking for other chanterelles. Since they fruit in groups, I often find others partially hidden in the leaves nearby. Contrast this searching style with morel hunting; there is a world of difference. Morels come into the world with all the camouflage of a motionless cottontail rabbit in the leaves. It almost requires that you feel one get crushed under your bare feet before your eyes can take it in. Even after spotting the first morel in an area, it requires careful, slow examination to see the others secreted in the nearby duff.

A third reason for chanterelles' popularity as an edible is their predictability. They regularly fruit in the same location in successive years. In a good chanterelle habitat, I know which tree to check in the forest and which side of the tree to examine in order to find the same patch of chanterelles I have collected there a dozen times over the past twenty years. This personal observation mirrors the results of a long-term study on the impact of chanterelle harvesting carried out in a coastal forest by the Oregon Mycological Society. They also have recorded regular fruiting of the Pacific golden chanterelle in the same small area over many successive years.[1]

TAXONOMY

The name chanterelle generally refers to the mushroom known as the golden chanterelle (*Cantharellus cibarius*; #7 in the color insert), but also is applied to the genus *Cantharellus* and the whole family of mushrooms collectively known as "chanterelles and their allies." This includes the genus *Craterellus*, home of the famous black trumpet mushroom in addition to several other notable edibles, and the genus *Gomphus*, home to the aptly named pigs ears (*G. clavatus*) and scaly vase chanterelle (*G. floccosus*). The final member of the chanterelle allies is the uncommon blue chanterelle (*Polyozellus multiplex*), a beautiful and fascinating mushroom of the northern fir forests. The best known and talked about are members of the *Cantharellus* and *Craterellus* genera, in part because almost all of the prominent edibles are here. With DNA research bringing into question taxonomy that has long held fast, the two main groupings of the chanterelles have been divided along lines that, fortunately, are primarily visible to any naked eye. Those mushrooms with a hollow stem are included in *Craterellus*. Those mushrooms that are vase shaped and solid are in *Cantharellus*.

Chanterelles are found worldwide, wherever the habitat supports tree species that form mycorrhizal relationships with fungi. Various species of chanterelles and craterelles are collected and widely eaten by people on all the world's major land masses except Antarctica and Greenland. There are about forty named species in North America and around ninety species of the two genera worldwide.[2] A more exact number would be dependent on a whole lot of learned and very opinionated taxonomists coming to agreement on what will define a distinct species within this cosmopolitan group. I, for one, will not be holding my breath waiting for consensus from a group of taxonomists.

The most prominent chanterelle in Europe and central and eastern North America is the golden chanterelle, *Cantharellus cibarius*. *Cantharellus* is a name derived from the Greek *kantharos*, meaning goblet or drinking cup, and refers to the funnel or vase shape of the fruiting body of members of this family.[3] The specific epithet *cibarius* is Latin for edible.

On the west coast of North America, the Pacific golden chanterelle, *Cantharellus formosus*, reigns supreme. Formerly lumped in with *C. cibarius*, it is now recognized as a separate species. Both are considered equally desirable and are nearly indistinguishable as they approach the sauté pan except that the Pacific variety lacks a distinct odor. When people in the United States speak informally of chanterelles, they are generally referring to one of these two species. In their comprehensive and detailed monograph on chanterelles, David Pilz et al.[4] included a table of some eighty-nine different common names in seventeen languages used for the golden chanterelles around the world. This wide recognition is a reflection of the high regard for the edible nature of this mushroom.

In the recent survey I sent out to gather information regarding the wild mushrooms collected, eaten, and most favored, the golden chanterelle was, by far, the most preferred edible mushroom. This held true for all levels of mushrooming experience, from beginner to seasoned. I talk about mushrooming with many people who attend the walks and talks I offer. For a significant majority, the reason they give for attending is to expand the varieties of mushrooms they know and are comfortable eating. If they collect and eat only one mushroom in Maine, it is generally the chanterelle.

DESCRIPTION

Chanterelles have several distinct characteristics that set them apart from other similar mushrooms. The first is the vase shape to the mushroom. Unlike the traditional mushroom with a thin long stem supporting a broad hamburger bun-shaped cap, chanterelles start with a stem that is narrow at the base and immediately flares out to the rim of the cap where, in a mature body, a depressed center gives the impression of a shallow drinking cup. (#7) There is little distinction between stem and cap as the blunted gills run down the stem. The rim of the cap is often regular and somewhat enrolled in a young mushroom and irregularly undulated or wavy in a mature cap. The second feature is the spore-bearing surface, known as the hymenium. In a "traditional" mushroom it would be composed of a series of closely arranged knife-like plates called gills. Chanterelles have what are described as rudimentary gills or blunted folds that run up the stem and then fork, often dividing into two as they climb the stem. The third area of distinction is the chanterelle color. Common names from around the world often refer to the color by comparing the mushroom to other yellow to golden-colored creatures in nature—egg yolks, chicks, or chickens. The color is not a true yellow, but a rich golden yellow, darker in older specimens or ones in greater light and paler in young and deeply shaded mushrooms. The last area of distinction is the aroma. I almost always smell a mushroom when I pick it, a habit so reflexive as to be almost unconscious. The rich apricot odor of the chanterelle amply rewards this habit; it is a smell that no other mushroom attains. The golden chanterelle typically grows to 3 inches wide, though occasionally much larger specimens are seen in ideal habitat. The height of a mature chanterelle is about one and a half times its width.

OTHER CHANTERELLES AND LOOK-ALIKES

Though the golden chanterelles are by far the best-known mushroom in this group, there are a number of other, generally smaller, eastern chanterelles that bear mention. There are no toxic members in the *Cantharellus* or *Craterellus* genera. The related *Gomphus flocosus*, scaly vase chanterelle or wooly chanterelle, causes gastric distress in some who have eaten it, though others eat this species with relish.

The winter chanterelle, *Cr. tubaeformis*, is very popular in northern Europe and is gaining in popularity with those Americans who have tried it. The small size of this species is partially made up for by its habit of growing in fairly dense troops. We find it predominantly in association with hemlocks from late summer through late fall.

The smooth chanterelle, *C. lateritius*, is common in southern New England and the mid-Atlantic region. It looks very like the golden chanterelle but without the blunted gills. Its hymenium surface is smooth to only slightly ridged. The choice flavor is little different from that of the golden chanterelle.

Cr. ignicolor and Cr. lutescens are two close look-alike small yellowish funneled chanterelles found, at times, in large trooping numbers warranting their mention here and in the collection basket for dinner. They often are called the yellow foot chanterelles.

CAVEATS

The jack o'lantern mushroom, *Omphalotus illudens* (see #8 in the color insert), is a somewhat vase-shaped bright orange mushroom found growing in dense clusters on the ground at the base of a tree or from buried wood. Beware! This toxic mushroom has been mistaken for a chanterelle by careless novice mushroomers. When eaten, it causes 12–24 hours of intense gastrointestinal distress. Differentiate it from chanterelles by the growing habitat of dense clustering and the fact that it has true, knife-edged gills that do not fork. (See more in Chapter 7.)

ECOLOGY, HABITAT, AND OCCURRENCE

The fortuitous fact that chanterelles appear in the same small area in successive years says a great deal about their lifestyle. Chanterelles are mycorrhizal fungi living in symbiotic relationship with trees, and more specifically with the roots of trees. This stable, long-term relationship is of benefit to both fungus and tree and helps to explain the consistency of fruiting. In New England we see them commonly in association with pine, spruce, and hemlock as well as the hardwood species of birch, oak, and beech. In a wet year, they sometimes fruit heavily under white pine. Though not able to support fruiting in an extremely dry year, the mycelium of the fungus lives on with the tree roots and sets fruit in the next wet season. Contrast this with a true saprobe such as the shaggy mane (*Coprinus comatus*) that might fruit heavily in an area for a year or two, but once the available food source is broken down by the fungus, the mycelium dies out and the hapless hunter is forced to find a new location for the main ingredient in shaggy soup.

For the past twenty years there has been an active debate regarding the best and most ecologically sound manner in which to harvest mushrooms. Is it better to pluck them from the forest duff or to carefully cut the stem, leaving the base still attached to the mycelium? In the study mentioned earlier regarding the long-term growth patterns of chanterelles in Oregon forests, after thirteen years the study did not find any decline in annual production of fruiting bodies on plots where the mushrooms were "plucked" from the ground when compared to an adjacent control plot where they were not harvested. The researchers did note a very slight decline in future mushroom production where chanterelles were cut at the base with a knife as a method of harvest.[5]

The question remains regarding the possible impact of over-harvesting contributing to a decline in chanterelle production in our forests. This debate has, at its root, the observed reduction in chanterelle production from forests in industrialized areas of Europe. This decline, reported since the 1980s, has likely been in place much longer. The causes of the diminished chanterelle harvest have not been proven, but several strong positions have received most of the attention. The first is the contribution of acid rain on the growth of mycorrhizal fungi. The second is the increased levels of nitrogen in the atmosphere and increased use of nitrogenous fertilizers on forests. In controlled studies, trees grown with additional fertilizer tend to reject their mycorrhizal partners because they no longer require the contribution of extra nutrients, so there's no reason for the trees to share their food pantry. One question remaining is what effect, if any, does an annual heavy harvest of the mushrooms have on long-term mushroom production? At this point the studies looking at this have shown no significant decline in mushroom production from regular harvesting of mushrooms. The removal of fruiting bodies does not diminish the refruiting in following years, and the reduction in spores released by mushrooms has not been shown to reduce continued fruiting. A study about to be published demonstrates that the vast majority of spores released by a mushroom fall within a few feet of the parent. The act of collecting and carrying mushrooms out of the forest in an open basket while they are dropping spores may vastly improve spore dispersal. A key factor in the future fruiting of mycorrhizal mushrooms seems to be the practice of minimal disturbance to the forest floor by avoiding packing down the soil surface or disturbing the duff layer when collecting mushrooms.

Look for your first chanterelles of the season as summer settles in to stay. In the northeastern United States that means generally by early July; earlier in southern interior sections; and later along the cooler downeast coast, up north, and in the higher elevations. There seems to be a positive correlation between a warm wet spring and a good chanterelle crop, though this is also contingent on the rainfall patterns in the summer. The peak of the season is in mid-August, and they will continue to fruit abundantly in good (meaning rainy) weather until mid-September and occasionally later. The golden chanterelle is a slow-growing, slow-maturing fruiting body. From the onset of a tiny button until the mature cap succumbs to rot may take well in excess of thirty days. One study showed an average life of the fruiting body of forty-five days with some living in excess of ninety days in cool moist weather.[6] Unlike the mega-dump of spores released in a few days as seen in most fleshy mushrooms, chanterelles mature spores slowly in successive layers over a longer period of time. Therefore, if you come upon a cluster of small buttons, leave them in place and return in a few days or a week to collect them in a more mature state. Fortunately, our chanterelles are somewhat resistant to insect invasion. I rarely see chanterelles infested with worms unless they are quite old and even then they are hardly ever riddled. Unfortunately, the same cannot be said of the abundant slugs that delight in finding the chanterelles a day ahead of me.

Chanterelles typically appear singly, loosely grouped, or scattered across an area of forest floor. Occasionally you will see them growing in small clusters, and in good habitat I also find them growing along a line or arc through the forest for several yards, perhaps following a tree root. In 2007, I came upon a 15-foot sweeping arc of closely spaced golden beauties. There were almost eighty mushrooms in that small arc. Compare this with the toxic jack o'lantern mushroom, a chanterelle look-alike, which grows in large dense clusters from a common base off of buried wood.

EDIBILITY, PREPARATION, AND PRESERVATION

Thoughts of the first breakfast of chanterelles begin just after I have eaten my last spring-collected morel. When the first russulas are out and the early amanitas are fruiting, I know the chanterelles are not far behind. Chanterelles are worth waiting for. Their bright golden color in a good split ash basket can be excelled only by their heady aroma when you place your face close into the basket. A basket of chanterelles evokes the scent of an equal weight of fresh picked apricots. For me they recall the sinful pleasure of jumping the fence as a child to raid the apricot tree in the neighbor's yard in Albuquerque, New Mexico, and to smell the sun-warmed fruit as I took the first bite.

Chanterelles have a delicate flavor, and shine when they are blended with food and spices that respect their understated character. Simple preparations are the order of the day: scrambled eggs or omelets, cream sauces, or dishes as simple as a basic sauté with butter, salt, and pepper. Begin by wiping away any lingering dirt and debris from the trimmed mushrooms using a brush or a dry or slightly moist towel. Never wash them under running water or soak your chanterelles! They have a tendency to take on water easily. I generally slice all but the smallest of the caps, though the size will depend on the dish to be made. Young caps are the most tender and they get slightly tough as they age. Unless they appear quite dry, I often start with a dry sauté in a pan over medium heat with a touch of salt. Heating the mushrooms will cause them to express their water and further cooking allows the moisture to evaporate. Add butter when most of the moisture is gone and sauté for 5 or so minutes, adding salt and pepper as desired. This is the starting point for almost any recipe and a fitting endpoint for a simple preparation. The flavorful components of the chanterelle are fat soluble, so the step of simmering in butter is vital to release and preserve the flavors. The alcohol in wine will release other subtle flavors. From there add simple herbs such as tarragon or cilantro, cream, and mild cheeses.

Chanterelles make excellent soufflés or quiche. If you use onion or garlic with them, use a light hand so as to not overpower the mushrooms. I sometimes combine chanterelles with other delicately flavored mushrooms. My favorite combination is with the sweet tooth, *Hydnum repandum*, with its light flavor and a distinctive, almost crunchy texture. The chanterelle is one mushroom that will not stand up to a tomato-based sauce.

If you face the enviable prospect of being overrun with excess chanterelles, resist any impulse to dehydrate them for future use. I often see dried specimens devoid of color, aroma, and character in gourmet foot stores. It is a sad and wasteful use of a scarce resource! Everything that makes this mushroom memorable is lost in the drying process. Instead, consider a light sauté in plenty of butter followed by sealing serving-size portions in freezer bags before labeling and popping them into the freezer. They retain their essential goodness for several months and will bring back warm memories of summer well into winter.

Chanterelles are about summer and recognizing the gifts of the season embodied in a strikingly beautiful fungal form. One of these gifts comes through the activity involved in the gathering of the mushrooms. A trip to the forest to immerse yourself in the cool, shaded woods will calm your mind and is just the therapy needed for the summertime rush. Chanterelles are not to be collected in haste, while dashing between meetings. Walk the dog, bring a friend and a picnic, and revel in the process. One of my favorite summertime collection sites is alongside a lake with granite ledges. I bring a suit and dive in when I get too hot. Once home with your catch, the process of preparation for the table need not take tedious hours. Chanterelles lend themselves to quick, light, summertime meals. A glass of wine, a chanterelle omelet, and—well, you provide the rest.

THE PERFECT CHANTERELLE OMELET

Chanterelles are to eggs what basil is to tomatoes; a pairing made by a generous and gastronomic God. For an omelet, there is no need to get too fancy with other additions—keep it simple and enjoy the blend.

1–2 cups fresh chanterelles, cleaned and sliced somewhat thinly
1–2 tablespoons butter
4 large eggs at room temperature beaten with the water
1 tablespoon water
Salt and freshly ground pepper to taste
½ cup of a mild-flavored cheese, sliced or grated
Chopped parsley as a garnish

In a shallow sauté pan or omelet pan with medium heat, melt the butter and add the sliced chanterelles with a little salt. Chanterelles can hold a large volume of liquid, so if they seem very moist, I often start with a dry sauté in the hot pan and add butter as the moisture is evaporated. Either way, the mushrooms will begin to release their water as they cook, and you want this to evaporate off. When they are done, remove the mushrooms to a dish and return the pan to the medium-low fire. Add additional butter if needed to coat the pan and pour in the eggs. Keep the heat low enough to cook the eggs slowly without scorching and as they firm, add back in the warm chanterelles and the cheese and a coloring of parsley. Fold over and give it enough time to melt the cheese and ensure that the eggs are fully firm.

CHANTERELLES AND CHICKEN IN CREAM SAUCE OVER FETTUCCINI

Because their flavor elements are largely fat soluble, chanterelles shine with cream sauces. Their understated flavor is also well suited to chicken. Putting the three elements together makes a very tasty and satisfying meal.

1 pound boneless chicken, in large bite-sized pieces
1 pound fresh chanterelles
1–2 tablespoons olive oil
¾ cup finely diced yellow onion or shallot
3 cloves garlic, minced (optional)
1 cup chicken stock, or ½ cup stock and ½ cup white wine
1 cup cream
Sea salt and freshly ground pepper
1 pound fettuccini
1 cup grated Parmesan or Romano cheese

Start with boneless chicken or bone out the meat yourself, saving the remains for great stock. I prefer thighs because they are more flavorful and tender than breast meat. Heat a large shallow pan with 1 tablespoon of the oil and brown the chicken on high, working in batches if needed. Once well browned, remove the chicken from the pan and save nearby.

Using the same pan (don't clean it out), add oil if needed and sauté the onions and garlic, if you choose, over medium heat. Once the onions are translucent, add the chanterelles and sauté until dry.

Return the chicken to the pan and add the stock, and allow the dish to simmer a minute before adding the cream.

Balance the flavors with salt and pepper and serve immediately over cooked and drained fettuccini with cheese as a garnish.

ECONOMIC VALUE

As mentioned earlier, chanterelles are valued as food throughout the world. In our global marketplace, wild mushrooms make a significant contribution to the commodity market. The demand for the highly desired, non-cultivatable edibles such as porcini, chanterelles, truffles, and morels in major cities around Europe, Asia, and the United States has created a market estimated at more than $12 billion per year for fresh and dried wild mushrooms. Into this vacuum have come the traders to fill the demand. This has resulted in the movement of wild mushrooms from rural communities into the cities, from impoverished third world countries into the developed countries of Europe, North America, and Asia, and from the Southern Hemisphere into the North. In some rural communities of Africa, Asia, and South America, the income generated from the collection and sale of wild mushrooms contributes a significant percentage of the total annual income for many families. The major importers of chanterelles are Germany and France, with other European countries also interested in the tasty golden mushroom. The largest suppliers of mushrooms to the European market are the Eastern and Baltic countries that comprise the former USSR, including Poland, Romania, Lithuania, Bulgaria, Russia, and Ukraine. In 1998, these regions accounted for more than 80 percent of the total European Union imports of chanterelles, some 28 million pounds of fresh mushrooms. The newest members of the export trade include some African countries such as Tanzania and Zimbabwe. There has been a suggestion that Pakistani villagers could bring in more income by taking advantage of the plentiful chanterelle crop in the mountain forests to develop an export trade to supplement the current trade in dried morels from the region.[7] This could have special significance at a time when there is increased pressure on available farm land.

In the United States and Canada, trade in chanterelles has become a significant part of what is now termed "non-timber resources" derived from our forests and is recognized as a major source of revenue for people in areas affected by the decline in the timber industry. As a result of environmental concerns, timber harvesting on public lands in some regions has been reduced, and many communities supported primarily by the timber industry have had to look for other sources of income. In these areas, some residents can make a significant portion of their income during the mushroom season. The heavily forested regions of the northwest United States, British Columbia, and Alaska constitute the epicenter of commercial mushrooming activity in North America due to the millions of acres of forest and a climate strongly conducive to mushroom growth.[8] It is estimated that in 1992, 515 metric tons of chanterelles were harvested from the forests of Oregon, Washington, and Idaho. The largest share of these went to the markets of Europe and Asia but 30 percent were used within the United States.[9] Wholesale buyers paid an average of $3.00 per pound to pickers, totaling 3.5 million dollars in income for mushroom hunters almost solely from chanterelles.

When you add up their cosmopolitan distribution, universal ease of recognition, excellent taste, and economic value, it is no surprise that chanterelles consistently make the high end of a list of best edible mushrooms. The novice mycophagist must sample chanterelles in order to establish a benchmark for all other mushrooms to follow.

∽ 5 ⌒

BOLETUS EDULIS

Ancient tradition has it that should you ever chance upon a lone Cep,
you should ask it quietly, "Where is your brother?"
since they invariably grow in pairs.
<small>CROATIAN TRADITIONAL SAYING</small>

*A*ny list of the world's most prized and desired edible wild mushrooms
would have *Boletus edulis* at the top along with morels, chanterelles,
and truffles. (I include truffles as a nod to their legendary mystique, but the
other three are more widely sought, collected, and eaten in most of the world
by many different cultures and peoples.) Like the chanterelle, *Boletus edulis*
has many different common names. In the United States, it is called the king
bolete, but even in America it is more often referred to by the Italian *porcini*
(little pig), a reference to the characteristic appearance of the young mushroom with a swollen fat stem and smaller cap nestled to the ground (see #9
and #10 in the color insert). For simplicity's sake, I will refer to it here as
porcini.

The porcini is a member of the boletes, fleshy basidiomycete mushrooms
that have a classic rounded cap on a central stalk and spores that mature in a
dense collection of sponge-like tubes (or pores) on the underside of the cap
where gills would be in many other mushrooms. In *North American Boletes*,
Alan Bessette, Bill Roody, and Arlene Bessette cover eighteen genera and
hundreds of species,[1] though they don't even come close to the 600 species
addressed in detail by Ernst Both in his 1993 compendium on the group.[2]
Though any beginning mushroomer can tell a bolete from a gilled mushroom, people have spent their lives learning all the mushrooms in this group.
B. edulis was the first described species and remains the type species of the
genus *Boletus*. This stout-stemmed, solid soldier is certainly the best-known
and most recognizable member of the boletes and, for many mushroom
enthusiasts, the species is synonymous with the whole group. The specific
epithet *edulis* translates as yummy.

To say that porcini is a prized edible is a bit like saying that Mozart is a really good composer; it gives you the basic information, but it belittles the reverence and encompassing passion that both inspire in their devotees. Nowhere is the passion for porcini more concentrated than in the mycophilic countries of Europe. When the summer and fall rains come and people across the region take to the forests, they always hope that a portion of the basket will be filled with porcini. In the Slavic countries, people pickle and brine many species of *Russula*, *Lactarius*, and other boletes, but the porcini often are reserved for eating fresh, at least until the first lustful appetite is sated. They are roasted with meats, fried with onions and garlic, and even eaten raw, sliced thinly as a main ingredient of a mushroom salad. Porcini is equally valued as a dried mushroom, and any surplus is quickly processed for drying to bring its rich mushroom flavor into dishes throughout the year. Many people value the flavor-boosting benefits of the dried mushroom over the fresh and, for them, all of the collection basket heads into the dehydrator. Unless you collect your own porcini in the United States, you will need to rely on dried mushrooms. Fresh porcini have a short shelf life and are rarely available for retail sale in this country, while the dried ones, at a very rich price, are available in most fine food stores. If your dried porcini are not very expensive, it is probably because there are other dried boletes making up the bulk of the product. This is not terrible, since many species of boletes have fine flavor dried, but they may lack the depth of flavor of true porcini.

TAXONOMY

I often refer to the porcini mushrooms as a complex, which is a way of acknowledging that there exists, in a given region or a given genus, a cluster of closely related species that are very difficult to distinguish without special-ized knowledge or equipment or both. In most regions where it grows, porcini is represented by a complex of several look-alike boletes that grow in similar habitats and fruit in overlapping periods during the season. Most are edible and it would take someone with a more refined palate than mine to distin-guish them on the basis of taste or texture. Mycophiles around the world, in Poland, Italy, and France to name a few examples, argue vehemently that the porcini look-alikes found in their region are superior to others. In the northeast United States, *B. chippewaensis*, *B. clavipes*, *B. variipes*, *B. pinophilus*, and *B. nobilis* are relatively common species that might be included in the porcini

A Sample of Common Names for
Boletus edulis from Around the World

Boletus, from Latin *boletus*;
derived from Greek *bolos* for clod or lump

Porcini (little pig) . . . . Italy
Cep (trunk) . . . . France
Penny bun . . . . England
King bolete . . . . United States
Steinpilz (stone mushroom) . . . . Germany
Borovik (forest mushroom) . . . . Russia
Beliy grib (white mushroom) . . . . Russia
Herrenpilz (gentlemen's mushroom) . . . . Austria
Hongo, boleto blanco (white bolete) . . . . Mexico

complex. There are some taxonomists who maintain that the only true *B. edulis* in North America are associated with imported seedlings of Norway spruce. If you are collecting for the sauté pan, there is no reason to beat your head against the fine-tuning of species here. All of the above-named species are edible. It can be a fun pursuit of knowledge, but not when the olive oil is heating in the pan.

The bolete family contains many edible species belonging to more than a dozen genera and quite a number are considered excellent edibles. Because of the number of related species and the challenge of accurate identification, I strongly recommend that beginners take a slow, cautious approach to grazing their way through the group. Even the best general field guides cover only a small percent of the species. Working primarily on my own with a few field guides in the early years of mushrooming, I enjoyed collecting and eating a few of the boletes in the genera *Suillus* and *Leccinum*. I cannot say they remain my favorite edibles, but they were a start. It took several more years and consultation with other mushroomers before I felt confident with the genus *Boletus*.

DESCRIPTION

Porcini are medium to large mushrooms that can be found growing in the forest, at the edge of the woods, or under mature trees in landscaped areas.

The caps range from 2 to 12 inches, and begin as rounded, but then move into a hamburger bun shape as they age (#9). A mature porcini cap becomes flattened to almost dish shaped. Cap color ranges from pale tan to dark brown with all variations in between. The surface is smooth to somewhat wrinkled and can become viscid when wet. The pore surface is white in a young mushroom and becomes yellowish and finally pale greenish brown in age as the olive brown spores mature and are released. The individual pores are round and small, 1–2 per millimeter, and never bruise blue. The stem of the porcini is often wider in the base and narrowing above, especially in a young mushroom (#10). The color is off-white to pale brown and always has some reticulate, or net-veining. The reticulations can cover the entire stem or be limited to the upper third. The flesh of the mushroom is whitish and never bruises blue.

CAVEATS

There is a myth that all boletes are edible. For me, beyond the old saying that all mushrooms are edible at least once, I reject any of generalities about edibility. There are no boletes that are considered deadly poisonous yet a number have sickened people over time. (My only sickening involved eating a lilac brown bolete, *Tylopilus eximius*.) In their thirty-year review of reported mushroom poisonings made to the North American Mycological Association (NAMA), Michael Beug and his colleagues listed twenty-two different boletes reported to have caused gastrointestinal distress in 118 people across the United States.[3] They acknowledge that the NAMA registry is not always notified about mild mushroom poisonings, so the actual number of sickenings is assuredly much higher. Know the species of mushroom you are considering eating and follow my guidelines for a new mycophagist about trying a new species. Within the genus *Boletus*, it is generally best to avoid any of the reddish-pored species that stain blue when bruised, as several of these are known to cause gastrointestinal distress. Again, if you are not 100 percent confident in your identification, don't reach for the sauté pan.

In the Northeast, one porcini look-alike has been implicated in several sickenings. It is *Boletus huronensis*, and though some guides call it edible, there have been a few cases of people becoming sickened following a meal of this mushroom. It can be differentiated from porcini by the pore surface that stains slowly blue upon bruising, the yellowish stem color, often with traces of red, and the lack of the fine net-like veining on the stalk. Don't eat these mushrooms.

ECOLOGY, HABITAT, AND OCCURRENCE

Porcini and almost all other boletes live in mycorrhizal relationships with forest trees and shrubs and, consequently, are an essential part of a healthy forest ecosystem. Because of their mycorrhizal lifestyle, it is unlikely they will be available as cultivated mushrooms anytime soon. *Boletus edulis* and the look-alike species of the complex form root relationships with a fairly wide variety of trees including species of spruce, pine, hemlock, and a number of hardwoods—most notably oaks. The generalist nature of their associations is quite different from some of the other boletes, especially those members of the genus *Suillus* that associate with only one genus of trees or even a single species. For a mycophage, mushrooms that are tree symbionts have both advantages and disadvantages. Mycorrhizal species often form long-lasting partnerships with the host; their underground mycelium are perennial. If you find a tree with porcini fruiting beneath it, place a pin in your mushroom map, and return to the tree in future mushroom seasons to collect again. Given this long-term monogamous relationship, the mycelium can wait longer between fruitings, secure in the awareness that it will not run out of food unless the host tree dies or is removed. For many mycorrhizal species, porcini included, this results in a feast-or-famine cycle of fruiting. There are many years in which I find a few members of the edulis complex to collect and eat but not enough to dry. Then will come the year in which I seem to trip over a profusion of caps in almost every stretch of forest I enter. I count on the feast years to provide me with a dried porcini supply to last through the lean years.

Because members of the *B. edulis* complex occur with a number of different tree species in a variety of forest types, they appear to pop up without rhyme or reason, especially to the novice eye. When you recall the long-term nature of the tree partnership, it should prompt you to look for patterns in what trees the mushrooms are associated with and when they are fruiting. Though not nearly as predicable in their pattern as chanterelles, in the right season with abundant rain, a few of your sites will surely produce mushrooms reliably. The fruiting season for porcini is extensive. I generally can count on a few appearing in early to mid-summer, along with chanterelles, and then in response to significantly wet periods throughout the growing season and into late fall. The heaviest flushes tend to come in September and early October and these cool weather crops are generally less prone to attack by larvae. In Maine I find the best crops associated with red oak or spruce, and the single most productive site I know is a planted spruce forest. This is one mushroom you do not want to let sit around maturing while you decide the perfect moment to harvest. The bugs and slugs are often ahead of you and at work!

EDIBILITY

When you are fortunate enough to bring home a basket of porcini, the first step is to look over your treasure with an eye to best use. If you didn't do this in the field, cut off the base of each mushroom, remove any bits of soil, and examine the mushrooms for signs of wormholes. Mushroom maggots are the larvae of flies that feed on mushrooms and they tend to start at the base and eat their way up the stem and into the cap. In the early stage, it is often easy to trim off the damaged portion. Some people do not mind minimal invasion. Separate the young mushrooms from the more mature ones. A young *B. edulis* has a pore surface that is still white or pale yellow and remains firm to the touch. As the mushroom matures, the pores change from white to yellowish to green, and become increasingly soft and squishy. Mature tubes should be removed, a task accomplished with a sharp knife or dexterous hands. I generally cook young, firm porcini fresh and dry older ones, though large firm caps do well roasted over a fire or in a hot oven.

Fresh porcini fare well sliced somewhat thickly and sautéed in good olive oil with a bit of garlic or your favorite form of onion. That basic start can become a simple dish by itself, lightly seasoned or part of a more complex sauce with additions. Roasted with garlic-infused olive oil, they are a great complement to meats or a satisfying addition to risottos or pasta.

PORCINI AND GARDEN TOMATO SAUCE

In the Northeast, porcini are often most abundant at onion harvesting time when I have more tomatoes than I can use fresh. I sauté liberal amounts of onions with sliced mushrooms, add chopped tomatoes, and appropriate herbs and spices. The resulting sauce is used freshly made or frozen for a wonderful winter treat.

As I mentioned earlier, dried porcini take on an entirely different dimension of flavor because drying concentrates and deepens the mushroom's essence. Clean and slice the mushrooms and place them in a dehydrator or on screens in a warm dry room such as an attic, or string them up in a warm room. Avoid using an oven for drying since they usually become too hot and the flavor is altered for the worse. Store your dried porcinis in glass jars or thick, well-sealed freezer bags; they will last for several years. Whenever I have the opportunity, I dry as large a supply of boletes as I can, knowing that their flavor will be great and never knowing when the next big porcini year will come. When you're ready to use them, place the mushrooms in a bowl and cover them with warm water to rehydrate. Save the water! It makes a wonderful and flavorful stock. Some knowledgeable chefs simmer the dried mushrooms with water to create extracts to enrich the flavor of soups and sauces. Jack Czarnecki, the proprietor of a famous, but now closed restaurant named *Joe's* in Reading, Pennsylvania, and the author of the seminal mushroom cookbook, *Joe's Book of Mushroom Cookery*, has mouth-watering details about the preparation and use of mushroom extracts.[4] Rehydrated mushrooms are renowned for flavor, but their texture leaves much to be desired. Chop them finely or the leathery texture will be too obvious. They add a dimension of rich flavor to many dishes. A dried porcini risotto is a wonderful repast on a cold winter night.

PORCINI RISOTTO

This dish is generally made with dried porcini, either yours from the last season's harvest or those purchased at a specialty food store. A little dried porcini goes a long way. I make the entire dish in a 4-quart enameled cast iron Dutch oven. The added fresh mushrooms are a great finish and do not need to be porcini; many cultivated or wild species will do nicely.

1 ounce dried porcini
2 cups hot water
3–4 cups chicken or other flavorful stock
Salt and freshly ground pepper
¼ cup good olive oil

1 medium onion in ¼-inch dice or 1 medium shallot, minced

2–4 garlic cloves, minced

2 cups Arborio rice (7 ounces)

½ cup dry white wine

2 tablespoons butter

1 cup freshly grated Parmigiano-Reggiano cheese (or mix with
  Romano cheese)

1 pound fresh porcini or crimini mushrooms, thinly sliced (optional)

In a medium bowl, cover the dried porcini with the hot water and let sit 15 minutes to reconstitute the mushrooms.

Remove the porcini and chop coarsely; add the soaking liquid to the stock to make 4 cups.

Heat the stock and the reserved soaking liquid in a separate saucepan to almost boiling.

Heat oil in the Dutch oven, add the onion, and sauté until translucent (5–6 min.). Then add the garlic, salt, some pepper, and the chopped porcini and sauté for an additional couple of minutes on low heat.

Add the rice and continue to sauté while stirring for an additional couple of minutes. Begin adding stock one cup at a time stirring the pot regularly. Add the wine after the first stock and then add additional stock as the last is absorbed. Stirring at this point makes for a creamier risotto. Cook until the rice is still a bit firm (*al dente*), adding additional stock to make a more liquid dish, if desired.

Stir in ½ of the cheese along with the butter.

For an added grand finish, add some small, firm, fresh porcini (or baby bellos or crimini mushrooms), sautéed in butter, and stirred in at the end or served on top of each portion.

The exact amount of liquid needed to cook the rice is inexact, and you may either have stock remaining or need extra stock to complete the cooking.

Serve with remaining cheese to top the portions and extra ground pepper and salt as needed.

THE *AGARICUS* BROTHERS

Life is too short to stuff a mushroom.
SHIRLEY CONRAN, SUPERWOMAN

*A*garicus is the genus of the western world's most economically important and widely used cultivated edible mushrooms. It is home to the nearly ubiquitous button mushroom, portabella, crimini, and other thoroughly domesticated mushrooms, along with some lovely wild cousins living in a suburban or rural neighborhood near you. The name is Latin, meaning gilled mushroom, and in the very early days of mushroom taxonomy, all gilled mushrooms were placed in the genus *Agaricus*. The system quickly became unwieldy and, as the recognition of related groups became more sophisticated, other genera and families were designated to accommodate the observed complexity.

TAXONOMY

It is estimated that there are more than 200 species in the genus *Agaricus* in North America, although there has not been a close taxonomic study of the genus in some time. Most good mushroom field guides include, at most, six to ten common species. Clearly there are many other, less common species that do not make the guides.[1] In the Northeast, the most common edible species are A. *campestris*, (the meadow mushroom or pink bottom), A. *arvensis* (the horse mushroom), followed closely by A. *silvicola* (woodland agaricus). Occasionally other species are collected and at least two have caused gastrointestinal distress. Along the West Coast, there are additional species and several more responsible for sickenings.

The most familiar agaricus by far is *Agaricus bisporus*, the domesticated white button mushroom. The brown crimini and portabella mushrooms are cultivars of this same species. The A. *bisporus* group is responsible for close to $1 billion in yearly sales in the United States and is heavily cultivated in

Europe, China, and many other regions of the world. The species accounts for 40 percent of the cultivated mushrooms currently sold worldwide and was the first mushroom cultivated in Europe. Farmers in France first began to notice the growth of A. *bisporus* in beds of melons cultivated in greenhouses around Paris in the mid-1600s. The melons were fertilized with aged manure from area farms and stables, which was the perfect medium for *Agaricus* to grow and flourish. The farmers began to encourage the mushrooms' growth and developed a local market supplying mushrooms to area eateries. For many years this technique for mushroom cultivation remained a closely guarded secret. By 1800, French mushroom farmers had learned that light in the greenhouses or field beds was not needed for mushrooms to grow and production began moving into the caves and catacombs surrounding the cities where there was more control over temperature and humidity. By that time, farmers in England, the Netherlands, and other countries in Europe also had begun to cultivate the popular mushroom and by late 1860s cultivation of mushrooms began around Philadelphia, Pennsylvania, as well. During the early years, piles of manure were inoculated using soil collected from areas where the fungus was fruiting. The technique was crude, and other mushroom species competing for the same food source would frequently appear in the beds. As people developed a better understanding of how mushrooms grow, an industry arose to produce spawn (mushroom mycelium) to provide as starter stock to growers. Initially, American mushroom farmers imported spawn from England until a spawn-generating industry sprouted in the United States in the early 1900s. In the 1920s, an American mushroom farmer, Edward Jacobs, developed a technique for making a pure spawn of *Agaricus* and thereby greatly reduced the number of competitive species in the mushroom beds. Around the same time period, an observant Pennsylvania mushroom farmer noted an almost pure white form of the mushroom in his beds and from this chance mutation sprung the development of the pale "supermarket mushroom" that now dominates the commercial *Agaricus* industry. From the relatively stable temperature and humidity conditions of caves and old mines, mushroom production has now moved into long, low production houses with exacting control over moisture, temperature, pests, and air circulation. Cultivation of *Agaricus* occurs in a number of places throughout the United States, most notably in Pennsylvania, the largest producer, and California the second.[2]

DESCRIPTION

Agaricus species share a few features that make them fairly easy to distinguish. All have gills, which start out light cream, become pink to reddish as the cap opens (see #11 in the color insert) to reveal them, and then mature into a dark chocolate brown. The spore color is also dark chocolate brown. The gills are free of the stalk, which has a noticeable ring (annulus) that can be single, double, or pendulous. At times the annulus is almost absent in mature fruiting bodies as weather and time wear it off the stalk. In dry weather or on mushrooms that fruit in open sunlight, the annulus can remain fixed to the margin of the cap and get pulled off in tatters that remain attached to the cap edge. There is one other notable characteristic of *Agaricus*; if you hold the cap firmly and give the stalk a gentle twist it will separate cleanly from the cap without any gill fragments. This underappreciated feature has spawned the creation and proliferation of the stuffed mushroom cap, a mainstay of the cocktail party.

COMMON EDIBLE NORTHEASTERN *AGARICUS* SPECIES

The meadow mushroom, *Agaricus campestris*, a short-stemmed stocky mushroom that has a whitish cap and stem and grows in open grassy areas. The cap is commonly 2–4 inches in diameter, imperfectly rounded, and becoming almost flat at maturity and smooth to somewhat fibrous or even scaly. Lest you confuse this with an amanita, be absolutely certain that the free gills are not white but pink in the button stage and quickly age to pinkish brown and then dark bittersweet chocolate brown. There is a ring on the stem that may disappear as the mushroom ages. The spore print color is blackish-brown.

The horse mushroom, *A. arvensis*, is the big brother to the more diminutive *A. campestris*. The horse mushroom is usually 4–8 inches in diameter, although 8–10-inch caps are not uncommon. The faint scent of almonds often accompanies this mushroom. The ring on the stem is more distinct and

Agaricus bisporus: the button mushroom, supermarket mushroom
Agaricus campestris: meadow mushroom, pink bottom, button mushroom
Agaricus arvensis: horse mushroom
Agaricus abruptibulbus and *Agaricus silvicola:* woodland agaricus

membranous than those in the meadow mushroom. Where the gills of the meadow mushrooms are pink, even in the button stage horse mushroom gills are cream-gray but then undergo the same color transformation as A. *campestris*, and become very dark brown. As with the meadow mushroom, the horse mushroom favors open grassy areas.

A. *silvicola* and A. *abruptibulbus* are two woodland species that are very similar to each other in appearance and habitat. Both are taller and more stately looking than the horse and meadow mushrooms and have fleshy, pendulous rings on long slender stalks. Each species has a swollen stem base, though it is more pronounced in A. *abruptibulbus*. In addition, the scent of sweet almond is often present in the flesh. Both are recognized as good edibles.[3]

CAVEATS

The risk of collecting toxic *Amanita* mushrooms mistaken for edible *Agaricus* is low in the Northeast and Midwest if you follow a couple of simple steps. Make sure the gills are developing the distinctive transition to pink and brown and avoid any buttons with white gills, seen when sliced open. Also make certain the stem base shows no signs of the distinctive *Amanita* swollen base and volva. Look for whitish mushrooms growing in open areas with free gills that transition from almost cream through pink to dark bittersweet chocolate brown and with a ring on the stem. A blackish-brown spore print is important.

In the northeast United States, we have few species of *Agaricus* that cause toxic reactions, but there are a couple of species that can cause distress for some people. A. *placomyces* and A. *meleagris* both tend to have a darker speckled cap with an umbo or darker flattened center. A. *meleagris* bruises yellowish and has a strong odor of phenol (a chemical smell like creosote) or ink. A. *placomyces* stains bright yellow on the base of the stem. *Agaricus xanthodermus* is another toxic species that bruises bright yellow, especially at the base of the stem, and has a chemical smell. Avoid eating any *Agaricus* mushrooms that stain yellow or have a strong chemical odor! On the West Coast, there are several common agarics that trigger gastrointestinal distress and tend to resemble edible species. According to David Arora, this has made *Agaricus* the most common mushroom genus causing gastrointestinal reactions in California and Oregon.[4]

One additional caveat regarding the genus *Agaricus*: Many mushroom species, including members of *Agaricus*, are able to concentrate heavy metals and take up some pesticides. The horse mushroom is especially adept at metal accumulation. For this reason, avoid collecting mushrooms from along heavily traveled highways or in areas where you know or suspect there has been heavy chemical treatment or possible chemical contamination. Many golf courses use extensive chemical management to maintain lush, weed-free grass. For this reason, I generally avoid collecting and eating mushrooms from golf course fairways. Beware the well-manicured lawn!

ECOLOGY, HABITAT, AND OCCURRENCE

Agaricus campestris and A. *arvensis* both favor grassy areas in lawns, ball fields, roadsides, and graveyards. I have noticed that they are more common in areas where the grass is not perfect and fruit even better in grassy areas that support a population of weed species. So seek them out in areas of stony soil, rough lawn, and the edges of roadside drainage ditches. They typically fruit gregariously in scattered groups. Agarics will, at times, develop large fairy rings of several dozen mushrooms, and you can often tell where one will pop up before the mushrooms appear by the deeper green color and lush growth of grass in a circle or arc. Be aware that other mushrooms can form fairy rings and stimulate grass growth in the same way, including edibles such as the fairy ring mushroom, *Marasmius oreades*, and toxic species such as the sweating mushroom, *Clitocybe dealbata*.

    Agaricus mushrooms have evolved as saprobes and most are what is known as secondary saprobes. They grow by continuing the breakdown of dead vegetative material that has already been partially decomposed by a primary saprobe. That is why they are commonly found in fields and farmyards and around composts and waste piles. The commercial mushroom industry follows a very carefully controlled process of composting horse manure and other plant matter to produce bedding substrate on which to grow button mushrooms.

    One trend I have noted over the years is that in a summer when we have abundant rain evenly delivered through the season, there is little fruiting of A. *campestris* and A. *arvensis* is also not as exuberant. I believe that this is due to the grass duff being consumed by other "rotters" such as slime molds, bacteria, and other fungi able to outcompete the *Agaricus* during wet periods. If my theory is correct, a few weeks of dry weather should yield a strong flush of meadow mushrooms when we have one of those tropical deluges come

September or October. The meadow mushroom fruits strongly during wet periods from August through September and can continue into October. The horse mushroom starts a few weeks later in a typical year but can continue to fruit through October and even into November in mild regions. Occasionally these mushrooms can be found in early summer during unusually wet weather.

EDIBILITY, PREPARATION, AND PRESERVATION

Most experienced mushroomers rate the meadow and horse mushrooms as good to choice edibles. I find their flavor to be distinctive and full, with the taste that most people associate with mushrooms. Young buttons have a mild flavor that increases in strength and depth as the mushroom matures. For this reason it is good to consider the dish you are cooking and determine whether you desire a strong mushroom presence or a lighter touch and use mushrooms matured to suit your needs. More likely you will collect the mushrooms and choose the dish based on the age of your mushroom bounty that day. You will find no better mushrooms for a hearty, creamed mushroom soup or mushroom gravy than the meadow and horse mushrooms! As with most of our edibles, the best way to start is to sauté cleaned, sliced mushrooms in butter or olive oil before proceeding with whatever recipe you choose.

In my copy of *The Mushroom Handbook*—that first guidebook I bought as a young man—Louis Krieger states the wisdom of his day regarding the poor nutritive value of mushrooms. "It is mainly as condiments that they are valuable. Beef, bread and beans are very nourishing, but who wants to eat these at all times?"[5] Contrary to our old beliefs, mushrooms are packed with great nutritional benefits. The *Agaricus* species contain 35 to 40 percent dry weight of protein including a relatively good amino acid complement. They are also a good source of vitamin D and several B vitamins as well as of potassium, phosphorus, and selenium.

In a good year it is easy to find and collect more *Agaricus* than you can use in a few meals and therefore preservation strategies need to be considered. Mushrooms sliced and sautéed in butter or olive oil can be frozen easily for later use. More mature caps with strong flavor can be dried and are great for use as a seasoning when powdered in a food processor. Store the powder in an airtight jar, and use it to flavor soups, sauces, and stews. One way that I preserve large quantities of agarics is to make a sauce duxelles.

WILD MUSHROOM DUXELLES SAUCE

2–4 tablespoons butter, olive oil, or a mix

2 pounds mushrooms, coarsely chopped

Salt and pepper to taste

3–4 tablespoons minced shallots (optional)

2–4 tablespoons white wine (optional)

A sprig or two of fresh thyme, tarragon, or dill (optional)

Mushroom duxelles is a preparation dating back to seventeenth century France. La Varenne, chef to the Marquis d'Uxelles around 1650, reportedly invented the mushroom paste. I like it with the distinctively strong flavor of mature *Agaricus* mushrooms, but it can be made with almost any mushrooms, though I would suggest not mixing species into one batch, as it muddies the flavors. Duxelles is made by coarsely chopping the mushrooms (which can be done in a food processor or by hand) and cooking them down in an open shallow sauté pan to concentrate the mushroom essence. When most of the liquid is evaporated and the mushroom paste is thick, it is ready for immediate use or can be refrigerated or frozen for later use. I spoon ½-cup portions of duxelles into muffin tins and freeze them. Later I pop the hockey puck duxelles out and into zip-lock bags for storage in the freezer. Duxelles also can be stored in the refrigerator for up to two weeks. I use it as flavoring in a vast array of recipes, as a garnish, or simply spooned on crusty French bread. Yumm!

CREAMY MUSHROOM SOUP

3 tablespoons butter

1 medium–large white/yellow onion, finely chopped

2 garlic cloves, peeled and crushed

1 tablespoon unbleached flour

5 cups vegetable/chicken/mushroom stock heated to a simmer

1–2 pounds meadow and/or horse mushrooms chopped in large chunks

½ cup white wine

¾ cup cream

Sea salt and freshly cracked black pepper

Chopped fresh parsley (for garnish)

Melt the butter in a heavy Dutch oven and add the onions to cook over low–medium heat till translucent (4–5 minutes). Add the flour and the chopped mushrooms and continue cooking until the mushrooms release their liquid.

Add the stock slowly and bring to a boil. Reduce heat and allow to simmer for 15 minutes.

Ladle half of the soup into a food processor, puree using steel blades, and return it to the soup pot.

Add the white wine and cream in separate batches and warm the soup thoroughly, but do not boil. Season with salt and pepper. Serve in bowls garnished with parsley and perhaps a nice grating of cheese.

Once again, this basic mushroom soup can be adapted to many different species of wild or cultivated mushrooms. The recipe works well with portobella or crimini mushrooms.

MUSHROOM COUSCOUS

Couscous is the primitive pasta almost ubiquitous in the North Africa and some Mediterranean countries. Like many pastas, it adapts to almost any combination of flavors. Though I have made this recipe for *Agaricus*, it can be subtly shifted to meet the needs of almost any edible species including chanterelles, porcini, morels, Maitake, chicken mushroom, and others. Have fun with the mix of other ingredients.

2 tablespoons olive oil

½ green or red bell pepper, chopped

½ cup chopped celery

½ cup onion

2 garlic cloves, minced

1½ pounds meadow mushrooms (or another compatible species)

Basil and parsley, finely chopped

2 cups couscous

2 cups boiling water or stock
½ cup white wine
Sea salt and freshly ground pepper
Grated cheese for garnish

I use a high-sided or deep skillet for this and do all cooking in the same pan. Heat pan over medium fire, adding oil followed by onions, garlic, pepper, and celery. Sauté for a minute or two and add the chopped mushrooms. After the mushrooms begin to lose their water, add the salt and pepper along with the dry couscous and continue to heat. Add the hot stock and the wine, briefly stir to evenly distribute the liquids, turn off the heat, and cover with a tight fitting lid. Allow to sit for 10 minutes and then serve with the chopped herbs as garnish. The additional garnish of grated hard cheese and freshly ground pepper is an added bonus.

PART III

DANGEROUSLY TOXIC, DEADLY INTERESTING

Introduction

POISONOUS MUSHROOMS
Not as Bad as You Fear

Fungi ben musheroms;
there be two manners of them,
one manner is deedly and
slayeth them that eateth them
and be called tode stoles,
and the other doeth not.

THE GRETE HERBALL, 1526

he horror stories abound: tragic tales of poor souls who mistakenly ate
the wrong mushroom and were found dead in their beds. People sometimes tell me anecdotal accounts of entire families that died following a meal
of mushrooms the night before. Even knowing that such stories must be false,
I still find them both frightening and compelling. The reality is that there
are cases of several members of a family dying from poisonous mushrooms,
though never within twenty-four hours. Deadly mushrooms have a delayed
onset of symptoms and take days to kill the victims.

Still, deaths by poisonous mushrooms are rare, in spite of growing concern
that mushroom poisoning is on the increase. The perceived risk far exceeds
the reality. Though medical providers see several thousand people each year
due to concerns regarding mushroom poisoning, almost none of those people
die and very few require medical intervention beyond activated charcoal and
anti-emetics, if medical intervention is needed at all. The national network of
Poison Control Centers handles 8,000–10,000 mushroom-related calls each
year, almost 80 percent related to toddlers or young children.[1] Of those mushroom calls made to Poison Control Centers, fewer than 5 percent develop
moderate or worse symptoms requiring significant hospital emergency room
intervention, and fewer than 1 percent are considered severe, requiring inpa-
tient hospital admission. For the thirty years ending in 2005, one or two people
per year, on average, died of mushroom poisoning in America.[2] There was a

surprising increase in 2009, when five people died of mushroom poisoning in the United States and Canada, according to preliminary reports compiled by the North American Mushroom Association (NAMA) Toxicology Committee chair Michael Beug. Four of the deaths were from amatoxins and the last, a man in his nineties, died from complications related to eating a type of bolete.[3] Still, despite the increase in 2009, compared to the number of people injured and killed each year by lightning (about 100), bee or wasp stings (30–50), or peanuts (up to 100), mushrooms are quite safe.

But while it's important to put the risk of mushroom poisoning into perspective, it's also important never to dismiss that risk. Several times over recent years I have identified poisonous jack o'lantern mushrooms in cases where a very sick person was certain that they had collected and eaten chanterelles. The green-spored *Lepiota*, *Chlorophyllum molybdites*, causes moderate to severe gastrointestinal anguish to several dozen people each year and consistently leads the list across America for the most frequent cause of mushrooming malaise.[4] If you never eat a wild mushroom, you'll never be poisoned by one, but if you aspire to eat wild mushrooms, it is vital that you acquaint yourself with this darker side to mushroom foraging.

If the emerging mycophagist acts responsibly, acquires good basic mushroom identification skills, and learns the common edible and common toxic species in his or her area, there is little risk of a bad experience. This is especially true for someone collecting and eating only common, easily recognized mushrooms like chanterelles, morels, or puffballs and avoiding the temptation to practice extreme mushrooming where the goal is to develop the longest list of different mushrooms eaten.

This section is in no way a comprehensive treatment of the toxic mushrooms in any region of America. There are plenty of great books, articles, and Internet sites that can fill that need. Rather, the goal is to look at commonly encountered scenarios in mushroom poisoning and suggested strategies for avoiding those pitfalls, as well as to underscore the worst-case scenario by looking at the death cap, the deadliest mushroom in the world. I'll also take a look at the ever increasing body of knowledge on the interaction of mushroom toxins in the human body. There are several mushrooms with significant histories as edibles, especially in Asia and Europe, that we now know are capable of triggering life-threatening illness and even death. When this happens with a mushroom that has an extensive history of collection and consumption, people's resistance to accepting the change in status can be significant. We will take a close look at three mysterious cases of mushrooms that have long edible histories and examine the information that has come to light and tarnished their status.

MUSHROOM POISONING

The Potential Risks and Ways to Avoid Them

I confess, that nothing frightens me more
than the appearance of mushrooms on the table,
especially in a small provincial town.
ALEXANDRE DUMAS

*M*ycologists, medical doctors, and poison control specialists who track mushroom poisoning cases have a pretty clear idea of what they consider a poisonous mushroom. A mushroom is considered toxic if it produces a predictable set of negative reactions in a significant percentage of the people who eat it.

It sounds straightforward, right? And for some species, it is. The death cap, *Amanita phalloides*, is responsible for at least 80 percent of mushrooming deaths in Europe and is increasingly problematic in the United States.[1] The related destroying angels, A. *bisporigera* and A. *virosa* (see #12 in the color insert), are less potent but equally dangerous. No one questions the universal toxicity of these amatoxin-containing mushrooms.

For most mushrooms, though, it isn't that simple. First of all, how do you define a predictable set of negative reactions? Second, how many sick people does it take to reach the level of significant? Some common and favored edible mushrooms cause problems for a small percentage of the people who eat them. A 2006 compilation of mushroom poisonings includes reported reactions to morels, chanterelles, and honey mushrooms.[2] Reactions to these popular mushrooms are generally fairly mild and occur only in a very small percentage of the many thousands of Americans who eat them, so they're not considered toxic by most mushroom experts, although as you can see in this book, responsible mycologists will note the existence of the small risk. Though estimates vary, there are up to 400 toxic mushrooms worldwide,[3] based on all reports of people's negative reaction to eating fungi, including reports on many mushrooms that most people eat without problems. A person can have or develop a bad reaction to a mushroom that the next 99 people enjoy without problems. These "idiosyncratic" reactions happen, but are difficult to use as an assessment of toxicity generalized to all people. The list of mushrooms with proven, consistent toxicity is much smaller, and many good mushroom field guide authors differentiate between a mushroom that has caused problems with a few people and those that sicken most people who eat them. The list of toxic mushrooms commonly found in any region—such as the following sidebar on common toxic mushrooms of the Northeast—will be even smaller. Many of the toxic mushrooms found in the Northeast, or related species, also are found in other regions of the United States.

In the classes I teach and the mushroom walks I lead, a few people regularly question my judgment regarding some mushrooms I refer to as poisonous. Their query is generally along the lines of "I've eaten that mushroom many times over the years without problems. It's not poisonous," they say. It's difficult to argue in the face of such persuasive first-person advocacy; however, mushroom chemistry is complex and people's food tolerances and vulnerabilities are equally complex with a number of variables coming into play. A mushroom earns the label of toxic over time, when a number of people report a bad reaction associated with eating it. Alternately, a mushroom may be labeled as poisonous if only a small number of people have died or suffered life-threatening illness due to eating it. The number of complaints needed to trigger the labeling has never been defined and there is a lot of folk wisdom involved, since the labeling of edibility and toxicity develops over generations and around the world.

For other species, including some with extensive histories of culinary use, the method of preparation can mitigate the toxicity. The false morel, *Gyromitra esculenta*, (see #13 in the color insert) contains highly toxic and carcinogenic hydrazines and is responsible for serious illness and deaths in Europe, and some cases of severe poisoning in the United States. Yet this mushroom and closely related species are eaten and highly prized by thousands in Europe and western North America. (See Chapter 9 for the full story.)

A couple of mushroom species are good edibles and people frequently eat them, but they can cause illness if the diner drinks alcohol during or after the meal. *Coprinus atramentarius*, known in England as tippler's bane and in the United States as the alcohol inky, causes a reaction similar to Antabuse (the trade name of disulfiram), which is used to treat chronic alcoholics by

Common Toxic Mushrooms of the Northeast*

Dangerously toxic:

Amanita virosa and *A. bisporigera*, destroying angels
Amanita phalloides, death cap
Conocybe filaris, deadly conocybe
Gyromitra esculenta, false morel and related species
Galerina autumnalis, deadly galerina and related species
Lepiota josserandi and *L. castanae*
Paxillus involutus, poison pax
Pleurocybella porrigens, angel wings

Moderately toxic:

Clitocybe dealbata, the sweating mushroom
Entoloma lividum (sinuatum)
Inocybe spp., especially *fastigata* and *geophylla*, fiber caps
Hebeloma crustuliniforme, poison pie
Naematoloma (Hypholoma) fasciculare, sulfur tuft
Omphalotus illudens, jack o'lantern mushroom

Mild to moderate toxicity (generally gastrointestinal):

Agaricus xanthodermus, A. placomyces
Amanita brunescens, A flavoconia, A. flavorubens, A frostiana
Boletus sensibilis and *B. subvelutipes*, red-pored blue
    staining boletes
Chlorophyllum molybdites, green-spored Lepiota
Gomphus floccosus, scaly vase chanterelle
Hygrocybe conica, black-staining Hygrocybe
Lactarius chrysorheus, L. rufus, L. torminosus, milky caps
Lepiota cristata
Pholiota squarrosa (toxic for some)
Ramaria formosa and some related species, coral mushrooms
Russula emetica, R. nigricans, R. densifolia, and other
    black-staining species
Scleroderma spp., earth ball or pigskin puffball

Tricholoma pardinum and others
Tylopilus eximius, lilac brown bolete

Toxic under certain circumstances:
Clitocybe claviceps, clubfoot *Clitocybe* (for some, if consumed
   with alcohol)
Coprinus atramentarius, alcohol ink cap or tippler's bane
   (with alcohol),
Morchella spp., morels (with alcohol, for a small percentage of folks)
Hygrophoropsis aurantiaca, false chanterelle, (edible, but causes
   problems for some)

Toxic unless completely cooked:
Armillaria mellea complex, honey mushroom
Lepista nuda, blewit
Morchella spp., morels
Laetiporus sulphureus complex, sulphur shelf

Hallucinogenic or inebriating:
Gynnopilus spectabilis, big laughing gym, *G. validipes*
   and related species
Psilocybe semilanceata, liberty cap, and other species
Amanita muscaria, fly mushroom, *A pantherina*, *A. crenulata*,
   and others
Panaeolus foenisecii, the lawn mowers mushroom, and other species

**Edible, even esteemed by some, but problematic for a very small
minority:**
Armillaria mellea complex, honey mushroom
Laetiporus sulphureus, sulphur shelf or chicken mushroom
Morchella spp., morel
Suillus luteus and other viscid-capped *Suillus*

* This table is in no way intended to be a comprehensive listing of
   toxic mushrooms[4]

helping them avoid the temptation to drink. The effects of drinking alcohol with tippler's bane include flushes, sweating, nausea, vomiting, racing heart, and general feelings of malaise, as with Antabuse. Symptoms generally abate within eight hours but can return if alcohol is again imbibed for up to seventy-two hours after a meal of these mushrooms. Interactions with alcohol also have been noted with morels, chicken mushroom, and a few others on very rare occasions. Although alcohol inkys are often categorized as toxic, it could be just as easily argued that the alcohol inky is edible and the alcohol is toxic.

There are mushrooms eaten and enjoyed by the overwhelming majority of diners, including the very popular edible honey mushrooms, *Armillaria mellea* complex, and sulfur shelf, *Laetiporus sulphureus*. Yet some people, probably less than 5 percent of the population, are unable to tolerate these mushrooms and have a mild to moderate gastrointestinal upset following a dinner with them. Does that make these species poisonous? If you happen to be one in the 5 percent, you might think so, but you would quickly learn to avoid the offending mushroom, as you would with strawberries, peanuts, or shellfish due to allergic reaction. The difference is that since the majority of people have a positive association with and a long history of eating strawberries, we do not paint all strawberries with the broad brush-strokes of suspicion as is often the case with wild mushrooms in the United States.

Finally, there are a few good edible mushrooms that will sicken most people who eat them raw or undercooked. These species contain a heat-labile toxin removed or neutralized by cooking. The popular edibles morels, honey mushrooms, and blewits are included in this group. When properly cooked, they cause no problems. The similarity is to foods like meat that are unsafe when eaten raw or undercooked.

Almost all mushroom field and cooking guides instruct the mushroom hunter to fully cook wild mushrooms before eating. In addition to those mushrooms with heat-neutralized toxins, this is necessary due to the structural make-up of mushroom cells. The combination of chitin and the long-chain complex polysaccharides that comprise the majority of the mushroom cell walls make them largely indigestible unless they are cooked. The heat of cooking starts to break down the complex cell structure and enables us to take advantage of the nutritious proteins, carbohydrates, and vitamins in the mushrooms. Even when mushrooms are fully cooked, our digestive tracts are unable to break down much of the mushroom cell wall components. Most of the glucan polysaccharides and chitin are passed through the gut as fiber, which is a necessary dietary component and helpful in lowering cholesterol, not to mention its assistance in maintaining regularity. (I love that word.) Some of these same polysaccharide glucans stimulate the functioning of the human immune system and are being used around the world as immune stimulants and as an aspect of cancer therapies.

Because they are basically indigestible, uncooked mushrooms are treated as unfriendly tenants in the gut, and overindulgence may trigger nausea and vomiting. It is generally accepted in the mushroom poisoning field that mild cases of gastrointestinal distress are often due to an individual's difficulty digesting the meal rather than any toxin in the mushroom. This is especially true if the mushrooms were not thoroughly cooked, but also can happen with good old-fashioned gluttony. If you come across a huge basket of honey mushrooms, remember that you don't need to eat them all in one meal.

A few years ago, a former neighbor of mine expressed her interest in trying wild mushrooms. I gave her a portion of a large fruiting body of hen of the woods, *Grifola frondosa*, and explained how I normally prepare it. Over the course of the day, as she passed the mushroom lying on her kitchen counter, she began breaking off small pieces of the firm, gray, spoon-shaped caps and eating them raw. She later reported liking the crispness of the texture and the mild flavor. Several hours later, she started to feel quite nauseous and became violently ill for a short time. After emptying her stomach, she fairly quickly recovered and, after talking to me and realizing her mistake, she cooked some of the mushroom the following day and ate it without problems.

As with an increasing number of people and foods, a few mycophagists develop allergic reactions to certain mushrooms, ranging from mild rashes to gastrointestinal disturbance or worse. A few people also develop an allergic sensitivity to mushroom spores. The risk posed by high concentrations of mushroom spores became known only following the increased cultivation of shiitake and oyster mushrooms in controlled indoor fruiting rooms during the 1980s. People employed to harvest the mushrooms are exposed repeatedly to high concentrations of spores when harvesting the mature fruiting bodies. Health officials began to note a rise in cases of this hypersensitivity pneumonitis in Japan and China where up to 10 percent of oyster mushroom workers develop symptoms.[5] This has also been reported among workers in the U.S. oyster mushroom cultivation houses.

My Inevitable Personal Story of Mushroom Poisoning

Sometimes a pattern of "idiosyncratic reactions" gives us enough cause for concern to re-label an edible mushroom as suspect or toxic. One example of this hit close to home with me, very close.

In August 1986, an abundance of rainy, foggy, overcast days made the tourists on the coast of Maine depressed and the mushroomers ecstatic. During those days, I embarked on regular mushroom hunting excursions and, one day, came upon several fine specimens of a bolete that was new to me. They were distinctive, large mushrooms with a purple-brown cap and a deep chocolate pore surface in place of gills. The inner flesh was pale lavender-brown throughout and firm. The mushrooms were fruiting singly in a mixed hardwood forest. I brought some prime specimens home in my basket and set out determining their identity. A spore print generously deposited showed pinkish-buff brown spores and confirmed that I was looking at a species in the genus *Tylopilus*. A review of several mushroom field guides including Gary Lincoff's *Audubon Field Guide to North American Mushrooms* and David Arora's *Mushrooms Demystified* left me little doubt that I had a basket of *Tylopilus eximius*, the lilac brown bolete. Both books reported the species as edible and Audubon indicated that the few look-alike species were not toxic. So being young (thirty-one) and adventurous, not to mention hungry, I cooked up the mushrooms by sautéing them in olive oil with garlic and salt and pepper, finishing them with a bit of cream and eating them over fettuccini with Romano cheese. Quite yummy!

Two hours later, while I was at work, I began to feel the rumbles and flip-flops of impending trouble. I immediately guessed it was the mushrooms not agreeing with me, and assumed that I would get sick, get rid of the offending contents, and then get over it. Several torturous and embarrassing hours later, I ended up in a local emergency room when my co-workers became so alarmed they called an ambulance. There I spent an extremely uncomfortable night on Compazine and IV fluids before being released in the morning.

I was interested in how I could have made such a painful mistake in identification or judgment, so I continued to seek collections of and information about this very distinctive mushroom. Both Louis Krieger[6] and Charles McIlvaine[7] agreed with the edibility call and noted that the specific epithet *"eximius"* means select. But in talking with other mushroomers, most notably Sam Ristich, the mycological guru of New England, I learned that several other people had ended up in emergency rooms around Maine after eating the same mushroom in 1986. I reported my case to the National Mushroom Poisoning Case Registry managed by NAMA as, I hope, did others involved with similar cases. When Roger Phillips published his popular guide *Mushrooms of North America* in 1991, he became the first field guide author to add a note of caution to the edibility of *T. eximius*. Over the intervening years the mushroom poisoning community in New England has become aware of perhaps a dozen or more cases of severe GI distress caused by eating *T. eximius*. I have heard of no cogent explanation for the toxicity of *T. eximius* in the Northeast when it has been eaten in other regions of the country for an extended period of time. The populations in the Northeast may have developed additional chemical toxins or we may have a slightly different variety of *Tylopilus*. In any case, I have not tried it a second time, thereby demonstrating my ability to learn from experience. Vomiting is not on my list of most desired activities.

A number of people assumed that, following my episode of mushroom poisoning, I would stop collecting and eating wild mushrooms. They expressed their surprise in varying fashion, but certainly some deepened their doubts about my judgment (or lack thereof) when I told them about my intention to continue eating wild mushrooms. My response to them was to ask if they have ever suffered food poisoning after eating out. The overwhelming majority replied, yes. I then asked if they continue to eat out. Generally they answered with some indignation, "Well certainly not at the place where I got sick!" Alas, I, also, no longer eat the lilac-brown bolete.

To put my personal saga of mushroom misadventure into context, I have collected and eaten wild mushrooms since the mid-1970s and over the years have tried more than fifty different species. During this period, I have been sickened only this once. Over the same period of time, I have easily enjoyed a thousand great meals of wild mushrooms and shared many of them with family and friends. Nobody has ever complained of more than an overfull feeling.

The risk of being sickened by eating wild mushrooms is real, but the potential for many fine meals of incomparably fabulous fungi is at least as real and much more likely to occur if you follow basic precautions outlined in this book. The task for the mushroom forager is to bring caution, preparation, and excitement into play in roughly equal proportions and to do your homework in order to learn about the potentially toxic mushrooms as you consider edible mushrooms for the table. Start slow, start small, and have fun.

Toxic mushrooms are generally grouped by the type of toxin they contain, and more specifically, the effects of the toxin on the human body. Officially, there are eight groups of toxins, though the incidence of poisoning in several of the groups is quite rare in the United States. The most dangerous and life threatening of the toxins have spurred scientists to understand their structure and mode of action. Thus we know a great deal about the amatoxins (see Chapter 8). We also have learned about the structure and action of gyromitrin from false morels (see Chapter 9). On the other hand, we know relatively little about the structure and specific mode of action for a range of compounds responsible for the most common presenting symptoms of mushroom poisoning, the gastrointestinal irritants.

The most frequently encountered set of symptoms in mushroom poisoning mimic those I experienced after dining on the lilac-brown bolete, *Tylopilus eximius*. They generally include mild to severe gastrointestinal distress including nausea, vomiting, diarrhea, and perhaps abdominal cramping generally lasting less than twenty-four hours and often accompanied by a general feeling of malaise. If the victim has poor health, the poisoning can further compromise their functioning and the very rare deaths have occurred under these conditions. In a healthy adult, the effects usually pass without lasting damage to any bodily system save to one's self-confidence regarding mushroom identification.

In general, the more quickly symptoms of mushroom poisoning develop, the less severe the outcome. Muscarine toxicity and the effects of hallucinogenic psilocybin and psilocin generally are seen within thirty minutes and pass within five hours. Most often they leave benignly, though there are occasional severe reactions to muscarine and it has caused a few deaths worldwide. Muscarine is the only mushroom toxin for which there exists an antidote. Victims recover rapidly when given an IV with atropine.[8] Muscarine is a toxin that causes profuse salivation, tearing of the eyes, sweating, and increased urination, among other symptoms.

The toxins responsible for more severe and lasting damage generally have a delayed onset of initial symptoms ranging from six hours to several days. I will not review all of the known classes of mushroom toxins in depth here. It seems more valuable to focus on the general paths to making unfortunate mistakes as a method to underscore how to avoid them. For an excellent and thorough treatment of mushroom poisoning, including clinical treatment recommendations, acquire a copy of Denis Benjamin's very readable book *Mushrooms: Poisons and Panaceas.*

The Most Common Mushroom Poisoning Scenarios

An arrogant fool from Muscongus*
Claimed he knew all there was about fungus
I need no advice,
I eat what looks nice.
So now he's no longer among us.
DIMITRI STANCIOFF

The range of decisions and actions resulting in a victim being evaluated by medical personnel to treat the effects of mushroom poisoning can result from a number of complex personal decisions and behaviors, including misinterpretation of mushroom descriptions, innocence based on naïveté or ignorance, faulty logic, belief in myths regarding mushrooms, and pure unadorned recklessness. To this list, I might add bad luck: the rare combination of the right mushroom, prepared in the right way, but eaten by a person who cannot tolerate the species, such as the honey mushroom. The good news is that most bad experiences can be avoided by following a few basic guidelines set forth in this section.

There are a few common mushroom poisoning scenarios that bear closer examination since the repeated and somewhat predictable mistakes of others can teach the rest of us what not to do. Though the specific examples given below come from my own experiences as a mushroomer and an identification consultant for Poison Control, they also represent common themes mentioned by other consultants and in the literature of mushroom toxicology

---

* Muscongus is a bay on the coast of Maine.

The Grazer

The regional Poison Control Center gets a call from a panicked parent, grand-parent, or caregiver of a two-year-old child found clutching a mangled mush-room in the yard or, even scarier, with a portion of the mushroom in his or her mouth. It is rarely clear whether the child actually swallowed any portion of a mushroom. Upon questioning by the anxious caregiver, the child becomes equally scared and anxious and gives conflicting information. The child shows no signs of poisoning, but after consulting with a regional Poison Control Center, or often on their own accord, the caregiver decides to take the child to a local hospital for observation, evaluation, and possible treatment. At this point, the poison control staff frequently contacts a consulting mycologist to aid in the identification of the offending mushroom(s). The family is urged to bring examples of the mushroom with them to the hospital for identification.

This example is an amalgamation of many "grazer" calls I have addressed as a volunteer consulting mycologist to the Northern New England Poison Control Center. The most extreme case involved at least nine children who had collected and sampled mushrooms in the woods as part of a group dare. After being tipped off by the most anxious child, terrified parents scoured the woods and brought all the mushrooms they could find to the hospital for examination. When I got the call from the hospital, the medical staff in posses-sion of the mushroom samples initially hoped that I would be able to identify them over the phone. One MD who claimed to know mushrooms said he believed that one of the mushrooms was an amanita, but it was soon evident that the staff had minimal familiarity with mushroom morphology and lacked the vocabulary to describe what they were holding. They also lacked the tech-nology to take and transmit accurate digital images of the mushrooms to me. It quickly became clear that my presence in the same room with the mushrooms was vital if I was to make sense of the diverse collection.

By the time I arrived, frantic parents and caregivers had brought the chil-dren and more than a dozen different types of mushrooms to the hospital. Several children had been evaluated by emergency department staff and admitted for observation and more were on their way in to the emergency department. At that point, no child was showing symptoms of distress beyond anxiety that was likely caused by seeing their parents so fearful. Several hours later I knew that there were no deadly amanitas or other seriously toxic mush-rooms involved and, of the rest, even *if* the kids had eaten any of them, the worst-case scenario would be moderate to severe gastrointestinal symptoms. In the end, none of the children involved developed symptoms, though several suffered through the process of ingesting activated charcoal and having gastric lavage performed on them. All, I am certain, were convinced to never eat a wild mushroom again.

In another case tailor-made for the coast of Maine, I received a call directly from an offshore island medical provider after a grandparent found her toddler grandchild in possession of a large yellowish mushroom with whitish patches on the cap and a ring around the stem. From the phone description of free gills and the base of the stem described as swollen, it appeared that we had a likely case of *Amanita* ingestion, but it was difficult to ascertain which species. It was late June, a time when few *Amanita* species fruit in Maine and not a time when I normally see any *Amanita muscaria* var. *formosa*, a known toxic species (see Chapter 12).

Murphy's Law peered over the horizon. It was a Friday night and the ferry had already made its last run from island to mainland. Since the child in question was asymptomatic, the situation did not meet the island's criteria for an emergency ferry run, so there was no way to get the mushroom to the mycologist. The solution came in the shape of a friendly lobsterman who traversed the ten miles of open sea with the mushroom carefully wrapped in wet paper towels and then caught a taxi and delivered the mushroom right to my door as evening ran into night. The mushroom proved to be *Amanita flavorubescens*, which is, at worst, mildly toxic, and the child remained symptom free under the vigilant eye of family and the island medical staff.

Of the thousands of calls to poison control centers each year regarding mushrooms, about 80 percent involve young children in the grazing stage of life. Before age five, and especially from six months to three years, kids explore the world and objects in their world by putting them in their mouths. When the object is a pretty little mushroom found growing at the edge of Nana's yard, it becomes every parent's nightmare. The overwhelming majority of young children evaluated for possible mushroom ingestion never develop symptoms of poisoning, but it is nevertheless prudent to identify the mushroom in question to ensure that the child is adequately treated. Due to their small body mass and developmental stage, young children can be seriously affected by a small amount of mushroom toxin. Some mushrooms that are benign to adults can have a dangerous impact on young children. The compounds psilocybin and psilocin, for example, which are found in several small species of *Psilocybin*, *Panaeolus*, and related genera, usually leave the average adult fully recovered from hallucinations and an altered mental state within six hours; in young children, however, the same toxins can spike elevated fever, trigger convulsions, and even lead to death in rare cases.[9]

As every parent or caregiver of a toddler knows, it is almost impossible to control what they put in their mouths. It is equally impossible to mushroom-proof the average backyard or park. As always, I recommend vigilance and either removing mushrooms from where toddlers might encounter them or removing toddlers from where they might encounter mushrooms. Rest assured that it is extremely rare for a toddler to be seriously sickened by poisonous mushrooms in the United States. If you suspect your toddler has eaten a mushroom, seek a phone consult with your hospital emergency department or poison control center.

The Case of Mistaken Identity

It was almost 1:00 AM, well past my normal witching hour, when the phone rang and jarred me from my sleep. The physician covering our local hospital emergency department was calling about a middle-aged man who was suffering from severe gastrointestinal distress. The man told a story of collecting a bunch of chanterelles, cooking them for dinner, and eating a fair-sized portion. His girlfriend, unsure of the mushrooms, his skills at identification, or both, declined the meal (much to her subsequent relief). Several hours after the meal, he began to feel sick and soon found himself in a painful gastrointestinal drama in which the bathroom played a starring role. He reported eating chanterelles in the past, supplied and cooked by a friend, and said that for a long time he'd been wanting to find his own. When he came upon the dense cluster of orange-yellow mushrooms on the ground at the base of an oak tree, he thought he'd stumbled on a bonanza of delectable fungi. The color and vase-shape, combined with the gills running down their stems, met his memory of chanterelles. (#7) Back home with his collection, he looked at the description of chanterelles in a popular field guide and made the mushrooms in his hand fit the description in the book.

Unfortunately, for his health and sense of mushrooming competence, the mushrooms that he actually picked and ate that late summer evening were jack o'lantern mushrooms, *Omphalotus illudens* (see #8 in the color insert).

The jack o'lantern grows in dense clusters around the base of hardwood trees, predominately oaks, and as a bioluminescent mushroom (see Chapter 16), glows in the dark with an otherworldly greenish light that emanates from its gills and can be seen in a very dark room. It is a beautiful and fascinating tree parasite, but it is toxic. Jack o'lantern mushrooms cause moderate to severe cramps, vomiting, dizziness, and an overall feeling of weakness and fatigue that can last for many hours or unusually, even days. Onset of the symptoms is generally within two to three hours of the meal. The individual in this case spent the night in the hospital for control of nausea and support of hydration and was released late the following morning.

As these stories show, the case of mistaken identity isn't always as straightforward as dissonance between a mushroom in hand and the description in a field guide. Especially for new mushroomers, there can be a strong temptation toward magical thinking. The desire to find a great edible can overwhelm rational judgment. If the collector has a strong preconceived notion of what the mushroom's identity is or, more importantly, what he wants the mushroom to be, his mind will be less open to objectively evaluating the specimen in hand. In the chanterelle case, the victim saw all of the relevant characteristics he *wanted* to see and ignored or downplayed the features that didn't fit. Eating wild mushrooms demands that the collector remain objective in seeing and evaluating identification features and not ignore or devalue characteristics that don't fit. Never eat a mushroom unless you are 100 percent certain of the identification. "When in doubt, throw it out!"

The situation above is a typical example of mistaken identity and there are several ways to avoid repeating it. First, know the characteristics of the most dangerous and most common toxic species in your area and avoid eating mushrooms with close toxic look-alikes. The classic example is the genus *Amanita*, the group of mushrooms responsible for the majority of serious poisonings and deaths in temperate climates. All members of this genus have a set of common features—free gills that give off white spores, a swollen stem base with remnants of a universal veil, and the presence of an annulus, or ring, around the mid-stem—that are apparent even to the untrained eye. It is the responsibility of anyone who wants to eat wild mushrooms to be familiar with the amanitas and their shared identification features. When these features are found together, it should place a mushroomer on high alert. The genus *Amanita* has some very edible and desired mushrooms in addition to the toxic species, but I strongly discourage novice collectors from eating from this group. In addition to amanitas, the genera *Lepiota* and *Macrolepiota* share many characteristics with amanitas, including the presence of some severely toxic species (as well as some great edibles). It is another genus to be avoided by all but the most experienced mushroomers.

Most good mushroom field guides include cautions about toxic look-alikes in their descriptions of edible mushrooms. Some guides, such as the *Audubon Field Guide to North American Mushrooms*, are particularly good at this. Again, my mantra about eating mushrooms that have toxic look-alikes or are known to cause problems for some diners is, "Why bother?" Why bother taking a chance when there are so many great, easily identifiable edibles growing in our forests, fields, gardens, and lawns? Start out with a couple of the common "Foolproof Four" and add to them as you become more competent at identification.

The Mycological Immigrant: Strangers (Eating Mushrooms) in a Strange Land

The mushroom poisoning literature is filled with stories of recent immigrants who collect and eat mushrooms found in their new homeland and who base their identification on knowledge and collection history from another region of the world. The most tragic cases in the United States have often involved Asian immigrants collecting and eating deadly toxic death caps, *Amanita phalloides*, believing they are edible paddy straw mushrooms, *Volvariella speciosa*. The result has been several deaths and serious illnesses that required life-saving emergency liver transplants (see Chapter 8).

Situations that result in less severe outcomes are far more common. A few years ago I handled a mushroom identification call from our regional Poison Control Center that involved two Central European sisters and one sister's American husband. The sisters, who had recently moved to the United States from Germany, had a long history of collecting and eating mushrooms as a normal part of their diet. It was late summer, there had been a prolonged period of rain, and the boletes were fruiting.

The sisters collected and cooked a meal of boletes and all three partook, though the sisters ate fewer mushrooms than the man did. After the meal, the man suffered from nausea and vomiting for about five hours before going to the hospital and, while there, reported that his wife and her sister also felt ill but had not developed his severe symptoms. Based on descriptions and photographs, it was determined that the mushrooms eaten were the lilac-brown bolete, *Tylopilus eximius*. The man was kept overnight, treated with IV fluids and something to control his nausea, and released the following day.

According to the patient and the emergency department doctor, the man's wife said she collected and ate a similar species in her native country. However, the lilac-brown bolete, which has been responsible for a number of cases of illness in New England and eastern Canada, does not occur in Central Europe. Many Europeans grow up learning that almost all boletes are edible with the exception of some of the red-pored, blue-staining species. Clearly, and unfortunately, the toxic nature of *T. eximius* in Maine was new to this recent immigrant.

Moving into a new area—especially if it involves a radical change in climate—challenges the mushroomer to learn new species and the ecological associations related to their growth. If the climates are similar, they will likely be home to many of the same major species. Many of the more common and popular edible mushrooms hunted for food in Europe, such as the golden chanterelle and the king bolete, are also common or have similar, related edible counterparts in the United States.

Like all strangers in a strange land, the immigrant mushroomer, whether moving from Michigan to Florida or Vietnam to Northern California, needs to learn the local mushrooms before eating them. The best option is to find an experienced guide in the new location. Others might get by with the purchase and use of a mushroom field guide covering the new region. As with many aspects of life, the danger is in assuming that nothing is different.

The Adventurer

Adventurers are characterized by a lack of rational concern about the identity of the mushrooms they eat. Another way of looking at it is that they share an affinity for dinner by mushroom Russian roulette. In my experience, they have included a sixty-year-old man who collected and ate the pretty white mushrooms growing near his compost pile and later reported to the doctor covering his case of gastrointestinal distress that the mushrooms looked "beautiful and benign." He cooked and ate them, making no effort to identify his dinner. Fortunately for him, those pretty white mushrooms were not the pure white destroying angel, and he recovered.

I've also seen a man in his mid-twenties who, while walking in the woods with a friend, found an unusually large cluster of robust brown mushrooms fruiting on a stump. He reported to me that he'd eaten raw mushrooms in the woods before without any difficulty and felt he had a good sense of what would be edible. Both he and his friend reportedly ate one or two caps of the mushrooms raw and, while his friend became quite ill within two hours and had violent gut-cleansing symptoms for about twelve hours, the other young man — the one I questioned — did not develop symptoms for about twenty-four hours, but reported ongoing difficulty holding down food for the next ten days with only a slow abatement of the distress. He said that eating the mushroom was an impulsive act; he'd had no intention of collecting mushrooms and has had no training in mushroom identification. He also assured me he did not collect the mushrooms to get high.

Adventurers tend to be people with a sense of invincibility, magical think-ing, and a dearth of common sense and judgment. Fortunately for them, less than 10 percent of the species of mushrooms they are likely to find are toxic and only a few of those possess toxins capable of severe damage or death. "God protects fools, drunks, and little children." Based on the literature of mushroom poisoning and the rarity of lethal events, this also seems to hold true for adventurers.

There is another sort of adventurer — those who seek mushrooms for the experience of hallucinations, visions and mind expansion, or the recreational high. Many adults have made rational, educated decisions regarding use of psychedelic mushrooms. They've done their homework to correctly identify the mushrooms they seek, as well as identify the risks involved, and many have had positive experiences, which, for some, have been life altering.[10] Paul Stamets in his 1996 revision of *Psilocybin Mushrooms of the World* gives a series of suggestions for the responsible and respectful use of hallucinogenic mushrooms.[11] Unfortunately, some young people using these mushrooms are seeking the high without the homework. When they are out collecting their own mushrooms, this can mean confusing toxic little brown mushrooms (LBMs) for the psychotropic ones. Some LBMs contain dangerous levels of muscarine. A few, found growing in the same habitat as certain psilocybin mushrooms, contain the deadly amatoxins.

Treatment challenges can arise from people who collect and eat mush-rooms but are unsure of their identification skills, or worse still, are not aware of how little they know until too late. The anxiety that sets in once the mushroom has been eaten is often enough to produce symptoms of panic in the anxious neophyte.

It was an early autumn evening in 2006 when I received the call regarding a twenty-something male who had ventured into the woods in search of the big laughing gym, *Gymnopilus spectabilis*. The laughing mushroom and a couple of related species contain hallucinogenic psilocybin and psilocin, though they are not well known or recognized as psychedelic mushrooms in the Northeast. The young adventurer, who apparently had read about the laughing mushroom online, collected a number of mushrooms and ate some of them before returning home. It was only when doubts about accurate identification began to settle into his consciousness that he, again, looked up the description, became increasingly unsure that he'd eaten the correct mushroom, and began to feel flushed, nauseous, and panicky. He arrived at the hospital emergency department in full panic and, following contact with the regional Poison Control Center, I was contacted to provide identification expertise. The digital images of the mushrooms collected and consumed proved to be a mixture of four different species, none of which were the laughing mushroom. Fortunately, none of the species presumably eaten were dangerously toxic either. The symptoms shown by the "victim" in this case could all be explained by his rising sense of panic over eating mushrooms he did not know compounded by his fear that they might be dangerously toxic.

Mushrooming is a great hobby and a healthy way to get out into nature. Eating mushrooms adds a richness and variety to the diet and focuses your mushroom education. For a careful person, the risk of eating a bad mushroom is very low and easily avoided by following my guidelines.

~⟩ 8 ⟨~

AMANITA NIGHTMARES
The Death Cap and Destroying Angel

Among all those things that are eaten with danger, I take the mushrooms may justly be ranged in the first and principle place; true it
is that they have a most pleasant and delicate taste, but discredited
much they are and brought to an ill name, by occasion of the poison
which Agrippina the empress conveyed unto her husband Tiberius
Claudius, the Emperor, by their means a dangerous precedent given
for the like practice afterwards. And verily by that fact of hers, she set
on foot another poison, to the mischief of the whole world and her
own bane especially (even her own sonne Nero, the Emperor, that
wicked monster).

PLINY IN THE NATURAL HISTORY OF THE WORLD, A.D. 23–79

*P*liny's description of the alleged murder of Emperor Claudius in the
first century A.D. is perhaps the oldest surviving record of a mushroom
being used as an instrument of murder and regime change. While the cause
of Claudius' death is a matter of historical debate, according to this version of
the story, the Emperor's fourth wife (and niece), the Empress Agrippina, plot-
ted to elevate Nero—her son from a previous marriage—to the throne. She
first convinced Claudius to adopt Nero, putting Nero in line for ascension,
and then laced the emperor's dinner plate with either the juice or chopped
fruit of the death cap, *Amanita phalloides*. Claudius, who was a well-known
glutton and inordinately fond of mushrooms, thought he was eating the colorful and tasty Caesar's mushroom, *Amanita caesarea*, a mushroom of high
acclaim across Europe, prized by nobility of the Roman Empire, and one of
his personal favorites.

According to the historian Tacitus (circa A.D. 55–117), the emperor finished
his dinner and enjoyed the evening without ill effect, but got sick during the
night and stayed sick for some extended time thereafter. He enjoyed a brief
recovery after emptying his system, but in Tacitus' next entry, the doctor

Xenophon was called to attend to the needs of the emperor and tried to make him vomit by sticking a feather down his throat. This seems to indicate that Claudius again became ill after his initial recovery, a course of illness consistent with amatoxin poisoning. Some historians suggest that Xenophon was part of Agrippina's plot and administered a second poison to the victim at this point, perhaps an enema of colocynth, a powerful purgative. Whatever the case, Claudius' condition deteriorated, and after a significant delay, the death of the Emperor Claudius was announced and Nero assumed the throne.[1] Once, again, the delay before death is consistent with amatoxin poisoning taking a number of days to kill a victim.

Sad to say, the story may be true and such tales are what give mushrooms a bad name. If the goal has been to vilify mushrooms, the choice of *Amanita phalloides* as the poster child of mycological villainy would be ideal. The death cap, which has long been upheld as the most dangerous and deadly of mushrooms, is responsible for the majority of serious poisonings and deaths by mushrooms across the world. In Europe, it accounts for an estimated 80–90 percent of mushroom-related deaths.[2] In the United States, serious poisonings by *Amanita* mushrooms have mostly involved the death cap and the closely related destroying angels, *A. bisporigera*, *A. virosa*, and *A. ocreata*. (See #12 in the color insert.)

The Amanitas

The death cap is a medium-large, beautiful mushroom with greenish-beige cap commonly found in forested regions across much of Europe and Asia. Though not native to North America, it was introduced to this country in the last century, most likely as an inadvertent mycorrhizal hitchhiker on the rootstock of imported trees, especially European oaks, pines, and spruce. In the United States, it has become naturalized and common in the West Coast states of Washington, Oregon, and Central and Northern California. The death cap is also found increasingly in the Midwest, Mid-Atlantic states, and southern New England. The mushroom was recently collected in Maine for the first time. Though it seems to prefer growing with species of trees in the oak family, it also is found with species of pine, spruce, birch, hornbeam, and horse chestnut, and reportedly now with hemlock. Rod Tulloss, one of the leading authorities on the genus *Amanita* in North America, reports that, in the western hemisphere, the death cap has been introduced into locations from Canada to Argentina, and, therefore, few forested regions should assume they are safe from this deadly mushroom species. Once established in an area on introduced trees, it can naturalize onto native trees and shrubs, a behavior that's been noted extensively on the West Coast. Such migration of an introduced mycorrhizal fungus onto native plant species is being increasingly referred to as mycorrhizal invasion. So far, in the Northeast the death cap has been more restricted, and has rarely spread from plantation sites where it's been initially established.[3]

The death cap is so dangerous, in part, because it resembles several edible members of *Amanita*, as well as edible species of the genus *Volvariella*. The paddy straw mushroom, *Volvariella volvacea*, is a popular edible mushroom of the tropics, especially in Asia, where it is widely cultivated on rice straw. It is frequently used in Asian cooking and is widely available canned in the United States. A second species, the common volvariella, *Volvariella speciosa*, is an edible mushroom regularly found in gardens and fields. Both of these species share the characteristic distinctive volva of the amanita, a cup of tissue surrounding the base of the stem that is the remnants of the universal veil, a sac fully enclosing the young mushroom in the button stage. Because the edible volvariellas are normally collected and consumed in the firm button stage, enclosed within or barely out of the universal sac, they look a great deal like young amanitas in the button stage. Several families who have mistakenly eaten the death cap have been recent Asian immigrants to the United States and naïve about the wild mushrooms in their adopted country, believing they were collecting edible mushrooms. This scenario — of new immigrants collecting and eating mushrooms resembling a known edible back home — is one of the most common situations in which deadly amanitas are eaten in America. A significant proportion of amatoxin poisonings in America in recent years involve newly arrived or first-generation immigrants.

As with many groups of mushrooms, the taxonomy of the genus *Amanita* is complex and the understanding of the relationships among species is in flux. Many current mushroom guides refer to the North American species of destroying angels as *Amanita virosa* or *A. verna*. Recent taxonomic studies suggest that both of these names refer to European species and that the majority of pure white *Amanita* species in our northeastern woods belong to the species *Amanita bisporigera*.[4] The genus *Amanita* is quite large world-wide, encompassing more than 500 "named species" according to *Amanita* expert Rod Tulloss, and mycologists generally agree that the North American amanitas are not well understood. I recall a conversation with Tulloss at the 2007 Northeast Mycological Federation Foray in Orono, Maine, in which he recalled his state of mind at the onset of his *Amanita* studies. He said that, at the time, he felt that it would be a good project of relatively short duration. Now, many years later, he regularly comes across specimens that don't correspond with any known species and admits that a revision of the group is nowhere near completion.

The Toxins: Amatoxins

Amatoxins, the liver-destroying toxins found in amanitas, are so potent that it takes as little as 0.1 milligram (mg) of alpha-amanitin per kilogram of body weight to kill a person. A lethal dose for the average-sized adult is only 6–7 mg. Analyses of mushrooms show that *Amanita phalloides* caps contain between 0.5 and 1.5 mg of alpha-amanitin per gram of tissue, with the greatest concentration in the gills of the mushroom. Since the cap of *A. phalloides* can easily weigh 50–60 grams, a cap that is four inches in diameter could contain enough toxin to kill several people![5] The cap of a destroying angel, *Amanita bisporigera*, contains, on average, about half the concentration of alpha-amanitin as a death cap, which makes it less potent, though still capable of causing death. Concentrations of the toxins can vary according to the age of the mushrooms, between mushrooms found in different locales, and even between individual mushrooms growing together in the same locale.

By way of comparison, consider the standard dosages of several common products: In general, it takes 200–400 mg of Ibuprofen or 325–650 mg of aspirin to treat a headache. To treat an infection like strep throat, we may take 200–500 mg of an antibiotic twice a day for ten days. And a 16-ounce Starbucks regular drip coffee delivers, on average, 320 mg of caffeine. Yet only 6 mg of amanitin will kill 50 percent of the adults who consume it.

Amatoxins kill people by shutting down protein synthesis in affected organs. More specifically, alpha-amanitin binds with an enzyme known as RNA polymerase II and prevents it from functioning. RNA polymerase II is responsible for assisting the body in building proteins as directed by our cellular DNA architecture. When protein production stops, cell division shuts down. When somebody eats a death cap, amanitins are absorbed through the gut, pass through the bloodstream, and end up concentrated in organs that need proteins to rapidly replace cells, primarily the liver and secondarily the kidneys. These organs bear the brunt of early amatoxin damage; death and near death experienced from eating amanitas is typically due to liver failure.[6]

The Course of Amatoxin Poisoning

By all accounts from the people who survived to tell us about it, the deadly amanitas are tasty and will be enjoyed in direct proportion to the skill of the cook. The first sign of difficulty begins six to twelve hours after eating the mushroom. A more rapid onset of symptoms of amatoxin poisoning often signals a greater intake of toxins and a poorer prognosis, as was the case with a woman in New York State who died in 2009 following a meal of at least a dozen Amanita bisporegera and who was reported to have the onset of illness in four to five hours. The delayed onset of symptoms is typical in amatoxin poisoning and a hallmark indicator of the potential severity of the poisoning.

With amatoxin poisoning, the initial symptom phase is marked by severe gastrointestinal distress including copious, watery, or even bloody diarrhea, cramps, nausea, and vomiting. These symptoms generally last 24–40 hours before slowly abating, leaving the victim weak, worn, and fragile. At this point, victims who have sought medical attention are sometimes sent home to complete their recovery, especially if the medical providers don't know they have a case of amatoxin poisoning on their hands. Thus begins the secondary latency period, a honeymoon phase lasting another 24–48 hours and ending with the onset of symptoms of organ deterioration or failure. The gastrointestinal symptoms start again with new bouts of cramps and diarrhea and the individual will appear jaundiced. Laboratory tests show signs of a compromised liver or liver failure and possibly compromised or failing kidneys. In severe cases, without proper and timely medical intervention, the course will progress to convulsions, coma, and death due to liver or multiple organ failure, which generally happens, on average, six to eight days after the person ate the mushrooms.[7]

Prompt medical attention is the key to saving lives. The appropriate blood tests to assess liver function can indicate early signs of liver distress during the initial gastrointestinal phase, giving medical staff the opportunity to support liver function as they work to prevent absorption of toxins and maintain hydration and healthy blood chemistry. Knowing the identity of the mushrooms that the victim ate greatly aids in the early treatment and improves their chances of survival. However, accurate identification can present a problem. Given the delayed onset of symptoms, there is often no remaining uneaten food and any that has been eaten has already passed through the victim's digestive tract. In some cases, mushroom identification can be made from an analysis of spores in the victim's vomit or stool samples. Treatment should never be delayed pending identification. Treat the symptoms present!

Synopsis of Treatment Priorities for Amatoxin Poisoning

The medical interventions practiced by alert and prepared medical teams reduce toxin intake and absorption and support bodily systems through:[8]

- Early monitoring of liver function through lab tests.
- Efforts to prevent or minimize toxin absorbtion through the use of:
  - Activated charcoal to bind toxins remaining in the GI tract
  - Silymarin (milk thistle extract sold under the trade name Legalon), shown to decrease the binding of the toxins in the liver and responsible for saving lives in Europe and recently in the United States[9]
  - Penicillin G in massive doses that helps to reduce toxin reuptake
- Support of adequate hydration through the use of IV fluids to replace fluids lost through gastrointestinal disturbance and increased urine flow.
- Liver albumin dialysis through the use of a Molecular Absorbent Recirculating System (MARS) to filter toxins from the blood and cleanse the liver, giving it an opportunity to regenerate or time to wait for a transplant.[10] This has been practiced primarily in Europe.

The initial latency period prior to the onset of symptoms also allows much of the toxin to pass beyond the gut and therefore beyond "recall" from gastric lavage or the use of activated charcoal to absorb the toxins. Studies have shown that the kidneys remove amanitin from the blood and it is excreted in urine. Therefore treatment always includes hydration to increase urine production and maintain electrolyte balance in light of the losses from gastrointestinal distress. In addition, massive doses of penicillin G have been shown to be effective in reducing the reuptake of the toxin from the bile, where it concentrates following passage through the liver.

Because the death cap is native to Europe and quite common there, and because far more continental Europeans than Americans hunt and eat mushrooms, European medical authorities have developed extensive experience and more sophisticated methods of treating amanitin victims than have North American doctors. For some years, Europeans have acknowledged the availability and use of injectable silymarin (milk thistle extract) for dramatic improvement in outcomes of severe amatoxin poisonings. Although it has not been approved for regular use in this country, the Food and Drug Administration granted approval for its emergency use in a 2007 California case involving four people who nearly died following the ingestion of death cap mushrooms. Although one elderly patient later died of kidney failure, the others experienced dramatic improvement in liver functioning following the silymarin treatment and recovered.[11] Mushroom poisoning experts and the medical personnel addressing the rare cases of amatoxin poisoning hope that injectable silymarin will be granted approval for use in the United States. The rare occurrence of such poisoning in the United States, coupled with the deadliness of amatoxin, does not lend itself to the clinical trials required by the FDA for approval of new drugs or the development of new intervention techniques.

As doctors and researchers begin to understand more about the remarkable regenerative ability of liver tissue, the Europeans have also increasingly been using a technique called liver albumin dialysis that uses a Molecular Absorbent Recirculating System (MARS).[12] MARS therapy assists in the removal of toxins from the blood, temporarily replacing the function of the liver, which has shown the ability to return to full functioning if bodily functions can be supported while it has time to rejuvenate. The MARS system was approved for use by the FDA in 2005 and should now become available for use in poisoning cases in the United States. The kidneys have far less regenerative ability than the liver, and amatoxin victims often live with chronic compromised kidney function following a poisoning.

Amatoxin Poisoning in the United States

Between 2003 and 2007, an unusually high number of cases of *Amanita* poisonings occurred across North America. Sixteen incidents involving seventy-one people poisoned by amatoxin-containing species were reported. These cases resulted in twenty-three deaths, a number almost unheard of in North America.[13] (Until 2003, there had been an average of less than one death per year from all mushroom poisonings in the United States.) Of the total number, four of the deaths were in the United States and Canada, and eighteen were in Mexico. Michael Beug of NAMA reported his concern that the markedly higher death rate in Mexico was due to the lack of availability of liver transplants and the intensive medical support reviewed above. A liver transplant is the final life-saving intervention when a person's liver function collapses and death is imminent. In countries with responsive and knowledgeable medical infrastructures, the death rate from amatoxin poisoning is around 10 percent. In countries where modern medical facilities are less available, the death rate, in the absence of intensive medical intervention, is closer to 50 percent.[14]

Any abrupt rise in the number of deaths attributed to mycophagy in North America is disconcerting, to say the least. Although it is too soon to discern a long-term trend or to make clear meaning from this recent increase, a few questions are in order. Does the trend reflect an increase in eating wild mushrooms and if so, are there specific groups of people that can be identified as at greater risk? Outreach is needed to educate recent Asian immigrants to alert them to the resemblance between edible paddy straw mushrooms and the death cap. In many European countries with extensive history of mycophagy and a larger percentage of the population collecting and eating wild mushrooms, the incidence of minor and severe poisonings is much higher than in North America. Are we likely to continue to see an upward trend in the number of poisoning cases as America increases use of wild mushrooms? It could be that the increasing cases of severe poisonings are due primarily to the spread of the death cap in North America. Over time we can gather the information needed to tell whether this is indeed a trend or just a tragic anomaly. Whatever the case, the good news for those worried about toxic mushrooms is that there exists a fairly foolproof way to avoid those amanitas containing amatoxins: don't eat any species from the genus or look-alike groups. For some people, it turns out, this can prove rather difficult.

A couple of years ago I got a call from my friend Dan one late summer afternoon. Dan had taken one of my mushroom identification courses and had quickly become quite seriously infected with the mushroom foraging bug. Dan was a cancer survivor and he incorporated many medicinal mushrooms into his diet to help maintain his health. Foraging mushrooms became a perfect complement to daily nature walks and as a practitioner of Qi Gong, his walking meditations served as an ideal way to be present in the moment and the beauty of the natural world. That summer and fall, however, Dan was often distracted by the presence of great edible and medicinal mushrooms along his walk routes.

On this day, he called to consult me about a batch of blusher mushrooms, *Amanita rubescens*, that he'd found that morning and was inclined to cook up for dinner. His description over the phone seemed clear and I agreed that he likely had a basket of blushers. According to most field guides, this is a good edible species, though most authors also caution readers to avoid this mushroom (and all other amanitas) due to its deadly cousins. Dan told me he intended to eat them, but his nervous tone belied his uncertainty. He quickly added, "What do you think I should do?"

Dan was caught up in an evolutionary phase that is part of the maturation most mushroom hunters pass through. "If the books call it an edible species, I should eat it" or "the more the merrier." As food-driven collectors become familiar with the common mushrooms and grow increasingly comfortable identifying different species, they often seem to feel an internal pressure to increase the number of edible mushrooms they've tried. Some risk-taking collectors develop an element of "extreme mushrooming," the need to collect and eat an ever-increasing number of mushrooms. When this competitive nature is applied to amanitas, Michael Kuo refers to it as amanita bravado, a behavioral disorder. "Sometimes, mushroom hunters with considerable identification skills are able to successfully identify and eat some of the non-poisonous amanitas without experiencing ill effects." Kuo goes further in expressing his concern that following a dinner of amanitas, the mushroom hunter brags of his exploits to more novice hunters who may lack the identification skills needed to safely collect and eat from this high-risk group of mushrooms. "This is a dangerous state of affairs for obvious reasons, and the people involved have made little social progress since high school. If you have enjoyed a nice meal of amanitas, keep it to yourself. Bragging about it only creates social pressure for others, with less identification experience, to make a potentially fatal mistake."[15]

I told Dan that even though I was quite confident in my ability to recognize blushers from many yards down a woodland path, I had never eaten them. In keeping with my painfully gained, somewhat conservative philosophy of foraging for edible mushrooms, I replied to my friend, "Why bother?" Why bother collecting and eating amanita mushrooms, no matter how edible, when they are so closely related to the deadliest mushrooms in the world? *Especially* during high mushroom season when there are great edibles practically leaping into the collecting basket. And *especially* if you have compromised health.

Dan took my advice about his basket of blushers and later told me that the conversation had taken root. He was, thereafter, less driven to convert every potentially edible mushroom into dinner. His wife, who had been growing increasingly alarmed with what she considered his risk-taking, was relieved and encouraged by the tempering of his enthusiasm. Being a good forager does not require an ever increasing "life list" of edible mushroom species.

∽ 9 ᢵ

FALSE MORELS
The Finnish Fugu

All mushrooms are edible,
but some only once.
TRADITIONAL CROATIAN PROVERB

*I*f I haven't made it obvious before, let me set the record straight: I live along the coast of Maine, and have made this beautiful state my home since 1981. Mainers have three seasons about which we can, and generally do, boast. Spring is not one of them. Winter is a postcard-perfect scene of ice, snow, cold wind, wet boots, and mittens. Summer, though slow to arrive and impatient to leave, is a blessed time of rain and sun, lush green hillsides, and perfect sailing, and it is not too hot except for perhaps three days a year. Autumn—what can I say beyond simply perfect? Fall is when the mushroom season peaks in both abundance and diversity. Fall is crisp cool nights and blustery sunny days, sweaters, and harvest. It leaves in a blaze of color.

Then there is spring, or what we note on the calendar as spring. March 23 came this year as it always does and, on that day, I looked out my window to a snow squall that was adding even more inches to a total that had already made the ski areas proud. True spring weather was still out of sight, around the corner of next month. Every year, before spring arrives, we go through a process of thaw that we affectionately call mud season, in which the surface of the earth transforms from a frozen solid to a non-frozen solid. In between the two solid states is mud—boot-grabbing, tire-miring mud—when you carry both an umbrella and a snow shovel. On the far side of mud season is May. May is when spring truly arrives in Maine, a month when life—put on hold all winter and restrained through mud season—explodes in an ecstatic burst of greenery and rushes on to summer. May is also the month we count on seeing our first mushrooms of the season.

Unlike the morel extravaganzas of Minnesota or Michigan, spring mushrooming opportunities in most of New England are not worth planning a vacation around. In general, saprobic fungi need the earth to be warmed in order to begin the active growth of their mycelial network. The mycelium feeding through the soil duff and dead wood debris generates the biomass reserves necessary to produce fruit. And mycorrhizal species growing in symbiosis with trees and shrubs generally do not start fruiting before early summer, when they begin receiving a boost of nutrients from their host trees. There are, however, a few notable exceptions. In the spring, a northeastern mushroomer might stumble across a few eager saprobic wood rotters such as the inky caps, spring oyster mushrooms, dryad's saddle, and later, as the spring days warm, we find wine cap stropharia fruiting on wood mulch or rich garden soil. Some beautiful and interesting cup fungi, such as the scarlet cup (*Sarcoscypha austriaca*), also fruit in the spring, although not in abundance. Of course, the spring mushroom that has every dedicated mycophagist holding her or his breath in anticipation is the morel. No other mushroom in North America has more widespread recognition and elicits more passionate anticipation. But to know the morel, one must also learn the cautionary tale of another spring mushroom: the false morel.

False morels and morels, sometimes collectively called sponge mushrooms, are both groups of sac fungi or, more scientifically speaking, members of a division of fungi known as *Ascomycota*. These fungi mature their spores in saclike mother cells (microscopic asci) from which they are forcibly discharged upon maturity. Asci line the surface of the pits of morels or the surface of the folded tissue on false morels. There are about twelve species of false morels in North America, all members of the genus *Gyromitra*. They fruit on the ground, and most species can be recognized by distinctive complexly infolded caps that resemble the surface of a brain. A few are more cup-like without a distinct stalk. The best known among them is *Gyromitra esculenta*, known simply in the United States as the false morel. I will refer to this species as "the" false morel to differentiate from the group as a whole.[1]

Description

The overall shape of the false morel is difficult to describe because it is so variable. The cap, up to 5 inches in diameter, is generally irregularly spherical, but it often has irregular lobes and ridges forming peaks and valleys (see #13 in the color insert). The cap color ranges from pale brown to a warm reddish brown, but gradually darkens in age or certain weather conditions. The cap surface is complexly folded into a series of ridges resulting in a brain-like effect of wrinkled convolutions. The surface is smooth and slippery and without hairs or scales. The cap curls under and attaches irregularly to a ¾–2½-inch-thick dingy white or buff-colored stalk that is also irregularly shaped and thickens toward the base. The stalk can be hollow or stuffed with cottony tissue and there is clear separation between cap and stem. Once seen side by side, one would never mistake the false morel for a true morel. The brain-like convolutions of the false morel's cap are very distinct from the pitted surface of the morel (see #2). Morels also have a distinctly hollow stalk that merges into the cap without clear distinction.

Ecology, Habitat, and Occurrence

Both false and true morels appear in the spring as the weather is warming. Occasionally, young false morels emerge along the receding edges of snow banks or shortly after lingering drifts melt. This is more common with the related G. gigas, called the snowbank false morel in the mountainous West where it is common. The false morels in New England generally appear around the same time as the early black morels, Morchella elata, and overlap with the initial flushes of the yellow morels, Morchella esculenta. I have found the false morel and yellow morels in the same area on the same day. In a region as geographically diverse and large as New England, there is considerable variation in fruiting times of both groups from south to north and as elevation increases. The most delayed appearance would be in the northern and western mountains where many emerging plants and fungi appear two to three weeks later than in southern locations. In the mountains of the western United States, sponge mushrooms fruit commonly throughout June at higher elevations.

The most common species of false morel in New England, G. esculenta, is often found in association with white pines. Long considered a saprobic organism, living off the decomposition of dead plant material, these false morels are now seen to have the ability to form mycorrhizal relationships with trees during at least a part of their life cycle.[2] This helps explain why they can often be found in the same location in successive years.

Toxicity and/or Edibility

False morels have been described as edible mushroom that sometimes kill.[3] They also have been called deadly poisonous mushrooms that are considered desirable edibles in Europe and parts of North America. John Trestrail, retired chairman of the Toxicology Committee of the North American Mycological Association (NAMA) and managing director of Spectrum Health Regional Poison Centre in Grand Rapids, Michigan, summed up the danger very nicely, "Persons who decide to continue this gastronomic gamble should have the number of their regional poison centers engraved on their eating utensils."[4]

The compound gyromitrin, the main toxic component in this species, was not isolated until the late 1960s and much of our understanding of its mode of action on the body and its physical characteristics come from the U.S. military. Why the military? Gyromitrin quickly converts to monomethylhydrazine (MMH) in the human gut, and MMH has been used as a fuel for rockets in this country and around the world, and we all know who uses rockets. The toxic and carcinogenic nature of the MMH prompted the military to seek a better understanding of how to handle the chemical safely and to care for workers exposed to MMH. A highly volatile liquid, MMH has a boiling point of less than 90 degrees Centigrade. It continues to be just as toxic in the vaporous state, making even the process of boiling off the toxin a risky act if done in a poorly ventilated space. In Europe there have been cases where people who dry commercial quantities of the mushroom have been poisoned by the fumes given off in the drying process. The suggested method to prepare false morels safely for food involves repeated cycles of parboiling. One must be certain to boil them in a well-ventilated space and to discard the water used in the boiling, because it also contains toxic quantities of MMH. The volatile, airborne MMH is able to enter the body through unbroken skin!

The Enigma of Gyromitrin Poisoning Cases

As I address in the section on mushroom poisoning, there is a significant idiosyncratic element to mushroom interactions in the human body. A group of people eating the same quantity of the same toxic mushroom will likely react in different ways. One person might become very sick, several mildly ill, and others will not be affected at all. With false morels, the challenge of predicting the circumstances under which a person will become sick after eating this mushroom is much more difficult and even less understood.

The difficulty seems due to a number of possibly interacting factors. The concentration of the toxin gyromitrin varies greatly in samples of false morels and seems affected by the specific strain of mushrooms, the age or maturity when they were picked, and how warm or cold the days have been. There have long been assertions that mushrooms collected in different countries or between in and North America might vary in toxin concentrations. This has been used, at times, to justify the ongoing use of false morels as food. I have seen no studies attempting to assay and quantify any such variation, if it exists. Specimens grown at high elevations have lower concentrations of toxins than those at lower elevations in at least one study.[5] This seems to be contradicted by another study from Finland showing that strains grown in warmer temperatures have lower levels of toxins than those grown at cooler temperatures. It would make some sense that, in warmer, sunnier conditions, a volatile toxin might be evaporated out of the mushroom. If the ultraviolet radiation from the Sun is responsible for volatilizing or neutralizing the toxin, higher elevations might result in lower toxin concentrations because of increased UV radiation in the thinner atmosphere at high elevations.

Studies on the toxicity of MMH using monkeys have shown that there is a very narrow margin between a dose causing no observable symptoms and a lethal dose. In humans (unwilling to undergo the same experiment to which we subject the monkeys), this also appears to be true though no studies have been attempted.[6]

There appear to be great differences in individual sensitivity to gyromitrin. This may explain why there is such marked difference in the response of individuals in a group after eating this mushroom. Some will be without symptoms, others will become very ill, and still others may die after the same meal. Most of these observations have been based on uncontrolled settings without the clear knowledge of amounts eaten. It does seem more certain that there is a dose-related threshold after which someone will become ill. People are more likely to become ill if they have eaten several meals of false morels over a short period of time. It is not clear whether this is related to a developing sensitivity to the toxin or if there is a cumulative dose at work.[7] The mushroom poisoning literature throughout the past century contains numerous accounts of people who ate false morels without any problems for many years only to become very ill after another meal of the species. Drying fresh mushrooms removes much of the toxin, but not all. Boiling the fresh mushrooms twice for ten minutes in a significant volume of water removes almost all of the toxin. Of course, given the toxic nature of vaporous MMH, this must be done in a very well ventilated room.

The history of gyromitrin poisoning has shown us that rarely is there a mild case. The threshold toxic dose of gyromitrin is only slightly higher than a dose producing no symptoms of illness, and many who become ill have serious symptoms that can include liver damage. Poisoning from gyromitrin-containing mushrooms can kill! A literature review of cases occurring between 1782 and 1965 showed a mortality rate of 14 percent in Europe.[8] According to NAMA's thirty-year review of mushroom poisoning cases, there were twenty-seven cases of poisoning by *Gyromitra esculenta* during the period ending December 2005.[9] In nine cases (33 percent) there was liver damage reported, and in three cases (11 percent), kidney damage. Michael Beug found no reports of deaths caused by gyromitra in North America over the thirty years, although anecdotal reports of earlier deaths in this country abound.

Symptoms of Gyromitrin Poisoning

In a pattern following the majority of potentially deadly mushrooms, the time between eating false morels and the onset of symptoms is typically delayed. Symptoms do not generally start for six to twelve hours, though in cases of severe poisoning they may start sooner (a bad sign). In cases of mild poisoning the symptoms last from two to six days, although those with kidney of liver damage can have ongoing chronic problems. The initial symptoms affect the gastrointestinal tract and include bloating, gas, nausea, and accompanying vomiting and cramps. Severe headache and fever also may be present in the early phase. After thirty-six hours, more severely poisoned victims can develop signs of liver failure including jaundice and swelling of the liver and spleen. The breakdown of red blood cells and corresponding increase in plasma proteins can overwhelm the kidneys at a time they are responding directly to the toxins, a combination of factors that has led to renal failure in some people. Those individuals ingesting a lethal amount of gyromitrin then enter a neurologic phase with potential convulsions, delirium, coma, and death.[10]

The Controversy of the Poisonous Edible Mushroom

Reconciling the former reputation of the false morel as a great edible mushroom and its newfound status as a potentially deadly species has not come easily or clearly in the mycological community. There can be little doubt why the general public would also be confused. I have reviewed numerous popular mushroom field guides written by a number of leading mycological authorities over the past 100 years regarding the edibility or poisonous nature of the false morel. They illustrate the split personality of this mushroom in the eyes of both the amateur and professional mushrooming world and the slow development of consensus regarding the risks posed by eating most species of false morels.

Charles McIlvaine was a passionate American mycologist at the beginning of the twentieth century, famous for his eager experimentation with, and comments on, the edibility of many mushroom species not normally consumed in this country. In his 1902 *One Thousand American Fungi,* he gives his input regarding the edibility of false morels, "Since 1882 friends and myself have repeatedly eaten it. In no instance was the slightest discomfort felt from it. It was always enjoyed." McIlvaine goes on to state, "but the species, though long ago esteemed highly in Europe and by many in America, now rests under a decided suspicion. It is not probable that in our great food-giving country anyone will be narrowed to *G. esculenta* for a meal. Until such an emergency arrives, the species would be better left alone."[11] McIlvaine penned these words without further information regarding the problems associated with eating the false morel—a case of being praised with faint damnation.

Writing some thirty years later in *The Mushroom Handbook,* Louis Krieger was equally ambivalent about the edibility of the false morel. "It is known to be deadly poisonous, yet many people, both here and abroad, consume it without the slightest trace of serious consequences. Against this stands the plant's record as the slayer of one hundred and sixty people. It would seem that either we are dealing with two distinct forms of a species, one edible, the other deadly, or such consumers as survive are possessed of a natural insensitivity to the poison."[12] Again, there is no clear statement about whether or not it is safe to eat.

In the early 1940s, Clyde Christensen seemed almost apologetic when he condemned the false morel to his blacklist in *Common Edible Mushrooms.* He praised it as an edible and then stated, "The fact remains that in both Europe and America it has been known with certainty to cause fatal poisoning. Many of these cases have been too well authenticated to permit reasonable doubt as to the identity of the fungus responsible. Such cases are rare, to be sure, and most of them have occurred among people who were sick or undernourished." In the end, the extent of the reported problems outweighed his regard. "Considering the extent to which the fungus is eaten and the general excellence of its reputation, it is with some misgiving that the author puts it on his blacklist, but the fact that it has been known, unquestionably, to poison people is sufficient justification for condemning it."[13]

In 1951, Canadian mycologist Rene Pomerleau took a clearer approach to the conflicting reality between safe edible and toxic killer by stating the steps to take to render the species edible. "In spite of its name, several authors claim that the Edible Gyromitra is not always safe and may sometimes cause serious troubles. Many individuals (the author himself) can eat this mushroom without harm. Its toxic component is eliminated when parboiled. However, one should try only a small amount for the first time."[14] This mixed message seems balanced to discourage the cautious soul and encourage dangerous behavior in a risk-taker.

In 1977, Orson Miller published his well-received *Mushrooms of North America* in which he divided out several species of false morels and classified *G. esculenta* as an edible western United States species. He reported that a closely related eastern American species was problematic and emphasized that he would eat only specimens collected in the Rocky Mountains or Pacific Northwest.[15] We now recognize the eastern species as *G. esculenta*. In publishing *The Audubon Field Guide to North American Mushrooms* only four years later, Gary Lincoff extended the cautionary note on all *G. esculenta* across the country while acknowledging that most reports of poisoning occur east of the Rocky Mountains. Both Lincoff and West Coast author David Arora, in his 1986 edition of *Mushrooms Demystified*, identify the toxins in *Gyromitra* as a derivative of monomethylhydrazine, the toxic and carcinogenic compound also found in some rocket fuels.[16] Knowing the identity of the toxin, they also wrote more authoritatively regarding the use of drying, parboiling, and cooking as historic methods for drawing off the volatile compounds and rendering the mushroom safer for consumption. They also carefully caution the reader to avoid eating the mushrooms.

In 1995, Dennis Benjamin, a pathologist and dedicated mushroom toxicological expert, published the book *Mushrooms: Poisons and Panaceas*, which has become an invaluable resource for all interested in mushroom poisoning. I greatly respect the line Benjamin has taken in his treatment of the false morel and his acknowledgment of the reality that, as toxic as the mushroom has proven to be in many cases, it continues to be consumed by many, many people, especially in the western United States, where he lives. (One estimate by John Trestrail indicated that over 1 million worldwide and up to 100,000 people in the United States eat false morels.[17]) Benjamin includes complete and accurate information regarding the toxins, the species known or suspected of causing poisonings, and a picture of the clinical course of the poisoning. In addition he explores recommended treatment and supportive measures for poisoning victims under medical care. Now here is where he tips his hat to the elephant in the room. He gives clear recommendations to avoid these toxic mushrooms and also includes a set of guidelines for the safe preparation of false morels for consumption.[18] I find myself caught between viewing this as a dangerous mixed message and a very thoughtful example of informed consent.

The Finnish Fugu

There is no other region of the world like Finland, where false morels are treasured for consumption and sold fresh, dried, and even commercially canned. Marianna Paavankallio is the author of the Web site Marianna's Nordic Territory, which features information on Finnish edible and poisonous mushrooms, as well as many mushroom recipes. According to Paavankallio, of the seventeen deaths in Finland attributed to mushroom poisoning between 1885 and 1988, only four were caused by *korvasieni*, as the false morel is known in Finland (although it's worth pointing out that four translates to almost 25 percent of the country's mushroom poisoning deaths). "Mushroom experts from outside Scandinavia are frequently shocked to discover that the deadly toxic false morel (*Gyromitra esculenta*) is regarded as a delicacy in the Nordic countries, where it is sold commercially and regularly consumed. Often they seem to think that their Nordic colleagues must be totally ignorant of false morel's toxicity. The truth is, however, that every single man, woman and child who was born in Scandinavia knows—at least in Finland—that the false morel is lethally toxic if eaten raw and that even inhaling its fumes can cause poisoning symptoms."[19]

The Finnish Food Safety Authority, Evira, recently published a brochure about the safe preparation of *korvasieni* and requires the information to be included in the packaging of any false morels sold fresh or dried in the country. It is available in many languages in part because the Food Authority believes that natives know of the risks, but that foreign visitors might either believe that the mushroom is deadly poisonous or don't know it is edible and most certainly need accurate information on ridding the mushroom of the toxin.[20] The care needed in rendering the false morel into a safe edible has led a few to dub the mushroom the Finnish fugu, in honor of the prized Japanese puffer fish of the same name and similar toxic nature. I am one American not inclined to eat false morels and caution the reader to avoid this form of mushroom Russian roulette.

A FALLEN ANGEL

Out mushroom hunting—
dangerously close to caught in
late autumn showers
MATSUO BASHO (1644–1694)

*S*eptember 2004 followed an unusually wet and warm summer in Japan. The Sea of Japan was in the path of an unusually large number of named typhoons that had come ashore in parts of the country that year and, as in all wet years, the beach-goers complained and the mushroom gatherers rejoiced. Mushroomers took to the forests and fields, and a variety of fungi were gathered and eaten with great enthusiasm by the locals throughout this highly mycophilic land. Along with many parts of China and Korea, Japan is one of the more mycophilic regions in Asia.

The first recognized victim sought help in mid-September. An elderly woman was brought in to a local hospital exhibiting slurred speech, unsteadiness of gait and balance, light-headedness, and an overall sense of malaise. Over the next days, her symptoms progressed to tremors in the extremities, seizures, and increasing disturbance in consciousness as she slipped toward coma, finally requiring intubation and ventilation. The patient died of symptoms associated with acute encephalopathy fourteen days following her admission to the hospital. Simply put, encephalopathy (literally brain death) is a deterioration or degeneration of the brain tissue.

There were more than fifty other victims spanning six Japanese prefectures that fall. Over the course of two months, at least fifteen deaths across the country were attributed to this outbreak of encephalopathy. Autopsies showed brain lesions, specifically in regions of the brain known as the basal ganglia and the insula.[1] The victims shared many things in common beyond their illness. Many lived in the prefectures of Yamagata, Akita, and Niigata along the northeast coast, almost all were elderly (the average age was sixty-nine), and each person had a history of moderate to severe kidney dysfunction, including many who had a history of kidney dialysis. The final unifying characteristic was that they all also had eaten one type of common wild mushroom within a month prior to the onset of their symptoms. In many cases, they had eaten the mushrooms as part of several meals in the weeks prior to the outbreak of their symptoms. Many reported a long history of collecting and enjoying the mushroom in question.

In North America, we know this mushroom as angel wings, or *Pleurocybella porrigens*. It is common across many cooler regions and habitats, can be found growing on coniferous wood, and is closely related to the common oyster mushrooms. In Japan, it is called *sugihiratake*, which is striking because the ending *take* on a mushroom indicates that something is edible, medicinal, or both. Angel wings always have been considered as a good edible species and is highly regarded in Japan, as a welcome addition to miso soups, and battered and fried as tempura. Many rural residents look forward to the cool, wet autumn weather when it appears, and surge into the woods to collect *sugihiratake*. In addition to being foraged in rural areas, it also is brought in from rural areas and sold in cities.

In New England, angel wing mushrooms seem to favor dead, decaying spruce and fir logs, especially when the wood is lying in contact with the ground. According to David Arora in *Mushrooms Demystified*, "It is to rotting conifers what *P. ostreatus* is to hardwoods—that is, common and cosmopolitan."[2] It does not appear to be common in Europe. All of the North American references I consulted about this species refer to it as edible, though the European guides refer to it as inedible, which is likely based on lack of familiarity and exposure. Roger Phillips, in his 1981 *Mushrooms and Other Fungi of Great Britain and Europe*, lists the species as rare, reported only from the Scottish highlands and with an unknown edibility, though ten years later in his *Mushrooms of North America*, he reports it as edible and good, a reflection of its familiarity among American mushroomers. As with many less-known edibles in the United States, there exists a range of opinions regarding the gastronomic quality of this mushroom. Where some authors rate it as good, others see it as bland, and its thin flesh as a deterrent to usefulness. I suspect that any author with a field guide published after 2004 and cognizant of mushroom toxicology will place a warning regarding the edibility of the "fallen" angel.

Since 2004, a number of articles have been published by Japanese medical authorities, either describing the clinical course of the victims of angel wings poisoning in 2004 or, later, investigating to discern the chemistry and mechanics of the toxic reaction. It seems clear at this point that victims' degree of renal failure has a direct correlation to their prognosis; the people with the poorest kidney function are the most likely to die or face severe long-term impairment. The search for the responsible agent began with the initial cases and, as of this writing, remains unsolved. One theory has pointed toward cyanide and related compounds that are found in small quantities in angel wings as causative agents of the syndrome.[3] Another group is exploring compounds related to vitamin D that may act as agonists or antagonists to the vitamin, triggering hypercalcemia or hyperammonemia.[4] These conditions are identified as a clinically significant excess of either calcium or ammonia (from protein breakdown) in the blood. Careful evaluation of a patient with known kidney degeneration secondary to diabetes and seen for severe encephalopathy showed an increase in the breakdown proteins that would suggest demyelination of brain nerve tissue. (Myelin is a protein coating on nerves and essential for normal nervous system functioning.) This may indicate that the undetermined mushroom toxins act to demyelinate nerve tissue.[5] Consensus seems a distant goal.

At this time, it's also unknown whether all populations of angel wings have the potential to poison and possibly kill individuals with impaired kidney function or whether this is due to a variation of the species in Japan. At least one study has looked at the differences in chemistry among mushrooms collected from areas where the Japanese victims foraged and areas without known poisonings. No recognizable differences were seen though the researchers did not have any known compounds they were assaying for. In order to determine whether this mushroom can again be eaten outside Japan, further study is in order. It's likely that individuals with normal kidney function can continue to eat the species without problem, but without knowing the mechanism of toxicity, we can base such a statement only on history. I have certainly revised my opinion of the gastronomic desirability of angel wings from bland to dangerously interesting—interesting from a toxicological perspective that will never again include eating this species. Again, my philosophy on eating risky mushrooms is, "Why bother?"

Angel wings, which are closely related to the common oyster mushrooms, were until fairly recently, included as another species in the genus *Pleurotus* along with the other widely eaten and cultivated species and varieties. In New England, these include the common autumn-fruiting *P. ostreatus* and the equally pervasive *P. populinus* fruiting on species of aspen and poplar in the late spring and early summer. Angel wings has now been placed in its own genus. Angel wings are aggressive primary decomposers of wood, feeding on the heartwood of dead and downed conifers. In our area of New England, that primarily means spruce, fir, and hemlock. The main visible distinguishing difference between angel wings and other species of oyster-like mushrooms is the choice of softwood host. Unfortunately, this is not always easily determined, since angel wings is primarily seen fruiting on wood in advanced stages of decomposition and often in contact with the ground. Another distinguishing feature is the very thin flesh of the cap, making it almost not worth collecting and cooking unless found in abundance. Other species of oysters have thicker, more "meaty" caps. Like other oyster mushrooms, angel wings has white spores. If you find a thin-fleshed whitish mushroom fruiting on wood and it has a brown spore print, it is likely a species of *Crepidotus*.

Consider this mushroom firmly off the recommended eating list until further information becomes available. Truly, the angel has taken a fall.

THE POISON PAX
A Deadly Mystery

Not being ambitious of martyrdom,
even in the cause of gastronomical enterprise,
Especially if the instrument is to be a contemptible, rank-smelling fungus,
I never eat or cook mushrooms.
MARION HARLAND, COMMON SENSE IN THE HOUSEHOLD:
A MANUAL OF PRACTICAL HOUSEWIFERY, 1873

What would you call a common mushroom widely eaten across much of Eastern Europe for many generations, which, in spite of its edibility, was the most common cause of mushroom-related sickenings in Poland? What would you call this same mushroom if every now and then dining on it triggered an immediate and severe reaction that included the breakdown of the victim's red blood cells causing anemia, kidney damage, and occasionally death? If you needed to factor in the reality that those people severely poisoned by the mushroom typically enjoyed an extensive history of eating it with impunity, you would be faced with a mycological mystery. This is the confusing tale of the poison pax, *Paxillus involutus*, also known as the brown rolled-rim mushroom.

The poison pax is one of the more recent additions to the ranks of mushrooms that were once thought to be benign—even esteemed—as an edible in some regions of the world and are now seen as seriously toxic. It has long been associated with the more minor toxic reactions of gastrointestinal distress in Eastern Europe if eaten raw or undercooked. For a number of years, mushroom experts were aware that this species caused problems when eaten raw, but had not implicated the cooked mushroom. Raw or undercooked *Paxillus* are frequently responsible for moderate to severe gastrointestinal distress, apparently due to the presence of a heat-labile toxin that is deactivated during cooking.

European mushroom-lovers have a very different attitude than Americans

about minor illness caused by mushrooms; they take it in stride as a manage-
able side effect of enjoying a diverse diet of mushrooms. On several occasions
I have talked to European mushroomers who, with a fatalistic shrug, normal-
ize the occasional gastric upset that befalls them in the course of mycophagy.

The recognition of the connection between the poison pax and dangerous severe hemolytic anemia was much more slow in coming. Even after
the tentative connection was made, the fact that the anemia struck people
following a successful history dining on this mushroom proved to be a major
barrier to connecting *P. involutus* as the causal agent to the hemolytic reaction. Though the mushroom was implicated in other deaths across Europe,
following the death of the German mycologist Dr. Julius Schaffer in 1944,
serious questions were raised regarding the level of toxicity of *P. involutus*.
Dr. Schaffer and his wife dined on a meal including poison pax after which
he rapidly developed vomiting, diarrhea, and fever. Following hospitaliza-
tion within twenty-four hours, his kidneys, apparently already compromised,
began to fail and he died two weeks after his last mushroom meal, despite the
fact that Schaffer and his wife had previously enjoyed many meals of poison
pax. (Dr. Schaffer is perhaps the only bonafide professional mycologist known
to have died of mushroom poisoning.[1] It's not unusual for people who are
passionate about mushrooms—either professional or dedicated amateur—to
get sick from eating a mildly toxic mushroom, but rarely will a knowledgeable
mycologist eat a really poisonous one.)

The first reports of sudden death by hemolytic anemia associated with
eating poison pax were published in the 1960s and attributed the illnesses
and deaths to an unknown toxin.[2] All of the victims who developed hemolytic
anemia had eaten poison pax before without any serious problems, although
many of them did report gastrointestinal distress after the pax meal they ate
immediately prior to the serious poisoning. In the 1970s, German scientists
determined that the rapid onset of severe poisoning was attributable to an
immune response, and in 1980, the German toxicologist R. Flammer discovered an antigen in the mushroom capable of stimulating a response in the
human immune system.[3, 4]

Here is what we now know about the course of poison pax poisoning
that ends with severe consequences. For some people, following repeated
ingestion of poison pax, the body responds to an unknown antigen in the
mushroom and produces immunoglobin-G antibodies that then circulate in

the bloodstream. When they eat their next meal of the mushroom—and it can be many months later—antibody–antigen complexes form in the bloodstream. These complexes attach themselves to the surface of red blood cells circulating throughout the body, triggering cell lysis. This rapid breakdown of red blood cells begins within two hours after the meal and what follows is a rapid rise in free hemoglobin in the blood and overall anemia. The resulting rapidly lowered blood pressure can, at times, induce shock, followed by blood clotting in the vascular system. Victims typically complain of lower back pain as their kidneys become overwhelmed attempting to clean the cell fragments and free hemoglobin from the system, which may eventually lead to kidney failure.[5] Severe cases have led to extensive hospitalizations and, occasionally, death. Rapid intervention to support kidney function and to flush the toxic components from the blood can assist in recovery. By the mid-1980s, central European doctors were using plasma exchange therapy to rid the blood of the antibody–antigen complexes as an effective life-saving method along with rapid response to mitigate the effects of shock.[6] Poison pax consumption has led to a number of deaths in Europe over the years. The antibody–antigen reaction does not happen often or in many of the people who historically have eaten these mushrooms. This intermittent negative reinforcement leads some rural people in countries such as Poland to continue to eat poison pax in spite of warnings regarding the danger involved.

No deaths have been attributed to poison pax in the United States. However, Michael Beug reports that at least two cases of serious poisoning involving three adults have been reported in the United States over the past thirty years. These cases involved kidney failure and associated symptoms.[7] One can ask why we would worry about a mushroom, rarely eaten in the United States and with only three reported serious poisonings in over thirty years? Beyond the need to save lives is the need to understand the course poison pax can take so we can treat the victims in these rare cases and because there is a risk that cases may become more frequent in the future. In the Northeast, poison pax is one of a large group of mushrooms and slime molds found growing in wood mulch in increasing numbers or with extended range. Though poison pax is a mycorrhizal species, growing in close symbiotic association with the roots of trees, it appears also to benefit from energy gained by the rotting organic matter in wood mulch. This combination of mycorrhizal and saprobic activity is likely the norm in many mushroom species. In the late fall, I have observed heavy flushes of poison pax fruiting in mulch, generally beneath birch trees or shrubs. In several instances, there were many dozens of caps present in a very small area. The increased abundance may pose a threat to recent Eastern European immigrants, toddlers, and people who eat mushrooms without adequate knowledge about the dangers.

Today, anyone who consults a recently published mushroom guide will learn about poison pax's toxicity. Field guides published prior to 1980 in the United States and perhaps even later in some Eastern European countries, however, may refer to the risk of gastrointestinal distress, but generally not report the risk of potentially fatal hemolytic anemia. In 1902, Charles McIlvaine stated that *P. involutus* was "considered to be edible throughout Europe and considered esteemed in Russia."[8] Rene Pomerleau refered to this mushroom as "edible" and is representative of mycologists of his time, though some emphasize the need for cooking. Following 1960, it is interesting to see the slow infiltration of initial caution, mixed messages, and finally, in the late 1980s, a clear message regarding toxicity. Here is a sampling of the recommendations of field guide authors over time:

- **1963:** "Harmless if cooked, of little value; slightly poisonous to some when raw."[9]
- **1972:** "There are conflicting stories about the edibility of this dull brown plant."[10]
- **1973:** "Good edible, but toxic in the raw state. It is recommended to blanch this mushroom in a very large volume of water for a long time and to throw away the strongly coloured cooking water."[11]
- **1974:** "Edible, but not highly regarded. Reported as highly esteemed in the U.S.S.R."[12]
- **1977:** " . . . poisonous . . . Nature of toxin—Type III, gastrointestinal. This should be considered as dangerous, since deaths have been reported from it. The toxin is apparently most potent in raw specimens. Other authorities cite poisoning by this species from a gradually acquired allergic sensitivity that can one day suddenly lead to severe hemolysis, shock and acute kidney failure following a meal of *P. involutus*."[13]
- **1981:** "Although this species is eaten in some places, in other parts of

its range it can have a decidedly acid-sour taste. There are reports that it can produce a gradually acquired hypersensitivity that causes kidney failure."[14]

- 1982: "Harmless if cooked, slightly poisonous if eaten raw; **best avoided.**"[15]
- 1986: "Dangerous! It is often eaten in Europe and by transplanted Europeans in America, but it can cause hemolysis and kidney failure if eaten raw and sometimes when thoroughly cooked!"[16]
- 1987: "There are conflicting reports regarding the edibility of this mushroom; because of reports of poisonings, we have listed it as a poisonous species."[17]

In general, North American and western European guides published after 1990 give clear cautionary warnings, but not all do. Luigi Fenaroli, the author of a 1998 Italian pocket guide to mushrooms called *Funghi*, states, "Edible mushroom of good quality (high value), not easily confused with other noxious species. It is also successfully used in the preparation of dried mushrooms. Some authors have signaled the potential toxicity if consumed in its raw state and they recommend eating them only after a cooking period of at least 25 minutes, even though this recurrence has never been reported in the Southern European countries."[18] Clearly this author has not kept abreast of European mushroom poisoning reports.

I can only hope, given the potentially severe nature of the toxic reaction, that we do not see an increased number of poison pax cases in our hospital emergency departments. As for me—let the record be clear—I do not recommend collecting and eating the poison pax.

PART IV

MUSHROOMS AND THE MIND

The Origin of Religion and the Pathway to Enlightenment

ENTHEOGENS
A New Way to View Hallucinogenic Mushrooms

To make this trivial world sublime,
Take half a gramme of phanerothyme.
ALDOUS HUXLEY

To fathom Hell or soar angelic,
Just take a pinch of psychedelic.
HUMPHRY OSMOND

*I*n most cultures around the world, wild mushrooms are best known either as food or as potential poison. However, mushrooms also have been sought out and used by indigenous peoples in many cultures around the world for the effects they produce above the shoulders—to open and expand the mind in religious ceremonies and as intoxicants during celebrations. On almost every continent, from the Aztec and Mayan cultures that the Spaniards discovered on their arrival and conquest in the sixteenth century[1] to the ancient Greeks use of datura, there have been examples of people using plants and fungi in religious and spiritual practices to engender a state of altered consciousness that helps them access clarity of mind, understand the will of God, or gain insight for healing. In most cases, the living organism that the psychoactive compound is derived from is treated reverentially and can even be considered as a gift from, or synonymous with, the gods. Many powerful hallucinogens come from species of indigenous mushrooms.

Since the middle of the twentieth century, there has been a surge in the investigation of mind-altering natural products as the western world began to explore the application of these powerful traditional medicines. The early western adopters sought to develop a language to refer to the compounds and the experience they unleash as a first step in talking about their effects and applications to a wider audience. Lysergic acid diethylamide (LSD), a synthetic drug initially isolated from the fungus ergot, was one of the first mind-altering drugs systematically studied in the West. The first group of modern researchers that sought to understand and describe the effects of LSD coined the word "psychotomimetic" to refer to a drug that induces psychosis. Psychiatrists in Europe who began to experiment with the use of psychotomimetics in therapy used the term "psycholytic" ("mind-loosening") in the 1950s to describe a form of therapy, the compounds used in the therapy, and the desired action of the compounds. Psycholytic therapists viewed LSD, psilocybin, mescaline, and other agents as having the potential to loosen the ego defenses, and used them as an aid to traditional psychoanalysis, especially with resistant clients.[2] In 1957, the British psychiatrist Humphry Osmond devised the term "psychedelic" ("mind-manifesting") in an effort to avoid the stigma of mental illness frequently associated with psychology. Osmond wanted to take "psyche" back to the word's Greek root meaning "soul," and therefore focused on the action of these drugs on the perception of self in the universe. The term "psychedelic therapy" was used in the same period in Europe and America and relied on higher doses of LSD, and later other hallucinogens, as a way to induce insight, acceptance, tolerance, and profound spirituality.[3] In later years, the term psychedelic was broadly applied in pop culture to music, art, and lifestyle and thereby was tainted in the view of Osmond's followers.

Because the use of mind-altering compounds produces an alteration in sensory perceptions, the drugs became widely known as hallucinogens. The word hallucinate is derived from the Latin "allucinari," which means to wander mentally or talk nonsensically and is synonymous with verbs indicating insanity or delirium.[4] Since we don't refer to shamans in an altered state as crazed or psychotic, this term seems inadequate to describe the traditional role of these powerful soul releasers. Aldous Huxley, who described his journeys under the influence of mescaline in *The Doors of Perception*, suggested the name "phanerothyme"—which means to make intense emotions manifest—to capture the deep significance of his experience while under under mescaline's influence. In a playful exchange of ideas with Osmond, Huxley wrote

> "To make this trivial world sublime,
> Take half a gramme of phanerothyme."

To which Osmond replied, marketing his own ideas,

"To fathom Hell or soar angelic,
Just take a pinch of psychedelic."

Since this is probably the first time you've come across the term "phanero-thyme," you know whose ideas prevailed in the search for a language to name this unique class of compounds.

While psychedelic describes the psychoactive compounds, it also quickly came to refer to an entire lifestyle and movement. In 1979, a small group of respected ethnobotanists, ethnomycologists, and others widely respected for their work in the culture and use of hallucinogens coined the term "entheogen" to describe those psychoactive plants, mushrooms, and extracted compounds used by shamans and priests in traditional ceremonial settings or others seek-ing to create a similar ritualized setting. They desired to "propose a new term that would be appropriate for describing states of shamanic and ecstatic posses-sion induced by the ingestion of mind-altering drugs."[5] Concerned about the rapid proliferation of popular use and abuse of a variety of psychoactive drugs including LSD, mescaline, and psilocybin throughout the 1960s and 1970s, the group felt strongly that there be a method of referring to psychoactive compounds that referenced their ritualized use as gateways to the soul and enlightenment rather than simple recreational use. Entheogen comes from the Greek terms "etheos," referring to the god within, and "gen," which is the root of our English word "generative" and connotes the idea of accessing or becoming the god within. The influential thinker and writer Stanislav Grof, MD, wrote of his own fundamental experience following the use of entheo-gens, "I had a completely atheistic background when I encountered entheo-gens. For me it was not so that my first entheogenic experience confirmed or deepened something I already believed in; it was a 180-degree turn."[6]

My intent in the research and writing of the following chapters is to underscore the history of, and potential for, the use of psilocybin-containing mushrooms as entheogens and to underscore the historic use of muscimol-containing Amanita mushrooms in the same light. The abuse of psychedel-ics in the 1960s and 1970s led to the end of legitimate clinical practice and research into their potential applications in a variety of psychological settings. The slow, deliberate steps toward rehabilitation of the reputation of these entheogens are under way, and the future holds great promise for their use in assisting people to make meaning and peace with their world.

In the process of adding chapters on mind-altering mushrooms to this book, I find myself feeling vulnerable to the charges leveled by the sober and earnest scientific community and by concerned parents of impressionable teenagers who populate the planet of my other professional life as a clinical social worker and suicide prevention specialist. The exploration and publication of information about psychedelic mushrooms, other than as clearly worded cautionary tales used to bolster the 'just say no' dogma of adolescent parenting, threatens to place me clearly in the crosshairs of teachers, substance abuse counselors, police, and other people whom we rely on to protect our children. As the parent of an adolescent, my intent is not to glorify or aggrandize the use of hallucinogenic drugs or to encourage their use in uncontrolled settings. At the same time, I don't want to dismiss the potential for personal enlightenment and self-revelation simply because of the excesses of an ill-informed and irresponsible generation of recreational abusers. We have trivialized historic and ritualized use by indigenous peoples and the legitimate potential of clinical applications of compounds such as psilocybin because of our fear about the wildest excess of group LSD trips. The comparison between indigenous use and clinical applications and the uncontrolled excesses of partying is unfair and blunt. Coming of age in the early 1970s, my life was shaped by the tenor of the times and the people who questioned and challenged the cultural norms and, in so doing, brought about both widespread dissent and needed social change. To many parents and societal leaders, the uncontrolled and stormy turbulence of the late 1960s and early 1970s—and its associated excessive drug use—looked like a forest fire that threatened to consume the society they had spent their lifetimes building. The reaction of the so-called "establishment" was to attempt to quell the storm, and drug use was one of the most visible targets. Looking back, however, it seems that much of the idealism that colored the 1960s has been quelled, and drug abuse continues.

The abuse of drugs—including alcohol, marijuana, and nicotine, along with the increasingly powerful and destructive concentrated and synthetic drugs, including opiates such as oxycontin, amphetamines (including methamphetamine), cocaine, and others—remains a major and legitimate concern in the United States and around the world. The ceremonial use of entheogens by indigenous peoples did not include the uber-potent synthetic derivatives, such as LSD, that are available today. LSD presents an increased risk for a bad trip, in part due to its potency, and also because people often use it without the shelter of proscribed ceremony and support. There's a good reason why powerful prescription drugs are prescribed under the care and supervision of a doctor or other professional. In an ideal world, our doctors act in the role of shaman, establishing the ceremonial "set and setting" by informing and preparing the patient in order to ensure that the medicine can do its work. Every explorer of unknown territory needs a knowledgeable and experienced guide. This is as true for the use of psychoactive mushrooms as it is in the application of insulin for a diabetic.

AMANITA MUSCARIA
Soma, Religion, and Santa

Ein Männlein steht im Walde
Ganz still und stumm
Er hat von lauter Purpur
Ein Mäntelein um.
Sag' wer mag das Männlein sein
Das da steht auf einem Bein?
Glückspilz!
Fliegenpilz!

Little man stands in the forest
very still and mute.
He has around him
a little coat of red.
Say, who may the little man be,
that stands there on one leg?
Happiness mushroom!
Fly mushroom!
TRADITIONAL GERMAN RIDDLE

There are few mushrooms capable of triggering a broader set of associations or a wider range of reactions in people around the world than the fly agaric, *Amanita muscaria*. It is an enduring symbol of good luck and holiday cheer in parts of Europe and one of the most widely depicted mushrooms around the world—one you have surely seen in fairytale illustrations, nature photographs, plastic gewgaws, and sculptures. Whenever an author, illustrator, or artist seeks a colorful iconoclastic rendering of a mushroom, the fly agaric is most likely to lead the list of contenders. You are probably already envisioning the candy-apple red cap covered with an artfully concentric accumulation of white "warts" that is the most commonly rendered version of *Amanita muscaria*. (See #14 in the color insert.)

The fly agaric has a contradictory and confusing reputation. *Amanita muscaria* is a visionary hallucinogenic mushroom used in several cultures across the world, most notably in Siberia and other Baltic regions where people use it as an intoxicant and as an aid to shamanic healing and ritual. It has a long history of reported application as an attractant and killer of household flies. Some consider it a deadly poisonous species, though it has claimed few lives over the past 150 years. Others have learned how to prepare it safely as food and esteem it as an edible mushroom. Good luck charm, intoxicant, insecticide, food, poison—wow!

The many common names of the red or yellow *amanita* reflect its rich history around the world. Like Americans, the British know this mushrooms as the fly agaric. To the French, it is the *tue-mouche* (fly mushroom or fly killer) or *crapaudin* (toadstool). And it is known as the *mukhomor*, or fly killer, to the Russians. In Germany and adjacent Central and northern European countries, the *fliegenpilz* (fly mushroom) and *glückspilz* (happiness mushroom) is a common theme of the Christmas season and is used as tree decorations and part of the traditional advent plate along with forest greens, a red apple, and red candles.[1] Beginning in the 1800s, printed holiday cards bearing prominent images of the fly agaric along with other symbols of good luck such as horseshoes, four-leaf clovers, and fairy folk were exchanged at Christmas or to mark the New Year. The bright red and white mushroom also has been linked with the Yule celebration.

As children, we believe that reindeer fly through the night sky hauling a sleigh bearing a red-garbed, white-trimmed Santa Claus who crosses the land spreading good cheer and gifts. Some believe the image of Santa in red and white is a representation of the fly mushroom. Others postulate that reindeer came to "fly" through our sugarplum-filled imaginations fueled by *Amanita muscaria*. Are the reindeer physically flying or are they high as kites?

Reindeer (*Rangifer tarandus*), as they're called in Europe and Asia, are herd animals of the tundra and taiga of northern regions. (This is the same animal known as caribou in North America.) They have been domesticated for centuries and their husbandry forms the basis of the nomadic lifestyle of Laps in present day Norway and Finland, the Cukchi of Siberia, and other nomadic groups in Mongolia.[2] Traditionally, for all the nomadic groups, reindeer skins provided the raw materials for the tents over their heads, the clothing on their backs, and the warm, tough boots on their feet. In many regions, they are still raised for their hides and meat, and their milk is used fresh and made into cheese and yogurt. Reindeer milk is perhaps the world's richest in fats and solids. Fresh, it is the consistency of cow's milk cream.

Reindeer are normally fairly docile and easily managed. In some regions, children as young as three learn to ride and handle the large beasts, and infants are carried in cradles on their backs as families travel to new grazing land. They are pack animals that can carry up to 100 pounds across tundra landscape and also are used to pull sleighs across the frozen landscape as the beast of burden in the far north.

The connection between reindeer and the fly mushroom has been reported many times, most famously from Gordon Wasson's work *Soma: Divine Mushroom of Immortality*, which sums up a number of historic references. Reindeer are fond of mushrooms and actively seek them out as a preferred food during the short arctic season when mushrooms abound.[3] They love the fly mushroom and have been observed selecting them preferentially over other types. Under the influence of the fly mushroom, the normally docile reindeer become quite frisky and difficult to manage and stories abound of their leaping and cavorting across the tundra after a meal of the bright red fruit. Reindeer not only seek out the mushrooms to eat, but also will seek out the urine of other reindeer or the urine of humans who relieve themselves after eating fly agaric. The mushroom's psychoactive chemical is excreted in urine and the reindeer can smell it. Accounts have described assertive tactics of the herd leaders seeking mukhomor-tainted urine, and the journal of an eighteenth century Russian explorer, Gavril Sarychev, described reindeer herdsman using sealskin containers of tainted urine to lure wandering animals back into the herd.[4] Men coming out of celebrations in which the fly mushroom was used as an intoxicant have reported being bowled over by reindeer seeking to share in the fun. So the leap (metaphorically) from reindeer "flying high" due to mushroom intoxication and flying reindeer harnessed to Santa's sleigh may not be too unrealistic.

Our modern image of Santa is an amalgam of northern European forest-dwelling pagan traditions coupled with early Christian beliefs and stories, and all abundantly leavened with twentieth century commercial spin. Early images of Santa from the 1800s showed him in forest browns and natural colors and not wearing red until later Victorian-era images.[5] Santa's current garb was epitomized in a 1931 advertising campaign by Coca Cola depicting the jolly man dressed in red, as bright as a newly emerging fly agaric cap. Clement Moore first depicted Santa being carried in a flying sleigh pulled by tiny reindeer in his 1822 poem *A Visit from St. Nicholas* and it is thought his ideas came from reports of the Saami people's use of reindeer to pull sleighs in northern Scandanavia. The red *Amanita* image has long been a symbol of good luck in the season of the longest night, a red light shining bright in the winter darkness.

Amanita muscaria as Intoxicant and as Visionary Vehicle

In 1730, a German-born Swedish colonel named Filip Johann von Strahlberg published a book about his experiences as a prisoner in Siberia that described his observations of the local village's use of mukhomer in celebrations, "Those who are rich among them, lay up large Provisions of these Mushrooms, for the Winter. When they make feast, they pour water upon some of these Mushrooms and boil them. They then drink the Liquor, which intoxicates them." He went on to relate the practice of those not able to secure their own mushrooms as standing by with vessels to collect and drink the urine of the fortunate ones, "as having still some virtue of the mushroom in it and by this way they also get drunk."[6] Strahlberg was one of several thousand Swedes sent to work in Siberia following their capture by the Russians during Swedish King Charles' disastrous invasion of Russia. During his twelve years as a prisoner, Strahlberg was nevertheless able to travel widely and made detailed observations of the people and customs that remain a valuable glimpse into the lives of native Siberian groups pushed out or disrupted by Russian expansion. There are a number of other early observations of the use of *mukhomor* as an inebriant throughout Siberia, mostly from Russian explorers and traders. Part of later Russian domination of this region included the introduction of vodka, a more universal inebriant that, over time, has replaced most *mukhomor* use.

Gary Lincoff, the contemporary mycologist and author of the popular *Audubon Society Field Guide to North American Mushrooms*, led a group

Native Siberians Adapt Use of Mushrooms as Food

The observation that most Siberian native peoples traditionally avoid mushrooms as food is further supported by the fascinating work of Sveta Yamin-Pasternak,[7] who studied and contrasted the mycological attitudes and eating habits of the native Yupiik and Inupiaq peoples along the shores of the Bering Straits in both Alaska and Russia. She noted that throughout the region and on both continents people shared common food preferences regarding meats, seafood, berries, and greens. However, she observed markedly different attitudes regarding mushrooms and each group's use of them. The people on the Siberian side collected, ate, and stored for winter use many mushroom species, especially *Lactarius* and *Leccinum* species, while on the Alaskan shores they feared and actively avoided mushrooms, maintaining a traditional assumption of their evil and poisonous nature. She found that the Siberian natives had no extensive history of mushroom use, but had adopted their strong mycophilic habits only during the past two generations, beginning in the 1960s. They learned to embrace edible mushrooms through their association with ethnic Russians who moved into the area heavily following World War II. As these teachers and government officials living in a new environment collected and used the local mushrooms, their passionate love of all things mushroom began to rub off on the local Yupiiks, especially those who lived along the coast and derived their living from the sea. Currently, there is a large proportion of the local people who avidly seek out the rich harvest of mushrooms during the very brief summer and autumn and preserve them for use during the nine months of winter that follow. The regional reindeer herders living in the same region continue to avoid mushrooms, though their four-legged charges avidly seek them out as a preferred food. Unlike the Koryaks to the south, the native peoples of the Bering shores have no reported history of *Amanita muscaria* use; it does not grow in their tundra region.[8] In contrast, the Alaska natives, without the recent Russian influence, continue to avoid all mushrooms, following long-held traditions.

of mushroomers to eastern Siberia on two occasions in 1994 and 1995 and spent time observing and interviewing residents of several native Koryak and Even villages on the Kamchatka Peninsula about their use of mushrooms in general and *Amanita muscaria* in particular. Their main informant was a seventh-generation Even shaman who reported on her use of A. *muscaria* as a medicinal mushroom to assist elders with sleep and as a wound poultice for its anti-inflammatory and analgesic effects. She also ate the mushrooms "as a device to allow her to visit the spirit world to seek, for example, the cure for an illness (physical, mental, or spiritual), or the place where a successful hunt could occur."[9] Interestingly, Lincoff reported that the Koryaks in the area used only two mushrooms, the fly agaric and chaga (*Inonotus obliquus*). Both were used medicinally; none of the local mushrooms were used as food. The ethnic Russian people now living in the area, in contrast, collected and ate many species of mushrooms, as is their custom, but did not collect or use the fly agaric.

According to some researchers, *Amanita muscaria* has had a significant impact on world cultures for at least 4,000 years and may be at the root of several of our major religions.[10] Gordon Wasson brought broad western attention to *Amanita muscaria* with the publication of his 1968 work *Soma: Divine Mushroom of Immortality* in which he postulated that A. *muscaria* was the substance, organism, and deified portal into insight and wisdom known as Soma. Soma is the plant/God described in written texts transcribing more than one thousand oral hymns of the Aryan peoples who migrated from northern lands of Eurasia, settled in an area now known as Iran, and became known as the Vedic people. An inebriant that produced visions, Soma was described as a liquid that could be squeezed out of a reddish plant and then drunk by priests in highly proscribed ceremonies. Unfortunately, Soma use in the Vedic descendents ended many centuries before Christianity, and written accounts of teachings passed down in an oral tradition without a clear description of the plant of origin are all that remain. Along with other hints, the description of Soma as a red plant without mention of roots, leaves, or trunk brought Wasson to the conclusion that Soma must be A. *muscaria*. This idea was met with strongly mixed reactions from Vedic scholars and the general public. It has been widely refuted by some scholars though it is still actively debated within the field. Many different plants have been proposed as Soma, though no broad consensus has been reached on the origin of this powerful religious symbol.

Following Wasson's work, John Marco Allegro, a British scholar of Oriental studies, published *The Sacred Mushroom and the Cross* in 1970. In 1953, Allegro had become the first British professional invited to join an international cadre of scholars to examine and translate the Dead Sea Scrolls, which were discovered between 1947 and 1956 in a series of caves along the ancient shores of the Dead Sea in what is now the West Bank of Israel.[11] Over the years, Allegro's studies and work with the scrolls led him to become one of the most public and outspoken members of a normally restrained field of scholars. He carried out his personal belief that the information on religion and culture contained in the scrolls should be made public for people to see and interpret on their own and that the scrolls contain information that would help us understand the shared origin of the three major religions, Christianity, Islam, and Judaism. Allegro was a specialist in the origins and derivation of language, a philologist, and worked to trace biblical language back to its roots. He developed a complex and involved argument that the roots of Christianity are connected to the development of myths, religion, and cult practices in a number of cultures. He further asserted that the roots of Christianity and other religions are intertwined with those of fertility cults that practiced the ritualized use of psychoactive mushrooms including *Amanita muscaria* to perceive the mind of God. Met with a strongly negative and skeptical reaction from the church and a variety of religious scholars, Allegro's work has been questioned and refuted by many and yet stands as a fascinating thesis into the origin of religion with a mycological twist.

The Fly Agaric in the 1960s

Following the publication of Gordon Wasson's *Soma*, the broader popular culture began to look more closely at *Amanita muscaria* as a source of enlightenment and psychic exploration. The hope that the fly mushroom could bring intense, sublime, soul-transporting experiences led a generation of seekers to try it. In the late 1960s and through the 1970s, thousands of people experimented with the effects of the fly mushroom as they experimented with and used other hallucinogens such as mescaline, psilocybin, and LSD. There are many accounts of these experiences, including one from Tom Robbins entitled "Superfly: The Toadstool that Conquered the Universe," published in *High Times* in 1976:

> I have eaten the fly agaric three times. On the second of those occasions I experienced nothing but a slight nausea. The other times I got gloriously, colossally drunk.
>
> I say "drunk" rather than "high" because I was illuminated by none of the sweet oceanic electricity that it has been my privilege to conduct after swallowing mescaline or LSD-25. On acid, I felt that I was an integral part of the universe. On muscaria I felt that I was the universe. There was no sense of ego loss. Quite the contrary: I was a superhero who could lick any archangel in town and the rusty boxcar it hoboed in on.
>
> I wasn't hostile, understand, but I felt invincibly strong and fully capable of dealing with the furniture, which was breaking apart and melting into creeks of color at my feet. Although my biceps are more like lemons than grapefruit, I would have readily accepted a challenge from Muhammad Ali.[12]

By many other accounts, the reality often experienced by fly agaric users has often not lived up to the advertised hype. The concentrations of the active ingredients of the mushroom vary widely with location, season, age of mushroom, and numerous other variables. People who imbibe it are often assured of becoming nauseous without the assurance of becoming high.

Gordon Wasson described his own experience of self-administered A. *muscaria* along with the experiences of his co-workers in the mid 1960s. They ate the mushrooms in a number of forms, including raw with and without food and the juice of the mushroom plain or with milk. The members felt universally nauseous and several became ill. They fell into deep slumbers and could not be aroused easily. According to Wasson, "When in this state, I once had vivid dreams, but nothing like what happened when I took Psilocybe mushrooms in Mexico, where I did not sleep at all."[13]

The author Frits Staal offers another description of Soma use, based on written accounts from oral Rigveda hymns. "The effect of drinking Soma is generally described by forms and derivatives of the verb mad, which has nothing to do with English 'mad.' It has a range of meanings including delight, intoxication, and inspiration. It also refers to the heavenly bliss of gods and ancestors and is, in the context of Soma, best translated and interpreted as rapture or elation."[14] Clearly, the historic record and the more recent, first-hand accounts differ markedly in both the tenor and content of the experience.

The Fly Agaric in Literature

When Lewis Carroll (Charles L. Dodgson) penned *Alice in Wonderland* in 1865, there is little doubt that he modeled the mushroom of amazing abilities after the attributes of the fly agaric. He likely read about the candy apple red-capped mushroom in contemporary mushroom literature such as Cooke's manual on British fungi that contained an account of the properties of *Amanita muscaria*. These were translated into the experiences of Alice when she encountered a prophetic caterpillar. The concept took on another, more pop flair in the mid-1960s release of Jefferson Airplane's "Go Ask Alice" with Grace Slick's haunting voice chanting about a mind moving slowly following having some kind of mushroom and the antics of a hookah-smoking caterpillar.

Other well-known popular uses of images of the fly agaric include the video game *Super Mario Brothers* and, for an older generation, the dance of the mushrooms in Walt Disney's production *Fantasia* to the accompaniment of Tchaikovsky's "Nutcracker Suite." In *Fantasia*, the mushrooms shake off their distinctive white warts within the first few seconds of the dance.

Amanita muscaria as a Poisonous Mushroom

Amanita muscaria is a poisonous mushroom and a few mushroom experts call it deadly poisonous. It is also an edible mushroom if properly prepared, regularly consumed in different parts of the world, and considered to be quite tasty. The simple act of writing these two conflicting statements in succession about the same mushroom makes me quite uncomfortable and sets the fellow mushroom poisoning experts in my head clamoring for rebuttal time. How can both of the previous two sentences be true—that the fly agaric is edible *and* poisonous? Even if they are both true, we risk giving a dangerous mixed message to the general public. Be that as it may, both statements *are* accurate, and A. *muscaria* is not the only example of such dichotomy. The tropical staples cassava, the source of tapioca, and the starchy taro root both require long specific preparations to render them edible.

Closer to home, pokeweed is a common wild plant with a long tradition as a spring green in parts of the southern United States. This deep green plant with red stems and enticingly purple sprays of berries contains a seriously toxic tuber, poisonous stems and older leaves, and edible, even esteemed new shoots. The deep red juice of the pokeberry has been used to make ink and, in fact, the Declaration of Independence was written using pokeberry ink. The roots of the plant are the most toxic, but even the shoots must be carefully boiled in two changes of water to leach out the low levels of alkaloid toxins they contain.

Charles McIlvaine (1902), famous in the mushrooming world for his cast iron stomach and effusive praise on the edibility of marginal mushrooms, considered the fly agaric "poisonous to a high degree." Though not very specific, he was right in that consumption of *Amanita muscaria* or the related species A. *pantherina*, A. *crenulata*, or A. *frostiana* generally results in onset of nausea and vomiting within ninety minutes, followed by confused thinking, loss of coordination or staggered gait, and, in some cases, euphoria, agitation, or both. This is often followed by a period of deep, coma-like sleep from which the individual may not be roused for some hours. During this sleep, the person might experience intense dreams or visions. The whole experience might also include tremors, muscle spasms, and cramps (perhaps from muscarine) and is generally fully resolved within twenty-four hours.[15]

Most authors acknowledge the toxic nature of this mushroom and qualify it as generally non-fatal. A very few will acknowledge that this mushroom is consumed as food in certain regions. In the *Mushroom Hunter's Field Guide*, the noted American mycologist Alexander Smith reports that "some people extract the poison and then eat the mushroom, apparently with no ill effects. They claim it is a most delicious species." He goes on to give general directions for the safe preparation including boiling in salted water. Smith finishes by giving the universal caveat emptor: Do so at your own risk.[16]

The food author William Rubel of Santa Cruz, California, began experimenting with preparing and eating *Amanita muscaria* after learning of a number of regions in Europe and Asia with a history of use of these mushrooms as food. He suggests boiling the mushrooms in salted water (1 teaspoon of salt per quart of water) and to discard the water before continuing to prepare the mushroom dish.[17]

That said, there also have been a couple of well-publicized historic deaths attributed to the consumption of the fly agaric, the most sensational of which was the 1897 death of the Italian diplomat, Count Achilles de Vecchj, in Washington, DC. De Vecchj considered himself an authority on all things fungi and, after talking with a vender at the K Street market, convinced the man to bring in some mushrooms found around his property. De Vecchj reportedly conducted some tests with chemicals and also cut the stem of the mushrooms with a knife, noting none of the blackening that would indicate (to him) poisonous properties. According to the vendor, the count considered these tests infallible estimations of wholesomeness. The count cooked up a large quantity of the mushrooms and served them for breakfast. De Vecchj himself ate several full plates, an estimated two-dozen caps. His friend, a Dr. Kelly, who consumed about half as many mushrooms, went on to work, fell ill, was briefly treated at a local hospital, and recovered fully. Count de Vecchj, who was known to be in poor health and weighed more than 300 pounds, fell ill shortly after his meal, collapsed and, after refusing an emetic, fell into a coma-like stupor. He developed violent convulsions and died the following day.[18] De Vecchj's death came at a time of Americans' growing interest in wild mushrooms and shortly after the establishment of the country's first mycological societies, and authorities used the publicity to sound the note of caution to would-be amateur mushroom eaters.

As in the nineteenth century, today severe illnesses and deaths from *Amanita muscaria* are exceedingly rare with perhaps three cases documented worldwide over the past fifty years.[19] In Beug's thirty-year review of mushroom poisoning cases in North America, 211 cases of toxic reactions were ascribed to the fly mushroom with one death attributed to freezing to death in a tent following *A. muscaria* ingestion. Other reported deaths worldwide have generally involved vulnerable people with already compromised health.

Dogs as well as reindeer find the muscimol-containing mushrooms attractive, and every year there are cases of pet intoxication and occasional death. Even cats, which normally have better sense about these things than dogs, are attracted to the fly agaric and panther cap and have become ill.[20]

Though the range of potential reactions from eating *A. muscaria* are broad and generally not severe, it is hoped that their recitation sounds the deep gong of warning to anyone considering their use as food or intoxicant. People generally get sick, and a very few dangerously so. A few people get high, and generally not wonderfully so. I recommend using them as good luck charms and avoiding them as food or recreation.

DESCRIPTION AND TAXONOMY

Amanita muscaria is one of the more striking members of the genus *Amanita*, an illustrious group of fungi notable for beauty and grace. The genus is home to both fantastically poisonous and famously edible members, including one of the better-regarded edible amanitas, Caesar's mushroom. Especially in Europe, Caesar's mushroom (*A. caesarea*) with its shiny orange cap and stem, is prized as an edible and known as a favorite food of the Romans as well their emperors, hence the name. The amanitas are even more famous as killers—the death cap (*Amanita phalloides*) reputedly killed Emperor Claudius. The truly dangerous nature of the amatoxin-containing species of amanitas has given rise to the common practice among mushroom field guide authors of recommending that no members of *Amanita* be considered as food. Others take a more nuanced approach but warn of the risks of misidentification.

The amanitas as a group have several features in common. All are upright classic-looking mushrooms with a central rounded cap that starts out almost spherical and matures into a flat or slightly convex shape. All have white or whitish gills free from the stalk and a white spore print. The cap sits atop a stem or stalk generally sporting a ring or annulus around the midsection that is the remnant of tissue covering the gills in a young mushroom. The base of the stalk is generally swollen and shows either scars or remnants of tissue that comprised a sac-like universal veil enclosing the entire mushroom in button stage. In several species, the cap of the mushroom is covered with scattered wart-like patches of tissue, the remaining bits of the universal veil. In other species, this universal veil splits open to allow expansion of the stem and cap and then remains cupped around the base as a sac-like volva.

After emerging from an egg-shaped button completely enclosed by the universal veil, *Amanita muscaria* assumes a traditional mushroom demeanor with a central stalk 4–8 inches high with a pendulous ring midway down and becoming bulbous at the base. This broadened stem base shows a series of concentric ring-like scars from the universal veil. The cap is perfectly round and central on the stalk, initially rounded and gradually becoming flat on maturity, generally up to 8 inches in diameter and covered with pyramidal whitish patches (warts) that are the broken remnants of the universal veil. The gills beneath the cap are whitish, closely packed, and free from the stalk. The spore print is white. In the northeast United States, we primarily see A. *muscaria* var. *formosa* with an orange to yellow cap and occasionally var. *alba*

The Fungal Invasion

Amanita muscaria is extending its range around the world due to man's intervention. Though its ancestral range is confined to the Northern Hemisphere, the movement of cultivated trees and shrubs as nursery stock into new environments and onto new continents has led to the introduction of mushrooms to new regions. Mycorrhizal mushrooms like amanitas, growing with desirable timber and landscaping plants, and saprobic mushrooms associated with livestock dung, have been especially mobile. The fly mushroom is now found introduced and naturalized on the continents of South America, Australia, New Zealand, and Africa.[21] In New Zealand, where conifers have been imported and planted in large numbers as a basis for their timber industry, there is concern regarding the presence and increasingly common occurrence of *Amanita muscaria*. The colorful mushroom thrives in plantations of imported Douglas fir (*Pseudotsuga menziesii*) and reportedly has adapted to live on some native species as well. There is some concern that this highly adaptable fungus poses a threat to native mycorrhizal mushroom species, and it is now considered invasive.[22] It is a new paradigm to consider mushroom-producing fungi as invasive along with plants such as kudzu, insects like the emerald ash borer, birds like the starling and pigeon, and mammals such as the Norway rat. Within the fungal kingdom, we are more accustomed to learning of invasive fungal pathogens of plants, memorable examples being Dutch elm disease and chestnut blight, which were transported to North America and are responsible for the death of millions of trees. Their swath of destruction has changed the forest and community landscape in fundamental ways across much of the United States. The idea that a mushroom is invasive has not yet settled into the public consciousness.

with a pale, off-white cap. (#14) West of the Mississippi River and in Europe, the classic red-capped form of the fly mushroom dominates.

According to recent genetic analysis and the work of Rod Tulloss, the yellow A. *muscaria* of eastern North America has been renamed A. *muscaria* var. *guessowii* in recognition of the genetic differentiation from the European variety *formosa*. At this time, most published field guides list the old name. West of the Mississippi River, the *Amanita muscaria* takes on the appearance of the red-capped form originally described from Europe and Asia, but is a different subspecies, A. *muscaria* var. *flavivolvata*. This variety is common from Alaska to Central Mexico and the highlands of Guatemala, while the original A. *muscaria* var. *muscaria* is known from Europe, Asia, and only far northwestern Alaska.[23]

Ecology, Habitat, and Occurrence

The fly agaric grows in symbiotic association with the roots of a number of tree species. It is commonly found fruiting around trees in lawns and parks as well as deep in the forest. Its association with trees is based on a lasting symbiotic mycorrhizal relationship between tree and fungus. The fly mushroom forms relationships with tree groups including spruce, pine, birch, and aspen. A dedicated mushroom hunter should be on the lookout for patches of A. *muscaria* fruiting because it often fruits in the same location and same time as the highly desirable and edible *Boletus edulis*. The statuesque fly mushroom is visible from a distance and worth stopping to appreciate for the eye-candy appeal alone, but while you are gawking, keep on the lookout for the less obvious porcini.

The combination of good rainfall and the cool weather in midsummer and autumn brings on the fruiting of the fly mushroom in the eastern and central United States. In Maine that means we see these brightly colored fungi anytime from August through early November. In a particularly wet year, the fly agaric also is seen occasionally in early summer though care must be taken to not confuse it with other yellowish amanitas. The typical rainfall and weather patterns on the West Coast trigger fruiting of the fly agaric in California, Oregon, and Washington from fall through the winter.

Active Components

Amanita muscaria in all of its forms and varieties along with a few related species including A. *pantherina*, the panther cap, contain ibotenic acid and muscimol, two closely related compounds responsible for the psychoactive response when this mushroom is ingested. The psychoactive compounds are in the flesh of the mushroom and concentrated in the skin and the associated underlying flesh of the cap. When ingested, both compounds are able to cross the blood–brain barrier and act on neurotransmitter receptors in the brain. Once bound to these brain serotonin receptors, muscimol tends to remain bound for longer periods than other neurotransmitters, thus accounting for its prolonged effects. There is some evidence that ibotenic acid is excitatory and muscimol is depressive, though in the process of cooking or drying the mushrooms, ibotenic acid is easily and quickly decarboxylated into the more active muscimol. This conversion also occurs in the digestive tract.[24, 25]

The mushroom toxin muscarine was first discovered in the fly agaric and was long held responsible for the effects of the mushroom when eaten. It has since been established that the concentration of muscarine is too small to cause significant effects. It has been suggested by some that small concentrations of muscarine might be responsible for the reported twitching and spasmodic movements that occur with some people who have eaten these mushrooms. Benjamin reports this with the caveat that real evidence is lacking to support the claim.[26] It is still possible to find recently published reports concerning the fly agaric and panther cap that attribute the toxicity to muscarine alone.

The extensive and conflicting history of these mushrooms will ensure that new information and theories regarding historic claims and attributions will keep mycologists and anthropologists busy for generations to come. For many, the beauty of these mushrooms alone is enough reason to stop and admire their presence in the world.

PSILOCYBIN

Gateway to the Soul or Just a Good High?

*I*n 1957, *Life* magazine published an article by the noted amateur mycol-ogist R. Gordon Wasson that introduced hallucinogens to the popular culture and gave us the term "magic" as a way to describe mushrooms. In "Seeking the Magic Mushroom," Wasson described his experience in a village in southern Mexico, where, accompanied by his friend Allan Richardson, he actively took part in a traditional ceremony that spanned the night and involved eating hallucinogenic psilocybin mushrooms under the guidance of a local curandera, or healer, Maria Sabina, identified in the article under the pseudonym Eva Mendez. Wasson, one of the first Anglo-Saxons to take part in such ceremony, experienced the visions and mind expansion these magic mushrooms induce. "I saw river estuaries, pellucid water flowing through an endless expanse of reeds down to a measureless sea, all by the pastel light of a horizontal sun." He reported seeing a female figure dressed in native costume and was struck by the inability to connect with that world he saw. "There I was, poised in space, a disembodied eye, invisible, incorporeal, seeing but not seen."[1]

For Wasson, an international banker and vice president of JP Morgan, it was part of a thirty-year quest with his partner and wife, Valentina Pavlovna Wasson, to explore the connections between people and mushrooms in diverse cultures around the world. The Wassons had first traveled to Mexico in the mid-1950s after hearing reports of indigenous peoples in the Oaxaca region practicing rituals with hallucinogenic mushrooms. They hoped and expected to find the people using *Amanita muscaria*, the fly agaric, in these ceremo-nies, which would further support their working hypothesis that *Amanita muscaria* was the Soma, the divine plant-god referred to in Vedic tradition. Though fly agaric was found growing in the mountainous region in nearby Oaxaca, people repeatedly denied using it. Later, the Wassons' continued exploration revealed that they were asking the wrong question: The people did use mushrooms, but the ones they used belonged to a group of species in the genus *Psilocybe* and related genera. This revelation led, after a period of investigation, to their nocturnal ceremony with Maria Sabina and the exposure of psilocybin mushrooms to the larger world. Valentina Pavlovna Wasson and her daughter participated in their own mushroom ritual five days after her husband's, and she wrote of her own experience. She died in 1958, and Gordon Wasson continued their life's work on his own.

History

Psilocybin mushrooms were being used by Mayans and Aztecs in ceremonies and sacrificial offerings long before the Spanish explorers first landed in the New World early in the sixteenth century. Following their arrival, a small number of Spanish priests and officials wrote accounts of these ceremonies, detailing their observations about the use of mushrooms in both ceremonial and religious contexts.

In the mid-1500s, a Franciscan friar named Bernardino de Sahagun described the use of magic mushrooms in several passages of his famous historical work, *Historia General de tas Cosas de Nueva Espana.* He observed natives eating the mushrooms with honey, partaking of nothing else but chocolate through the night, and recounted some people's visions of good fortune and long peaceful lives and other people's visions of violent death. "All such things they saw. . . . And when [the effects of] the mushroom ceased, they conversed with one another, spoke of what they had seen in the vision."[2]

Around the same time, a Dominican friar named Diego Duran also noted the use of mushrooms as inebriants during the festivities of the Aztec emperor Moctezuma II's ascension to the throne in 1502. And in a report on religious use from the seventeenth century, Don Jacinto de la Serna wrote of a fellow priest who gave the mushrooms out to festival participants "in the manner of a Communion so that they all went out of their heads, a shame it was to see. In Nahuatl, the language of the Aztecs, these mushrooms were described as *teonancatl*, which can be translated as 'sacred mushroom.'"[3]

The Aztecs' use of the name *teonanacatl*, which is translated as "God's flesh," reflects the belief that the hallucinogenic mushrooms were part deity, God's flesh, or a gift from the gods. This theme endures in several cultures where mushrooms are used ceremonially, including the northern European use of *Amanita muscaria*. The European Christian priests and missionaries witnessing these rites and celebrations reacted strongly to what they saw as the pagan nature of the ceremonies and condemned the practice as idolatry. As the Spaniards tightened their control on the native peoples of Mexico and Central America, the practice of their religion, the sacrifices, and the ceremonial use of mushrooms disappeared or were forced deep underground.

At the beginning of the twentieth century, it was widely believed that there was no remaining ceremonial use of mushrooms in the Americas. In 1915, the American botanist W. E. Safford reported, in a talk to the Botanical Society of Washington and in a journal article, his belief that magic mushrooms weren't being and never had been used in the Americas and that early reports to the contrary were mistaken and should have been attributed to the use of the hallucinogenic peyote cactus.[4] A Mexican physician who openly disagreed with Safford later found evidence of mushroom use in isolated mountain villages in southern Mexico. In 1938, anthropologists and botanists from the United States (with the help of local informants and experts, I imagine) "found" the mushrooms and observed a nocturnal ceremony in which the mushrooms were used.[5] Although World War II interrupted further exploration, this early rediscovery of the indigenous use of hallucinogenic mushrooms paved the way for the Wassons' work in Mexico in the 1950s. Interestingly, although the sixteenth-century Spanish Catholics considered the use of hallucinogenic mushrooms to be a pagan ritual, when Wasson participated in the ceremony, the curandera Maria Sabina included many Christian images and symbols. Likewise, several local villagers spoke about their ongoing belief in the Godhood of the local mushrooms and the marriage of indigenous beliefs and Christianity. "To eat the mushrooms, you must be clean: they are the blood of our Lord the Eternal Father."[6]

Throughout the 1950s, scientists in the United States and in Europe began to look more closely at a number of plants and fungi purported to contain psychoactive compounds and to study the chemistry of psychedelics as well as their potential for use in medicine. Roger Heim, a noted mycologist of the time and a friend of Gordon Wasson, accompanied Wasson on some of his explorations into Mexico and Central America in the mid-1950s. Heim collected, described, and named a number of the mushroom species used by indigenous people in Mesoamerica and was soon able to cultivate the hallucinogenic *Psilocybe mexicana* in his laboratory. In 1957, Heim approached the Swiss chemist Albert Hofmann with a request to identify the active components in the magic mushrooms that he and Wasson had collected in Mexico the previous year. Hofmann, who is best known today as the man who discovered and synthesized LSD in 1938, was working for the Swiss pharmaceutical company Sandoz, had read of Wasson's work in Mexico, and was already interested in magic mushrooms before ever being approached. He readily accepted the challenge. Hofmann isolated and named the active components—psilocybin and psilocin—from specimens of *Psilocybin mexicana* that Heim had cultivated. Hofmann quickly determined a method to synthesize psilocybin, and Sandoz marketed and sold it in pure form for research studies into its potential clinical use and later for sale to psychiatrists and other clinicians around the world.

In the early 1950s, average Americans were busy putting the deprivations of the Great Depression and the horrors of World War II behind them and were working hard to build a homogeneous and conventional society. The possibilities of psychic exploration and spiritual expansion were seen as foreign and threatening. To the seekers for whom the bland conformity of the 1950s and early 1960s felt stifling, however, the possibilities possessed a powerful allure.

The *Life* magazine article and the subsequent identification and synthesis of psilocybin and psilocin as the active agents came at a time when psychiatrists were beginning to use lysergic acid diethylamide (LSD) as a therapeutic tool. Hofmann had been working for a number of years studying and synthesizing some of the chemical compounds made by the fungus ergot (*Claviceps purpurea*). Several important medicines came from that research, including a very powerful medication called Methergine to staunch postpartum hemorrhaging that is still commonly used today.

Hofmann initially synthesized and isolated what we now call LSD in 1938 and it was referred to as LSD-25, one in a series of lysergic acid diethylamides that was initially thought by the company Sandoz to show little promise. At the time, Hofmann hoped that the lysergic acid derivatives would be heart stimulants like the chemically similar digitalis. No one had any idea that it was a powerful psychoactive compound. On a hunch, Hofmann returned to work on LSD-25 in 1943 and on April 16 of that year, he accidently absorbed a small dose through his skin and experienced a mild "weird state of consciousness." Three days later he conducted the first planned experiment on himself by ingesting 250 micromilligrams of LSD and became famous for having the first LSD hallucinogenic experience. This was also the first bad trip on LSD. Hofmann later described the experience as horrifying, believing that his body was possessed by a demon. In a speech that he delivered to the World Consciousness Conference in 1996, Hoffman described the difference between LSD and psilocybin by comparing the potency of LSD to an atom bomb and psilocybin to conventional strength weapons.[7]

From the 1950s through the 1960s, scores of studies and clinical trials were conducted using different hallucinogens to address such diverse areas as physical and mental illness. They included modeling psychosis through the exploration of induced hallucinatory experience as treatments for depression and anxiety disorders, and some promising applications for chronic alcoholism. During the mid-1960s, a small number of researchers also sought to use hallucinogens as a means to facilitate mystical experience, recognizing the commonly experienced perception of the breakdown of the ego boundaries between self and the universe described by many who had taken various hallucinogens.

Walter Pahnke, a physician and doctoral student at Harvard's School of Divinity, conducted what has become known as the Good Friday Experiment in 1962.[8] Seeking to examine the claim that the effect of taking a psychedelic drug can resemble a mystical experience, he conducted a double-blind experiment using purified psilocybin with twenty volunteer divinity students. He chose to use psilocybin due to the much milder and controlled experience it imparts compared with the significantly more potent LSD. The students were all of similar Protestant, middle class backgrounds, and none had previous experience using hallucinogens. A deliberate and conscious effort was made to prepare the subjects for the experience by careful screening, interviews, and psychological tests. Pahnke encouraged positive group dynamics through group interaction and matching the subjects into small compatible pods. The preparations were planned in an effort to reduce fear, build positive expectations, and encourage trust and confidence. The setting, which was carefully chosen for the experiment, was a small private chapel in the basement of a large church.

Ninety minutes after they took their capsules, the volunteers listened to a 150-minute Good Friday service of music, readings, prayers, and meditation broadcast from the church upstairs. Half of the subjects were given 30 mg of synthetic psilocybin and half 200 mg of nicotinic acid, which was used as a control because it causes increased agitation and a small "rush" without any hallucinogenic effects. In a departure from good research protocols (perhaps influenced by Pahnke's doctoral advisor, Timothy Leary), the five supervising group leaders also were given 15 mg of psilocybin.[9] Following the session, the subjects were asked to write about their experiences and complete an extensive questionnaire, and were interviewed about their responses. Follow-up interviews were held over the next six months.

The results of the Good Friday Experiment showed a significant difference between how the experimental and the control groups self-reported about their sense of internal and external unity, transcendence of time and place, objectivity and reality, and the presence of positive changes in attitude and behavior toward self, others, and life. The test subjects who were given psilocybin reported a greater sense of oneness with the universe, a lessening of the barriers between self and others, and an increased sense of peace. Pahnke didn't conduct any long-term follow-ups though he may have intended to; unfortunately, he died in 1971, the victim of a scuba diving accident in Maine.

In the mid-1980s, Rick Doblin, who later worked with Harvard's Kennedy School of Government as a drug policy researcher, began a long process to locate and interview the original test subjects in Pahnke's study and succeeded in locating and interviewing seventeen of the twenty original volunteers. Panke's original notes and uncoded subject list were lost and Doblin had to conduct an extensive investigation to find most of them. Doblin met with the subjects between 1986 and 1989 and gathered data using interviews and the same written questionnaire that Pahnke used in the 1962 study. He found a significant correlation between the results of Pahnke's six-month follow-up and his own long-term interviews. As with the six-month follow-up, the interviews more than two decades later revealed that the people who were given psilocybin felt strongly that the experience increased their sense of internal and external unity, transcendence of space and time, the perceived ineffability and transience of the universe, and a general sense of the sacredness of the experience. In addition, they reported persistent positive changes in their attitudes and behavior over the long term. Many reported that the experience helped them resolve career decisions, deepened their relationship to Christ, and heightened their sense of joy and beauty.[10] According to Doblin, these results support Pahnke's hypothesis that when people who are religiously inclined take psilocybin in a controlled setting, the experience can induce a deepening of their faith, just as cross-cultural mystical literature suggests. "All seven psilocybin subjects participating in the long-term follow-up, but none of the controls, still considered their original experience to have had genuinely mystical elements and to have made a uniquely valuable contribution to their spiritual lives. The positive changes had persisted over time and had deepened in some cases," according to Doblin. In contrast, many of the control volunteers had very little memory or strong impression of the experience when they were interviewed twenty-five years later.

In his discussion of the experimental results, Pahnke, in a clear moment of prescience, warned of the inherent risks, both ethical and psychic, of human subject experiments with psychedelics. He urged the use of carefully controlled conditions to establish the "set and setting" and screening to protect those study subjects vulnerable to psychic damage. Pahnke also warned of the risk of trivializing the hallucinogenic experience. "The intense subjective pleasure and enjoyment of the experience for its own sake could lead to escapism and withdrawal from the world. An experience, which is capable of changing motivation and values, might cut the nerve of achievement. Widespread apathy toward productive work and achievement could cripple a society."[11]

In the years following the Good Friday Experiment, the use of psychedelics became widespread and increasingly uncontrolled as a generation of youth sought release from a society whose values they neither understood nor supported. Timothy Leary became synonymous with the rebellion and his "turn on, tune in, drop out" message was adopted by many promising minds. Leary began his own experimentation with hallucinogens carefully and using responsible protocols, but his later abuse of hallucinogens in the name of experimentation, as well as the negative press surrounding him, led to the end of most legitimate research into the use of hallucinogens and their classification as illegal controlled substances in the United States in 1971.

Many of the therapies and research protocols using several hallucinogens in the United States and Europe during the early years focused on the treatment of alcoholics, believing that the psychedelic experience would facilitate the "bottoming out" phase of the addictive process and lead to a change in perceptions of self and associated behavior. Other areas of research and promising practice were devoted to understanding schizophrenic psychosis, and the therapeutic application of hallucinogen-facilitated therapy for a wide range of disorders including substance abuse, depression, neurosis, and anxiety. Many of these early psychotherapeutic trials resulted in published papers extolling their success, but the work lacked the use of controls and experimental rigor capable of providing it with lasting efficacy.[12]

During the 1950s and 1960s the U.S. military and the CIA spent years and an unknown amount of resources exploring the weaponization of hallucinogens for potential use to debilitate enemy soldiers and as a means of mind control during interrogation.[13] The now infamous project, code named MKULTRA, subjected thousands of military "volunteers" and unwitting civilians to doses of LSD and a number of other mind-altering drugs without their knowledge or consent. To this day, relatively little detail is known of the tendrils of this decades-long project because in 1973, CIA head Richard Helms ordered the destruction of all records of the project. Author John Marks, using the power of the Freedom of Information Act, was able to access some 20,000 pages of preserved documents that were previously thought to be destroyed. This discovery enabled him to write his 1978 book, *The Search for the Manchurian Candidate: The CIA and Mind Control*, describing much of the program's known efforts but lacking a sense of the overreaching goals of the project that could only come from open disclosure by the principal figures who have remained silent over the years.

Gordon Wasson, in his ethnomycological quest for psilocybin knowledge, became inadvertently caught up in these larger Cold War issues. Indeed, apparently unknown to Wasson, one of the early supporters of his psilocybin studies was a little-known front for the CIA known as the Geschickter Fund. The fund provided $2,000 to help pay for Wasson's trip to Mexico in 1956 to further the exploration of psilocybe mushrooms with curandera Maria Sabina. James Moore was a chemist at the University of Delaware and also in the employ of the CIA, manufacturing an array of mind-altering, and at times deadly, chemicals for them. He contacted Wasson in the winter of 1955 and expressed interest in studying the chemistry of the Mexican psychoactive mushrooms and further sweetened the deal by connecting Wasson with the funding from Geschickter. Moore himself benefited by accompanying Wasson on the trip to Mexico. Once there he was able to secure a bag of hallucinogenic mushrooms with the goal of isolating the active component to supply the CIA with another weapon for their psychoactive arsenal. Unfortunately for Moore and the CIA, Albert Hofmann and the Sandoz Company won the race to isolate and synthesize psilocybin.[14] Of course, the CIA could now purchase purified psilocybin from the same source as the LSD used in the infamous MKULTRA project.

The Mushrooms Behind the Controversy

Psilocybin-containing mushrooms can be found within a number of different genera of primarily saprobic mushrooms. According to Paul Stamets in *Psilocybin Mushrooms of the World*, more than 100 species in a diverse mix of genera have been found to be psychoactive due to the presence of psilocybin. A recent worldwide review of the group lists 186 reported psilocybin-containing species in 14 different genera of mushrooms.[15] The "neurotropic fungi," as Gaston Guzman refers to hallucinogenic mushrooms, have a worldwide distribution ranging from Siberia and Alaska in the north, to Chile, Australia, and New Zealand in the south, as well as one island in Antarctica. They occur from sea level to 12,000 feet in an amazing variety of habitats. Mexico has the greatest number of described species (43), but the reported distribution and abundance of species seems to follow the tracks of active mycologists who have interest in these small, brown, easily overlooked mushrooms. Guzman, an expert on the taxonomy of the genus *Psilocybe*, reports that when he examines collections from regions where there are few resident mycologists (including areas in the United States), he regularly finds collections of new psilocybin-containing mushrooms. The supposition is that as they are more closely studied, more species of hallucinogenic mushrooms will be described and named, as is the case with almost all groups of small, cryptic mushrooms.

The psilocybin mushrooms fall into the ecological niche of primary saprobes, relying on a diet composed of dead plant material that they break down and use as food energy. In the process, they recycle the nutrients bound up in the dead tissue. Stamets further organizes them into different groups based on their preferred habitats.[16] The habitats include dung, grasslands, moss lands, woodlands, riparian areas, gardens, and burned land. The most common denominators are habitat disturbance and the opportunistic nature of the mushrooms colonizing and exploiting recently created pockets of organic matter, whether they be a fresh load of dung or the disturbed soil of an avalanche site, road bed, trail, farm field, or building construction. In riparian areas, the debris deposited by cycles of flood and receding water creates islands of organic debris in often-moist conditions, perfect for rapid colonization and fruiting. Like with most primary saprobes, other than those on rotting large trees or logs, most psilocybins grow and fruit ephemerally, only as long as their food source lasts, and tend to be typified by short prolific bursts of fruiting. In small dung deposits, they may have a season or a small portion of a season to exploit the resource; in disturbed ground and gardens, perhaps a few seasons, and in landscapes with wood mulch, it is the same. Their lifespan can be prolonged by the addition of more organic matter, whether by further disturbance like flooding or adding more mulch or manure to landscaped sites.

As you might imagine, humankind's rise as a dominant species and our subsequent massive reshaping of the landscape has been a boon to the growth, expansion, and proliferation of psilocybin-containing mushrooms. Many areas that would rarely see these diminutive species are now visited by troops of them fruiting in homeowner's lawns and gardens, public landscaping, and disturbances along roads and trails.[17] Though this is one group of mushrooms most homeowners would be horrified to imagine fruiting in the mulch, the reality is that they might already be supporting the growth with their landscaping. Keep in mind that while the mushrooms grow, their mycelia is releasing the nutrients in the mulch for the garden plants' use.

Several of the better-known psychoactive species of *Psilocybe* and *Panaeolus* are referred to as dung-rotters or more formally as coprophilic mushrooms. These have evolved to colonize and break down the dung of herbivores and can be found on domesticated animal dung from cows, horses, sheep, and goats as well as dung from wild animals such as elephants, deer, and moose. I came upon a likely bed of *Panaeolus* or *Psilocybe* fruiting in porcupine dung deposited inside a deep granite overhang last year. The very wide distribution of *Psilocybe cubensis* in tropic and neotropic regions of the world is attributed to the movement of domesticated cattle across the globe. Other species have been spread through the export of nursery stock worldwide.

In the Northeast, the more common mushrooms containing psilocybin include the lawn mower's mushroom (*Panaeolus foenisecii*), several species of *Gymnopilus* and *Psilocybe*.

The Lawn-Mower's Mushroom
The almost globally ubiquitous haymaker's or lawn-mower's mushroom (*Panaeolus foenisecii*), is found on most lawns through the wet periods of

1. The shape and color of morels can vary depending on where they grow.

2. Lilac and apple blossoms tell you when the yellow morels are fruiting.

3. A pair of young giant puffballs at the perfect stage for eating

4. Shaggy manes are best eaten before they begin to mature and blacken.

5. A young sulphur shelf cluster at the perfect stage for eating

6. A mature sulphur shelf cluster on an oak tree

7. *(above)* A cluster of chanterelles with their blunted forking gills

8. *(left)* Compare the unbranched, knife-edged gills of the jack o'lantern with the chanterelle.

9. *(above)* A stately mature *Boletus edulis* with a characteristic hamburger bun cap and net-veined stalk

10. *(right)* These young porcinis are ready for cooking.

11. *(above)* Meadow mushroom gills change from pink to dark brown as they age—an important idenfication feature.

12. *(left)* The pure white destroying angel is common and deadly.

13. *(above)* False morels show great variation in the shape of their caps.

14. *(right)* Don't be fooled! The squirrel nibble on this fly agaric doesn't mean it's edible.

15. A cluster of prime young honey mushrooms

16. A fairy ring of *clitocybes* deep in the woods

summer. Chemical analysis of this species has found variable amounts of psilocybin and psilocin and the species is generally viewed as mildly psychoactive, at most, with many collections reported as lacking in psilocybin or psilocin. As I mentioned in the common mushroom poisoning scenarios section earlier in this book, the problem is that the suburban backyard niche that this small brown mushroom inhabits is also home to a most common and indiscriminate mushroom grazer: the human toddler. I handle several calls per year, on average, from the Northern New England Poison Control Center involving a child under age five who has ingested or is feared to have ingested this mushroom. As is the case with about 80 percent of calls involving children and mushrooms, almost none of the kids ever develop symptoms, but occasionally there have been reports of agitated children seeing things not present in the exam room, including one recent case in Maine. There is real risk here. Unlike the normally benign course of adult psilocybin intoxication, infants and young children can react strongly and spike a high fever or—more dangerously—develop convulsions with a high dose of psilocybin.[18]

The *Gymnopilus* Group

Another relatively common and psychoactive group of mushrooms in New England belong in the genus *Gymnopilus* and the most notorious or best known is the laughing mushroom or big laughing gym (*Gymnopilus spectabilis*). Not all members of this relatively common genus are psychoactive, and identification to species is not easily done without a microscope. Several years ago, I spent part of a lovely fall day in the woods with a high school class, teaching them about the beauty and ecology of Maine's mushrooms. We came over a small rise and there on the rim of the hill stood the branched stump of a large white birch. Sprouting from cracks in the bark and along the broken edges of the stump were at least a dozen clusters of a golden-tan mushroom with a distinct ring stained orange-brown from released spores. One of the more robust and prolific flushes of the big laughing gym that I'd ever seen was staring me in the face. My dilemma, of course, was whether or not to tell this impressionable and very interested group of kids about the more controversial characteristics of the mushroom, or to simply stick to the ecology of a wood-rotter. I decided to leave the decision in the hands of the teacher.

The *Psilocybe* Group

Several years ago I visited a site that had recently been subdivided for sale as housing lots, and where the developer had cleared most of the understory and used a chipper to reduce the slash to chips. He then used the chips to create several inviting paths through the woods and down to the edge of the sea. As I walked along one of these paths, collecting a few honey mushrooms and *Stropharia*, I saw a troop of tiny golden brown mushrooms fruiting from the chips. I looked more closely at them and realized I was seeing a species of *Psilocybe*, one I had never before encountered. As I handled the fragile stems, I noticed that they bruised a faint blue, an indication of the likely presence of psilocin, the more active ingredient in magic mushrooms. As I continued walking, I saw hundreds of the 1-inch caps along the trail in troops through the wood chip carpet. I later tentatively identified the species as *Psilocybe quebecensis*, a hallucinogenic species originally described from collections in the Jacques Cartier River Valley in Quebec[19] and never before reported from Maine. This may be yet another species extending its range thanks to our environmental disturbance and use of wood mulch for landscaping. Or it could be that it has been in the area in small numbers for many years and current landscape practice has increased the numbers.

Other *Psilocybe* mushrooms containing measurable amounts of psilocybin and psilocin include *P. semilanceata*, the liberty cap, found in pastures and fields throughout much of the world in temperate climates, though not reported from Maine until 1993, when a young man here disappeared and was later found drowned following consumption of a large quantity of liberty caps. Local youth had known of the presence of the mushrooms in wet fields in the area for some years, but had neglected to tell the mycologists. Undoubtedly, there are additional species of hallucinogenic mushrooms growing in our woods and fields, but these are the better known of the northeastern species.

Psilocybin as a Toxin

Psilocybin and psilocin are the two main active ingredients found in magic mushrooms and are responsible for the high most recreational users seek. Psilocin is a breakdown product of psilocybin and the compound quickly formed in the body of anyone eating psilocybin mushrooms. The compounds trigger a sense of relaxation and detachment from reality. At higher doses there is a change in the person's perception of both time and space. Increase the dose yet again and a person begins to experience hallucinations, with prominent features including distortions of time, space, and the perception of colors and form.[20] Cardiac symptoms can occur with increase in heart rate noted in about 50 percent of people. A 1996 clinical study reported that people showed an increase in heart rate of about ten beats per minute and a mild increase in blood pressure, both peaking within two hours.[21] Some people experience numbness and headaches. The emotional and psychic effects of psilocybin intoxication can include confusion, euphoria, exhilaration, and uncontrolled laughter or giggling. Visual hallucinations marked by vivid colors and moving images occur, but these are not common. Closing one's eyes to block out external stimulation increases the visual and psychic manifestations.

The type and emotional content of the perceptions can be quite variable and are heavily contingent upon the mindset of the person and the setting in which the experience takes place. This is where the emotional and psychic vulnerability of the person can play a large role in determining whether he or she will have a good or a bad "trip." Anxiety can rise, especially for an emotionally vulnerable or constitutionally anxious individual, and anxiety can be further heightened in a person not prepared for the experience. Frightening images and intrusive beliefs can overwhelm the person, contributing to a profoundly terrifying experience. The sensations generally peak within two to three hours of ingestion and gradually diminish with complete return to normal function within four to eight hours after eating psilocybin mushrooms.[22]

What is perceived as toxicity to a physician is viewed as potency by the recreational or clinical user of magic mushrooms. Chemists, mycologists, and toxicologists have over time attempted to evaluate the general levels of psychoactive psilocybin and psilocin in the various species. A sense of potency is needed in order to have some indication of the number of mushrooms needed to trigger a positive effect and avoid being overwhelmed by the sensations. Stamets notes the percentage of the two main components psilocybin and psilocin, when known, for the species covered in his guide. He gives a range of likely content based on the results of multiple analyses. It is clear that the growing conditions, substrate, genetic variation, and methods of preservation and storage all affect the level of active components.[23] Psilocybin mushrooms are most potent when they are consumed fresh and potency, though not affected by drying, diminishes over time in stored mushrooms as the active ingredients break down. Mushrooms growing in or dried in the sun have more rapid degradation of the psilocybin than those dried in shade.[24] The variability requires some caution when deciding how many mushrooms to use. Unfortunately, many illicit recreational "shroomers" are often young, impulsive, and decidedly not cautious.

Caveats on the Recreational Use of Psilocybin Mushrooms

One vexing problem with people who seek experimental dalliance with psychoactive mushrooms is the challenge of accurate identification. Remember the young adventurer described in Chapter 7 whose identification skills lagged behind his desire for the big laughing mushroom? His symptoms could easily have been caused by his deepening anxiety as he realized the dangerous depth of his ignorance.

In the mushroom identification classes that I've been teaching for twenty years, I occasionally have students whose primary goal is to learn the psychoactive mushrooms available in the area in order to expand their repertoire of recreational entertainments or avenues to spiritual enlightenment. The first time a young man expressed his keen desire to learn what *Amanita muscaria* looked like, I froze, and thought, "OK, now what do I do?" Caught between my desire to awaken a broad interest in mushrooms and my concern over safety and liability, I came down on the side of education. I welcomed him in and happily taught the skills needed to recognize the common mushrooms of Maine and to begin the lifelong process of identifying the less common species. As a normal part of the class, I also give an extensive lecture about mushroom toxicity and the potential for harm with misidentified mushrooms. I don't make it a goal to find a psilocybin-containing mushroom or, in the example above, the fly agaric to show the magically inclined, but I do hope they learn good basic identification skills from the class. Some very dedicated professional mycologists started out in the 1960s and 1970s primarily seeking psychedelic mushrooms. They may have started their mycological fascination with mind expansion, but the long-term consequences have been a whole different form of mind expansion and some very gifted professionals adding to the font of knowledge about mushrooms in the United States and the world. Much of our knowledge and many of our techniques of exotic mushroom cultivation have been furthered by the work of early pioneers seeking to find or cultivate magic mushrooms.

It is important to note, however, that there is a very real danger in confusing a psilocybin-containing species for a poisonous and potentially deadly mushroom such as species of *Galerina*, *Conocybe*, or *Inocybe*. All four groups are populated with little brown mushrooms (LBMs), small, undistinguished mushrooms with dark gills and brown to black spore prints found growing on lawns, in gardens, and in the forest. LBMs lack truly distinctive features that set them apart from the crowd, just like most *Psilocybe* mushrooms. The deadly *Galerina* (*Galerina autumnalis*) and a few related species can be found fruiting on wood in spring and fall and are called deadly for a good reason. They contain small amounts of the same amatoxin found in the flesh of the death cap (*Amanita phalloides*). Though by some estimates it would take upward of fifty *Galerina* to kill the average adult, those who use psilocybin mushrooms recreationally often consume many mushrooms in seeking a high. The small, ring-stalked *Conocybe filaris*, or deadly *Conocybe*, is similarly deadly poisonous, easily confused with other LBMs, and found growing in grassy areas or in landscaped beds. Though not common in northern New England, I found this deadly species growing in the wood mulch at my local health club one recent autumn.

The Legal Status of Psilocybin in the United States and around the World

U.S. federal law in 1971 classified the two primary active components in magic mushrooms, psilocybin and psilocin, as Schedule I substances under the Controlled Substances Act without specifically mentioning the mushrooms containing those compounds. Later case law clarified that the mushrooms are considered containers of the active compounds and are therefore also illegal to possess, buy, or distribute without a specific DEA license. An interesting loophole developed, however, with the recognition that the spores of psilocybin-containing mushrooms do not themselves contain psilocybin.

That means people who pursue these mushrooms for recreational use have access to the raw material needed to cultivate the mushrooms. Starting with viable spores and some basic mushroom cultivation skills, it is relatively easy to grow some species of psilocybin-containing mushrooms. As with almost anything from solar plumbing to nuclear submarines, the information is readily available on the Internet. Although California, Georgia, and Idaho have made possession of psilocybin mushroom spores illegal, most states have not, and a thriving underground trade has developed in the sale of spores, cultivation materials, and the social networking to support the activity. Just how the purveyors of spores manufacture or otherwise obtain a salable product without breaking federal law by possessing psilocybin-containing mycelium and fruiting bodies is a bit confusing, but the trade continues nevertheless. Under a strict interpretation of federal law, many suburban homeowners could face charges of possession based on the wild mycoflora in their lawns and gardens. My own efforts to collect and identify the new species found recently in Maine also would be illegal based on an inflexible interpretation of law. The good news is that there is no history of law enforcement taking such an aggressive stance, and few police have the skills in mushroom identification to support it.

Unlike many other illicit drugs, hallucinogenic fungi and plants were not covered in a broad U.N. action on drugs enacted in 1971, in part due to the recognition that a number of these plants are commonly found growing in public places and enforcement would be a nightmare. It was left up to individual countries to create legal language and enforcement to cover their needs. Following the U.S. ban, several European countries remained fairly open to mushroom use and possession, most notably the Netherlands, where mushrooms could be purchased at licensed Cannabis Cafes and "Smart Shops" that also sell marijuana.[25] Over the past five years, however, in response to some alarming reports of abuse of psilocybin and other hallucinogenics in the club scene across Europe, almost all countries have banned possession or sale of psychedelic mushrooms. The Netherlands became the final European country to enact such laws in October 2008. In the United Kingdom, hallucinogenic mushrooms became illegal to possess or sell in 2005 and approval of the law hinged on the inclusion of language clarifying that homeowners would be protected from prosecution for the chance natural occurrence of magic mushrooms in their bit of garden.

Psilocybin Research Coming of Age

Three decades after psilocybin and other hallucinogens fell from grace amid the crazy days of the late 1960s, there has been a resurgence in research into the use of psychedelic compounds in the United States and Europe. In 2006, a report was published detailing the results of an elegantly designed and carefully executed study involving the application of a controlled dose of psilocybin as a method to induce profound mystical experience. The study, which was carried out at the Johns Hopkins University School of Medicine, involved thirty-six adult volunteers, all without prior experience of hallucinogens and carefully screened for psychological stability and the regular practice of some form of religious, contemplative, or meditative practice.[26] The protocol included careful preparation to set a stage for the subjects to have a positive experience and was held in rigorously controlled circumstances involving a carefully designed, living room-like setting, medical monitoring, and the use of two trained and experienced guides to accompany the volunteers and support them during their experiences under the influence of the drug.

In many ways, this study was an updated replication of Pahnke's Good Friday Experiment with a more rigorous set of controls, evaluations, and standards. Volunteers were randomly chosen to receive either synthetic psilocybin or methylphenidate (Ritalin) as a control. The sessions were repeated at two-month intervals with the other compound so each person experienced both active drug and control. Interestingly, in this study, neither volunteers nor their guides knew that both compounds would be administered or the order of administration. The control group volunteers received two sessions with Ritalin followed by a third, unblinded session with psilocybin. In this way the controls were the only participants who knew without doubt they had received psilocybin and when. All sessions were conducted individually with the single subject monitored by both a male and female monitor. The primary monitor was a clinical psychologist who had previously monitored more than 500 sessions of entheogen therapy dating back to the 1960s. He met with each volunteer several times before the initial session to build comfort, a clear set of expectations, and a sense of confidence, all of which have been shown to reduce the incidence of negative experiences.[27] He also met with volunteers after the session to assist in the processing of their experience. All volunteers completed several standardized questionnaires immediately following the experience that were used to measure a number of aspects of each session including those related to mystical experience and the degree to which the experience compared to others they had. In addition, each volunteer was asked to designate three adults in their lives to rate changes in the participant's attitudes and behavior following the experience. A graduate assistant who had not met the participants and therefore had no biased impressions of the individual volunteers interviewed each designated adult following the experiment.

The results of this study as measured in interviews and questionnaires at a two-month interval from the experience revealed that 67 percent of the participants rated their experience of the session in which they were administered psilocybin as either the single most meaningful experience of their lifetime (10 percent) or among the top five experiences of their life (55 percent). The Ritalin experiences rated top five for less than 10 percent of participants and none rated the experience as the most meaningful. In addition, 33 percent rated the psilocybin experience as the most spiritually significant experience in their lifetime and 38 percent among the top five spiritual experiences.[28] From the control group, 8 percent rated their experience among the top five and none as the most significant spiritual experience. In a fourteen-month follow-up, the participants continued to score the experience with similarly high significance and all but one person was accurately able to identify their psilocybin session as reflected in a question about which session produced the most profound change in ordinary mental processes.[29] In addition, the psilocybin experiences scored significantly higher on a scale measuring mysticism at both the two-month and fourteen-month follow-up. At the two-month point, twenty-two of thirty-six volunteers met the criteria for having experienced a "complete mystical experience" as did twenty-one of the thirty-six at fourteen months, a result that speaks to the temporal endurance of the participants' reflection on their experience.

In addition to the renewal of psilocybin research into mystical experience, there have been a small but growing number of studies using psilocybin as an agent to address anxiety disorders such as post-traumatic stress disorder and obsessive-compulsive disorder,[30] as well as major depression and various addictions.[31] There is a growing interest in the use of hallucinogens to assist people with the anxiety and fear that can often accompany the end of life. Roland Griffiths and his team at Johns Hopkins are involved in such a study involving cancer patients. The idea is that a single dose of psilocybin or a similar hallucinogen can elicit an experience to greatly reduce the boundaries between self/ego and the whole of the universe. In many people, this instills a sense of oneness or unity with a greater whole or with God. This has had the effect of greatly reducing the fear of death for some people.

The field of psychedelic research, tainted by the abuse and negative press of the 1960s, is making a slow and very deliberately cautious comeback. The design of the studies, including safeguards for the participants and the use of double-blind controlled conditions, has added to the respect for and validity of the work. Because of the occasional occurrence of a "bad trip" in the 1960s, the concept of set and setting was developed describing a clinical context within which hallucinogen research and therapy should be done. Early on in the exploration and development of hallucinogen use in clinical settings, the most common negative events were the surge of anxiety, fear, and loss of control by people under the influence of hallucinogens, especially the very potent LSD. The more gentle and benign high produced by psilocybin or mescaline led to fewer "bad trips." From the mistakes of the early years, an appreciation developed for the need to prepare people carefully for what to expect from being under the influence of a hallucinogen, referred to as the "set" or mind set, and the need to structure the physical environment, psychological, and social support for the journeyer carefully through the process, referred to as the "setting."[32] Though a number of pioneers contributed to this development, Timothy Leary and other members of the Harvard research project published the early work in the United States,[33] detailing the need to attend to the "set and setting" of psilocybin or other hallucinogen use. Researchers have found that adequate support and preparation of their study subjects before, during, and after the administration of a hallucinogen leads to reduced events of paranoia and panic attacks and an increase in positive, valued experiences. Following their acclaimed recent study, the staff of the Johns Hopkins Psilocybin Research Studies Group developed a set of guidelines and suggested protocols for those designing human hallucinogen research that details the areas to consider and address when doing responsible studies with psilocybin. Following these guidelines may enable the new era of positive clinical applications of hallucinogens to continue.

PART V

MUSHROOMS WITHIN LIVING ECOSYSTEMS

HONEY MUSHROOMS
The Race for the World's Largest Fungus

You cannot find a mushroom without leaving the house.
TRADITIONAL RUSSIAN SAYING

*I*n April 1992, an unexpected headline shone from the pages of the *New York Times:* "Twin Crowns for 30-Acre Fungus: World's Biggest, Oldest Organism."[1] The story that followed was based on an article published that day in the journal *Nature,* detailing the results of four years of research by a team of three biologists studying a plot of forest near Crystal Falls, Michigan. The researchers, Myron Smith and James Anderson of the University of Toronto and Johann Bruhn from Michigan Technological University, claimed to have discovered a mushroom-producing fungus of enormous proportions.[2] Before long, this single colony of the common honey mushroom, *Armillaria bulbosa,* growing beneath the surface of the forest soil, garnered attention from around the world.

Although they initially set out to determine the genetic diversity of fungi growing within a given area of forest, and specifically to determine how to differentiate between individual colonies of a species of fungus in the forest, the team discovered that all the samples of *Armillaria* in an initial plot of 120 × 60 meters belonged to the same individual mycelial network. The team extended its sample area along a transect and still did not reach the limits of the genetic individual, referred to as a genet. Over the following years, they determined that the mycelial network of this single genet extended over a thirty-acre area. After estimating—conservatively by most accounts—the annual growth rate of the mycelium, the team determined that the fungus was between 1,500 and 10,000 years old, making it the oldest known living creature on Earth. They estimated the combined weight of all the fungal growth by weighing the mass of the honey mushroom mycelium contained in a measured area of soil and then extrapolating to the amount of soil in the surveyed area. They determined that the fungal mass was about 100 tons, approximately the same weight as a blue whale.

The biologists were completely unprepared for the barrage of media attention following publication of their results, as calls from media and glory-seekers came from around the continent and from across the world. According to Wisconsin mycologist Tom Volk, one Japanese businessman wanted to fund a boardwalk exhibit and charge people fees to view the giant fungus and CNN called to report that a jet was en route to the site and requested that one of the researchers be on the ground for aerial photographs of the mammoth fungus![3]

Of course, what anyone standing in the midst of the world's largest fungus would have seen was . . . a forest. With trees, shrubs, grasses, and flowers, it would have looked indistinguishable from any other thirty acres of forest in the area. If they happened to be there the previous September or October after a good soaking rain, they might have seen honey mushrooms fruiting singly and in scattered clusters across the forest floor—a sight nowhere near as impressive as a blue whale. Thrill-seeking customers touring a honey mushroom boardwalk exhibit would likely have been just that: bored.

Almost immediately following publication of the findings, rival claims to the title of the world's oldest and largest fungus came flooding in. Almost twenty years earlier, two forest pathologists, Kenelm Russell and Terry Shaw, working in southwestern Washington studied a genet of a related honey mushroom, *Armillaria ostoyae*, which they reported as covering perhaps 1,500 acres. Russell and Shaw, who completed work on *their* humongous fungus in the 1970s, based their claim on a study of incompatible mating types, working from the premise that strands of mycelium from different individuals will not combine when growing together on agar medium, whereas strands from the same individual will grow together into one unit under the same conditions. The two collected sexually compatible samples of the fungus over an area encompassing a huge swath of forest—almost one and a half square miles. Some scientists reviewing the competing claims noted that Russell and Shaw had excellent aerial photos to support their claim but lacked the convincing genetic evidence of the Wisconsin study.[4] Even today, the race for the biggest fungus continues. In 2000, another team of forest researchers reported the discovery of an individual fungus growing in the mountains of Oregon that dwarfs both prior claims. In a 2008 updated report on the area, the largest genet of A. *ostoyae* is reported to cover more than three and a half square miles or 2,385 acres and to be between 1,900 and 8,650 years old.[5]

These big fungal genets have raised even bigger questions about what defines an "individual," especially in a fungus that spreads by mycelial growth through the forest soil when those almost-invisible colonies of mycelium have no defined shape or boundary. In other words, where does the growth of one individual end and a new individual begin? In the case of the Michigan honey mushroom, the researchers acknowledged that there were interruptions in the mycelial network of the fungus; it was not a continuous interconnected web. Though the islands of mycelium proved to be identical, they challenged the normal definition of an individual, which is characterized by a defining and limiting boundary. In humans, the limiting boundary is our skin. In a tomato plant, it encompasses all the roots, stems, leaves, flowers, and fruit. But if an organism doesn't have skin or a stem, and in fact, doesn't even have a determined growth pattern or shape, where does singularity end and plurality begin? It's obvious where an elephant begins and ends and, if there were two genetically identical elephants, we would call them clones or identical twins, but they would certainly be considered separate individuals. The distinction is much less clear in the case of a fungus that grows outward in all directions as it seeks out available food and moisture, but might, over time, become isolated islands of growth in a larger sea of the forest ecosystem. If the space between these genetically identical or sexually compatible islands of growth is widely spaced with no known contiguous connection, are they still one individual? The questions raised by the thirty-acre fungus are monumental indeed and will likely provide rich fodder for debate for some time to come.

Taxonomy

Honey mushrooms comprise a small group of closely related species of forest fungi. Not too long ago, most were lumped into *Armillaria mellea*, but taxonomists today generally recognize them as a complex made up of at least six species and perhaps up to fourteen, based on chemical, ecological, and morphological differences.[6] In the Northeast, honey mushrooms growing on conifers are usually *A. ostoyae* and on hardwoods, either *A. mellea* or *A. gallica*. Most amateur mycologists or casual mushroom foragers will have a difficult time differentiating between these closely related species. To identify a honey mushroom, the best bet is first to determine whether the host tree is conifer or hardwood deciduous.

DESCRIPTION

(The following is a general description for all honey mushrooms and may not closely fit some varieties. The species in this complex are often difficult to distinguish using simple field characteristics alone. Consult a good field guide to your area for more detail.)

Honey mushrooms are tan to yellow-brown to brown mushrooms fruiting singularly or, more typically, in clusters on wood or on the ground from the buried wood of roots. (See #15 in the color insert.) The caps are generally 2–4 inches across and convex, becoming flat with maturity and with a region in the cap center with a number of dark, coarse hair-like scales. In the emerging button, the entire cap may appear covered with these scales. The gills are light tan, and attached to the stalk or slightly decurrent. The stalk is colored like the cap, generally twice as long as the cap is wide and may taper at the base. Each has a thick, fleshy whitish ring and often is irregularly scaly. The spore print is white.

LOOK-ALIKES

One mushrooming myth says there are no poisonous mushrooms that grow on wood and, therefore, any that you find on wood are safe to eat. Wrong! This myth, like many, contains a germ of truth. None of the polypore bracket fungi, which often fruit on wood, are poisonous. Although it's more accurate, even this generality should never form the basis of a decision to eat a new mushroom. Never eat a mushroom unless you are 100 percent certain of the identification and the edibility of the species. When in doubt, throw it out!

There are several poisonous wood-rotting mushrooms with gills, none more notable and toxic than the deadly *Galerina*, *Galerina autumnalis*, and its cousins, which also grow singularly or in small clusters on wood. Unlike the honey mushrooms, it is smaller and produces a brown spore print. As its name implies, the deadly *Galerina* is a potentially deadly toxic species, containing the same cyclopeptide toxins that are found in death cap amanitas. *Galerina* mushrooms typically fruit in the same cool wet autumn weather that honey mushrooms favor.

Another famous and notable clustered wood-rotter is the jack o'lantern, *Omphalotus illudens*, which usually grows in dense clusters on the ground at the base of trees infected with its mycelium. (#8) Jack o'lanterns cause severe gastric upset in anyone mistaking them for edibles. A last potential problem mushroom is the brown-spored big laughing gym, *Gymnopilus spectabilus*, which grows on wood during the same autumn period and is generally quite bitter and also hallucinogenic.

A number of smaller mushrooms superficially resemble honey mushrooms but generally fruit singularly rather than in clusters. Be certain your collection contains the hallmark identification features of clustered growth, a white spore print, the presence of small dark scaly hairs on the cap, a thick fleshy ring, and attached or slightly decurrent gills.

ECOLOGY

The various species of honey mushrooms function as saprobes and parasites in the forest ecosystem. As saprobes, they are known as a "white rot" fungus because they consume the brown lignins in wood as a food source leaving only the white cellulose. In the process, they recycle the nutrients bound up in the wood. As parasites, honey mushrooms have earned a reputation as virulent pathogens, attacking, weakening, and killing a wide variety of tree species. Generations of foresters and land owners have regarded *Armillaria* root rot with a mixture of awe, fear, and loathing for the damage it causes to forest, orchard, and landscape plantings. As the mycelial network becomes established, it forms thick, dark-skinned rhizomorphs of densely compacted hyphae. These hyphae, which look like bootlaces or shoestrings, grow through the soil and search out the roots of new trees to invade, making the fungus capable of rapidly finding and attacking weakened trees over a broad area. The rhizomorphs, extending from an area of established infection, also act as effective conduits of moisture and nutrients to regions of an expanding mycelial network as the fungus moves into new territory.

An infected tree shows signs of distress within a year or two as the root function is compromised and the tree suffers from lack of nutrients and water, but sometimes trees can live relatively unaffected until they come under stress and the fungus overcomes the tree's weakened natural defenses. On heavily infected trees or trees killed by *Armillaria* root rot, you can see a network pattern of the black bootlace rhizomorphs growing between bark and heartwood. The stump of a tree killed by root rot continues to house living mycelium for many years, serving as a site of inoculation for a new generation of trees planted in an area infected with honey mushrooms. For this reason, careful foresters mechanically remove infected stumps prior to replanting forests in areas where an aggressive honey mushroom infection has been active.[7] Though honey mushrooms have a reputation as aggressive tree pathogens, some species live primarily as saprobes in the soil or become parasitic only when the trees are dying or under stress due to drought, insect infestation, logging, or other factors.

Another fascinating and eye-catching feature of honey mushrooms is occasionally seen by nocturnal visitors to the rain-moist summer forests. Wood colonized by honey mushroom mycelia occasionally exhibits bioluminescence, a faint ethereal light that glows in the dark to the fright or delight of unwary nighttime sojourners. (For more information, see Chapter 16 on bioluminescence.)

EDIBILITY

The late Dr. Richard Homola, a former professor of mycology at the University of Maine, was an avid collector and photographer of Maine mushrooms and an enthusiastic fan of honey mushrooms. He told me that he preferred them to most other edibles and collected and preserved a supply of them for winter use. During the autumn months, usually after mid September in Maine, honey mushrooms will respond to a good period of rain by producing incredibly abundant flushes of fruit during a short intense period. This is a mushroom you can collect almost by the truckload in a good fruiting year. For the best eating, collect young firm caps before they become completely open. The tough stalks tend to be fibrous and are better left behind, although Tom Volk recommends peeling away the fibrous skin and eating the pithy inner flesh of the stalk. This seems a bit labor intensive for my style of cooking.

Honeys regularly fruit with abandon. Huge numbers will grow in clusters of young tight buttons interspersed with mature and over-mature individuals and the whole tableau can seem a bit overwhelming. It can also over-excite the greedy part of our psyche and lead to indiscriminant collection as we bring as many mushrooms home as we can carry. Once home and in the kitchen, make certain that as you prepare your collection for cooking or preservation, you again review each individual to be certain you have only honey mushrooms and that each is firm and healthy. Discard any questionable specimens or any that appear old or potentially spoiled. Many cases of mushroom sickening are due to the consumption of old mushrooms infected with bacteria.

Caveats

Whatever age or portion of the mushroom that you choose to eat, be certain that you fully cook your honey mushroom meal! Honey mushrooms contain a heat-labile toxin capable of causing mild to moderate gastrointestinal distress in unwary diners who value undercooked veggies. Dine on crisp broccoli or green beans and take a chance on rare beef, but feast only on well-cooked honeys!

I have a friend, a local chef of German descent, to whom I love to bring mushrooms. Following his friendly open smile at seeing the basket, he almost invariably will tell a story of his family's use of mushrooms as survival food during the lean years in Germany following World War II. Unfortunately, he bought some honey mushrooms from a collector and, either not warned or unaware, lightly cooked them for his family. He awoke in the night to an uncontrollable urge to visit the bathroom and found it a popular room shared through the night with two other family members. All recovered before noon the next day, but learned the hard way to completely cook this species.

In addition to those stricken by undercooked meals, a very small percentage of people are unable to tolerate honey mushrooms and develop mild to moderate gastrointestinal distress after eating them regardless of the cooking. There are many theories regarding the cause of this phenomenon: mushrooms growing on conifers, over-indulgence, and allergic reactions to name a few. Because of this rare reaction, I recommend that the first time you eat honey mushrooms, try a small amount and see how it suits your system. I would not serve honey mushrooms to a crowd of mycologically naive diners without adequate warning. That said, I happily serve it in many forms to my family and generally dry a supply for off-season use in soups and stews where its robust flavor shines.

Walking through a forest picking the occasional cluster of tight young honey mushrooms, I rarely consider the mass of mycelia growing through the soil duff and colonizing the wood of the tree where the mushrooms have fruited. That this interconnected mat of fungal growth might cover several acres and have a combined mass that dwarfs me doesn't intrude on my complacent collecting as I enjoy the fruits of all that labor. I certainly never consider building a boardwalk to exhibit the sight.

~⊃ 15 C~

FAIRY RINGS AND FAIRY TALES

You demi-puppets that
by moonlight do the green sour ringlets make,
Whereof the ewe not bites . . .
SHAKESPEARE, *The Tempest*

And I serve the fairy queen,
To dew her orbs upon the green
SHAKESPEARE, A *Midsummer Night's Dream*

*I*magine that you are a shepherd leading your flock of sheep and goats to
good grazing ground on the high downs in southern England 350 years
ago. In the fresh morning light, on the dew-covered downs, you come upon a
sight new to your eyes and wondrous to your mind. A large sweeping circle of
small mushrooms is fruiting along the outer edge of a grassy ring. The inside
of the ring seems trampled; the grass is patchy and sparse with areas of almost
bare ground. The rim of the circle, where the mushrooms peer above the grass
blades, is just the opposite. Here the grass is growing more luxuriantly than in
any of the surrounding area—tall, dense, and with a deeper green hue than
the surrounding turf. You are certain that you have been past this spot before
and have never seen this remarkable sight. It is as if some magic were at work.
Could this be one of those fairy rings your grandfather has told you about?
Quickly you gather the sheep into a tighter knot lest one stray into the circle
seeking that rich grass. Your grandfather has told tales of the fate that awaits
man or beast wandering onto such a fairy-blessed place.

There are certain experiences that serve to remind us all that there is an
organizing force overseeing the universe, no matter what your religious affili-
ation. The thrill of coming upon a large fairy ring of mushrooms fruiting in
the middle of a lawn or field is one of those moments for me. The almost
unnaturally rich, tall, green grass surrounding a center of scrabbly grass and

bare ground is equally thrilling. It's no surprise that fairy rings have inspired awe, myth, and mystery throughout time and around the world.

Simply put, a fairy ring is a group of mushrooms sprouting together in an easily discernable circular pattern. The rings or arcs can range in size from a few inches to several hundred meters and are found all over the world in areas of temperate or subtropical climate. The largest known ring—located in France and created by the growth of the fungus *Clitocybe geotropa*—is more than a half mile in diameter and thought to be as much as 800 years old. It is common to see fairy rings that are 10–20 feet in diameter in lawns, ball fields, and parks.

The rings, or sweeping arcs of interrupted rings, are easiest to see on tended lawns or hay fields and are less obvious in pastures or in the woods. Fairy rings of mature mushrooms sometimes can be found in forests, especially when made up of larger fruiting species such as the fly amanita, giant puffballs, or white *Clitocybe* growing on smooth conifer needle duff. (See #16 in the color insert.)

Before scientists developed a good understanding of the fungus life cycle and growth patterns, many explanations—mundane, fantastical, and super-natural—were put forth in an effort to explain the strange and striking presence of fairy rings in our midst. Here are some of the better known beliefs associated with fairy rings around the world.

In a number of regions in England and continental Europe, it's said that fairy rings appear in places where the fairy folk meet, hold their balls, and dance. The mushrooms that appear around the edge of the rings are resting seats for the tired fairies. In Sussex, England, fairy rings were called hag tracks, while in Devon it was believed that fairies would catch young horses in the night and ride them round in circles. Also in England, it was long thought that the dew on the lush grass at the edge of the fairy ring was collected by country lasses and purported to improve the complexion, or used as the base of a love potion. In Denmark, elves traditionally have been blamed for the rings and in Sweden, a person entering a fairy ring passes entirely under the control of the fairies. The Germans and Austrians believed the bare patch in the center of the ring is where a fire dragon rested after his nightly wanderings. In many regions, it was thought that fairy rings marked the location of treasure, which could not be secured without the help of the fairies.[1, 2, 3, 4]

And here in the United States, *The Monadnock-Ledger* of Jaffrey, New

Hampshire, supposedly reported a large fairy ring found during the summer of 1965 and attributed its presence to having been left behind by a flying saucer. That same summer, sightings of UFOs were reported from the nearby the town of Exeter, New Hampshire.

Natural phenomena also have been used to explain fairy ring formation. Over time, people have attributed them to ants, termites, and moles, cow or horse urine, the result of haystack placement, and the action of thunder and lightning. In 1791, Erasmus Darwin in his epic poem *The Botanic Garden* postulated that the causal agent was "cylindrical lightning" that burned the grass in a circular pattern and was responsible for the resulting increase in soil fertility. Darwin wrote: "So from dark clouds the playful lightning springs, Rives the firm Oak or prints the Fairy Rings."[5]

We now know that fairy rings result from the unrestrained growth of fungal mycelium through its grassy growing medium and the equally unrestrained fruiting of the fungus along the outer rim of the ring of growth. Consider a pair of spores of a mushroom such as the meadow mushroom, *Agaricus campestris*, or fairy ring mushroom, *Marasmius oreades*, germinating in an open grassy field. These mushrooms are saprobes that feed off the dead grass blades and roots in the top layers of the soil. Once the spores germinate, the hyphae begin to grow outward and, in the absence of any breaks in the continuity of the food source and moisture, the network of hyphae will grow and feed its way through the grass duff at an equal rate in all directions.

Once established, the rate of fairy ring growth can average 5 to 9 inches per year depending on the consistency and amount of rainfall. If the fungus produces mushrooms the first year, it likely would be a small cluster at the point of origin, and any increased growth of the grass could be easily passed off as a result of animal defecation in the absence of fruiting mushrooms.

As the mycelium grows outward, the area of maximal feeding moves outward as the mycelium encounters new organic matter, and the interior portion of the expanding circle becomes depleted of nutrients. The soil in the center of the ring is therefore less fertile and the grass there looks stunted with bare patches of ground. (This retarded grass growth also has been attributed to the mat of mycelium blocking the uptake of water into the soil.) Along the leading edge of the ring, the fungus is actively "feeding"—breaking down the dead plant matter into basic nutrients. With more available nutrients, the grass grows more luxuriantly than either the grass inside or beyond the growth

Mushrooms Commonly Found in Fairy Rings

Marasmius oreades	Fairy ring mushroom	edible
Agaricus campestris	Meadow mushroom	edible
Agaricus arvensis	Horse mushroom	edible
Clitocybe dealbata	Sweating mushroom	poisonous
Chlorophyllum molybdites	Green-gilled *Lepiota*	poisonous
Macrolepiota procera	Parasol mushroom	edible
Macrolepiota rhacodes	Shaggy parasol	edible
Calvatia gigantea	Giant puffball	edible
Amanita muscaria	Fly agaric	poisonous

of the fairy ring. It is unusual for a patch of ground to be perfectly homogeneous and free of obstacles; therefore it's unusual to see a fairy ring of any size that isn't interrupted in some way. Most grow out as one-sided arcs or curved lines and others become misshapen as one area grows at a different rate than another due to variations in soil moisture, food availability, rocks, ledges, or other factors.

As a mycophile always in pursuit of good edibles to grace my table, I seek out fairy rings as both a curiosity and a potential source of food. Although I know that some mushrooms growing in fairy rings are toxic, many are edible, so I keep an eye out for the lush grass growth in summer and fall that tells me I might find some mushrooms when they're fruiting.

When I look through the literature and on the Internet for information about fairy rings, I'm somewhat surprised and amused at the number of references to them as a disease of lawn and landscape. There are how-to Web sites devoted to ridding well-tended lawns of this troublesome scourge. (I am constantly amazed at the lengths some people will go to in pursuit of the perfect-looking lawn.) The remedy generally involves intensive aeration, application of herbicides (often not effective), extra nitrogenous fertilizer to mask both the bare spots and the lush growth and, if all else fails, the removal and replacement of the topsoil in an "infected" area. Seems like a whole lot of work to kill off a fascinating backyard exhibition of fungal growth and a source of potentially edible mushrooms. Besides, if we rid ourselves of the fairy rings, where will the poor fairies dance?

THE FAIRY RING MUSHROOM
OR SCOTCH BONNET
(*Marasmius oreades*)

This is the best known among the many mushrooms that are capable of form-ing fairy rings (hence the common name) and is a regular sight in almost any grassy area that isn't overly fertilized and manicured. Evidence of the rings is common throughout the growing season in the form of expanding bands or rings of stimulated green growth at the leading edge and retarded growth inside the ring or arc. Mushrooms fruit throughout the growing season, but most predictably in early summer and again in the early autumn in the Northeast and similar climates. I find it easiest to spot the lush green growth of the ring in late spring or mid- to late autumn.

DESCRIPTION

The common name Scotch bonnet comes from the typical shape of the mush-room's cap. In the early stages, it is rounded and develops a distinctive broad central knob called an umbo on the cap as it opens fully. The caps and gills are generally the same color, off white to pale tan and darkening to tan with age or repeated "rehydration resurrections," which refers to a mushroom's ability to dry out and then return to a fully active moist state when wet weather returns. (See more on this below.) The surface of the cap is bald and smooth without any scales, hairs, or slipperiness. The gills are free to attached (but never decurrent), broad, and widely spaced. The spore print is creamy white. Caps are generally 1–2 inches in diameter when mature. The stems are thin (⅛ inch) and long (up to 3 inches), fibrous, tough, and pliant. A mass of caps is said to have a faint odor of almond extract, but I have not noticed this.

ECOLOGY

The mycelium of the fairy ring mushroom can remain dormant for long peri-ods of time as it awaits the proper moisture conditions for growth. Because it has evolved as a persistent perennial in a favored environment, you often can count on the Scotch bonnet to fruit yearly or several times yearly over many years.

One fascinating feature of this mushroom is its ability to produce fruit-ing bodies that are capable of completely drying out, only to rehydrate later and continue to grow and produce new spores. For a mushroom that grows and fruits on open grassland under the full onslaught of the Sun and faces the vagaries of intermittent rain showers, this represents a great reproductive advantage. For years, observers were aware of this rehydrating ability, but scientists were unsure whether spore production and cell division continued after the mushroom dried out; in other words, it was unclear whether the mushroom truly remained alive when rehydrated. More recent observations and studies have confirmed that this is indeed the case. The mushroom remains alive, though inactive, when it's desiccated and returns to full active spore production when it rehydrates. Scientists have been working toward a better understanding of the mechanisms that allow living organisms to seemingly return to life following this "rehydration resurrection."

Sea monkeys are perhaps the best-known example of rehydration resurrection. They arrive in the mail as a packet of powder that is actually a herd of encysted brine shrimp—tiny shrimp-like crustaceans native to salt ponds and salt flats all over the world—that, due to the feast-or-famine water cycle of their natural environment, have evolved adaptations that enable them to go into "suspended animation" or dormancy when their desert environment dries up. During the encysted state, there are no measurable signs of life and they can survive for long periods of time, enduring extreme temperatures both hot and cold. But sea monkeys quickly return to normal functioning when salt water is added to the powder.

Resurrection ferns and other such ferns exhibit similar patterns in feast-or-famine environments where there is not enough moisture. I remember the first time I collected the fronds of the Stanley's cloak fern in the foothills of the Sandia Mountains outside of Albuquerque, New Mexico. These ferns grow in microclimates created by overhanging granite ledges or under the protection of huge granite boulders where any rain that falls flows off the rock into these protected oases. Growing at an altitude of 6,500 feet in an area that receives less than 10 inches of rain per year, the small fronds of these ferns curl up upon drying into tight ball-like clusters with powdery white, waxy undercoated surfaces facing out. In times of wet weather, the fronds unfold and photosynthesis begins anew.

Studies of organisms able to manage rehydration resurrection, including fairy ring mushrooms, show that as they dry out there is an increase in the production of certain sugars such as trehalose. As the dried organisms rehydrate and reactivate, they consume the trehalose. It seems that the increased levels of these sugars play a significant role in preserving the integrity of cell walls as the tissue dries.[6] Studies confirm that the fairy ring mushroom has been shown to increase and decrease levels of trehalose as it dries out and rehydrates.

LOOK-ALIKES

There are a few mushrooms that grow in grassy areas and can resemble fairy ring mushrooms. A few brown-black spored members of the *Panaeolus* or *Psilocybe* genera prefer this habitat, so avoid any mushrooms without off-white gills. The poisonous sweating mushroom, *Clitocybe dealbata*, also grows in grass and easily can grow along with the fairy ring mushroom. It has a dirty-white cap and closely spaced white gills attached to a white stem or slightly decurrent. The sweating mushroom contains muscarine and will produce markedly unpleasant symptoms, including copious sweating, tearing, and salivating within thirty minutes in anyone who has eaten it.

CAVEATS

Because fairy ring mushrooms thrive in domesticated lawns, there are a couple of specific caveats regarding their collection for food. I have made the mistake of *not* collecting this mushroom several times, thinking I would return in a day or so to gather the bounty. There were two mistakes in that assumption; the first had to do with the unfortunate habit we suburbia dwellers refer to as mowing the lawn. Uncountable delectable mushrooms succumb to those rapacious whirling metal blades each season. The second mistake was perhaps more pernicious and had to do with other alert mushroom collectors (including many who have learned the art at one of my classes) getting the bounty ahead of me. The final caveat involves the reality that, like many other mushrooms, the fairy ring mushroom is able to absorb and retain some pesticides and heavy metals. This mushroom grows best in unpampered lawns anyway, so avoid collecting them from a well-manicured lawn where there is a good chance that chemical treatments have been in use.

EDIBILITY

Marasmius oreades is considered by many mushroom fanciers to be a good to choice edible. Though small in size, it is common to find many individual fruiting bodies in an arc or fairy ring, so a sizable quantity can be collected on a good day. The tough fibrous stem is best removed, as it doesn't add much to the quality of the dish. I find that if I pinch the upper stem between my thumbnail and first finger, the cap will easily and cleanly pop off the stem. David Arora suggests bringing scissors along when collecting for clean stemless Scotch bonnets. Not surprisingly, given its ability for rehydration ressurection, *M. oreades* dries easily and drying is the preferred method of preservation. This is one mushroom I wouldn't hesitate to collect in a semidry state. The fairy ring mushroom cap is the perfect size and shape to use whole in a number of dishes. Several years ago I used a jar full of dried caps in a Thanksgiving bread stuffing for our holiday turkey to great reviews. Cooked, this mushroom retains a chewy texture and has a mild distinct flavor, making it a welcome addition to many dishes.

Fairy rings present us with an opportunity to meditate on the wonder and the intricacy of the natural world. They also offer a phenomenal opportunity to teach children about nature and the life cycle, ecology, and mythology of these fascinating fungi. Fairy rings can be formed by a number of mushrooms, and in every instance they evoke a whiff of magic.

> Of airy elves, by moonlight shadow seen,
> The Silver token and the circled green.
> ALEXANDER POPE, *Rape of the Lock*, 1712

~⊃ 16 C~

FUNGAL BIOLUMINESCENCE
Mushroom Nightlights

Some things which are neither fire nor forms of fire
seem to produce light by nature.

ARISTOTLE

*W*alking along a forest path at night is a magical pastime and an exercise in awareness. As your vision shrinks, your awareness of the sounds, smells, and tactile impressions grows. Any cone of light emanating from a flashlight is quickly absorbed by the black hole of darkness. For people who aren't at home in nature, a mature, dense forest can seem intimidating even in the daylight with its limited vista, enveloping intimacy, and dense canopy. But at night it is altogether more intense. The crowded crush of the trees seems like its own universe and the slightest sound of a twig snapping underfoot is both magnified and insignificant. Scary childhood fairytales—with their ravenous wolves, huge hairy spiders intent on our doom, and strange wizened characters offering fruit that appears too good to be true—actually seem plausible. There is a reason that ghost stories are told around a campfire deep in the forest. We are descended from forest-dwelling ancestors, and back when we hunted in the forest, other creatures in the forest also hunted us. It was not a particularly safe place. At night we feel more strongly connected to those roots. They seem to be only one coyote howl away.

Twenty-five years ago, when I was teaching environmental ecology in a great program offered by the Tanglewood 4-H Camp and Learning Center in Lincolnville, Maine, we would liberate kids from the confines of the classroom and bring them into the living laboratory of the forest to offer hands-on education about our connections to nature. For middle schoolers, we offered an overnight program where, in the late evening following dinner, we led small groups on hikes into the night-shrouded forest. Entering a mature white pine forest at night with a group of thirteen-year-olds is like escorting them into the Cathedral of St. John the Divine. Knowing adolescents, at first I expected giggles, gibes, and horseplay, but the majesty of the dark forest always elicited a quiet reverence in groups of normally restless kids. When we had them turn off their flashlights and sit in the dark forest, the reverence deepened into a profound, though nervous, respect for their insignificance. And if we knowingly planned our nocturnal respite in an area with a stump covered by honey mushroom mycelia or colonized by the fruit of the luminescent *Panellus* or jack o'lantern mushrooms, the reverence turned to wonder. It always took a minute for to the kids to adjust their eyes to darkness, but then someone observant would whisper, "Hey, what's that weird light there?" If it was honey mushroom mycelia, they were referring to streaks or patches of greenish glowing light across the surface of dead wood on damp ground. If we were lucky enough to be next to a patch of fruiting jack o'lantern or *Panellus*, then a pale greenish light would emanate from the gills of a dense cluster of caps.

Bioluminescence, foxfire, fairy sparks, torch wood—whatever you call it, it is a wondrous and sometimes frightening sight to come upon unexpectedly along a dark path in the forest. The word bioluminescence literally means "living light." Close to fifty different species of fungi worldwide have demonstrated luminescence, including the three common and widespread North American mushrooms mentioned above. The number of identified luminescent species continues to grow as we explore the fungal diversity of the tropics. Recently five new species of luminescent *Mycena* were discovered in Brazil.[1]

People always have been captivated by the phenomenon of living fungal tissue giving off light in the night. In some folk mythology, glowing wood was seen as a sign of fairy revelry, which is what gave bioluminescent fungi the name fairy sparks. And although I believed for years that the name foxfire came from the Appalachian mountains (it is, indeed, used in that region), the name originally comes from the French "faux fire" or false fire and is used to describe glowing fungal light.

There are many stories of people using luminous fungi, including accounts of soldiers in the Pacific Islands jungles in World War II who used clumps of glowing fungi for light when they wrote letters home.[2] These same soldiers would lace a bit of glowing mushroom onto the barrel of their rifles during night patrol or guard duty, to signal friendly status. In Europe, there are accounts of the use of clumps of torchwood to mark pathways through the forest. Perhaps Hansel and Gretel did not use breadcrumbs to mark the path out of the forest from the witch's house. If they used Foxfire in the night, they would still be as lost in the daylight as they were if the birds ate up their trailing crumbs.

Foxfire also has earned a footnote in the annals of marine history. The first submersible boat designed to attack another ship was built in 1775 by the colonial American patriot David Bushnell and was used during the Revolutionary War. Though unsuccessful in its attempt to attach an underwater mine to sink the British naval vessel *HMS Eagle*, the small submersible boat marked a milestone in naval warfare.[3] In early trials, Bushnell realized that use of a candle for light in the enclosed boat would quickly deplete the oxygen and shorten the boat's underwater time limits. He turned to another great inventor of the period, Benjamin Franklin, for ideas. Franklin suggested use of foxfire, which was used to give out enough light to view the compass and depth gauge.[4]

Although no amount of knowledge can take away from the magic of sitting next to a pale, glowing bit of wood in a dark forest on a quiet fall night, scientists *have* made great strides in their understanding of bioluminesence—a mystery found not only deep in the dark forest in fungi, but deep in the dark ocean among other organisms as well. A mile or more deep in the ocean, where no surface light penetrates and perpetual darkness is the norm, anglerfish and dragonfish have evolved the use of luminous organs and appendages to attract unwary prey and potential mates. At depths in excess of 5,000 feet, many deep-sea inhabitants depend on dead or dying organisms, mostly microscopic in size, to filter down from the fertile surface for their food. While the deep ocean floor offers as much shelter and habitat as shallower waters do, locating a mate and, for larger carnivores, finding prey is not so simple. Among the range of remarkable adaptations to this dark sea life is the evolution of specialized light-emitting organs in a number of species of vertebrate fish and a range of invertebrates like shrimp and marine worms. Many have patterns of light-emitting organs along their heads and the sides of their bodies. Others, specialized predators with plus-sized mouths and an array of teeth sure to give young children nightmares, have developed glowing appendages that hang off their snouts in front of their gaping jaws. These inviting beacons lure the unwary to dinner. The adaptive advantage in easier access to food or to reproductive success in a completely dark world can explain the energy devoted to develop and maintain such specialized, light-emitting organs.[5]

Far from the ocean bottom, a similar wonder takes place across dark summer fields in New England. Growing up in the Southwest, I never witnessed the marvel of fireflies winking across dark fields until I spent the summer of 1971 in upstate New York. North America has no species of luminescent beetles living west of Kansas. I call fireflies beetles because that is what they truly are: They are members of several families of predaceous beetles native to many parts of the world, but most common in tropical regions of Asia, Central, and South America. Though adult fireflies are not always luminescent, the larvae and the eggs are. In larvae, the presence of luminescence is thought to communicate to potential predators that their glowing target possesses certain chemical defenses making a meal of "glowflesh" an unpleasant experience. (I have found no explanation for the glowing eggs, but perhaps they too advertise their toxic nature.) The various patterns of light emitted by the adult males as they fly serves as a bright signal to potential mates and helps in differentiating both among species and among members of the same species. The females watch the male antics and signal who they like the most with single bursts of light, like flashing a dazzling smile across a crowded dance floor.

The chemical reaction that produces light in deep-sea creatures, fireflies, and luminescent fungi is essentially the same. It involves a reaction between a substance known generically as luciferin and a generic enzyme luciferase, which in the presence of energy-releasing ATP and oxygen breaks down, thereby releasing light. Unlike the more common light-emitting reactions in nature, such as fire, almost all of the energy used in the bioluminescent reaction is released as light with almost none wasted as heat and, as a result, is sometimes referred to as cold light. In comparison, the incandescent light bulb wastes about 90 percent of its energy as heat.

There are few written records of bioluminescence from the time of Aristotle and Pliny the Elder until the mid 1600s, in part because of deep suspicion and superstition related to any strange or unexplainable phenomena. The Italians historically believed that the dancing lights of fireflies were the souls of their departed loved ones and dreaded their coming. In the late 1600s, a more thoughtful and scientific approach swept across Europe. The famous philosopher, early chemical genius, and relentless observer Robert Boyle determined that air was needed in order for luminescent fungi to glow. Using an enclosed jar, he determined that when the air was pumped out, creating a vacuum, the fungal glow stopped, and restarted only when air was reintroduced into the jar. At the time, it wasn't known that air is composed of a mix of gases; later studies determined that the chemical reaction is dependent on the oxygen in the air. Two hundred years after Boyle's experiments, Raphael Dubois, a French marine scientist working with luminescent clams and a species of beetle, determined that there were two components in the clams responsible for the light emission when mixed. He named these luciferin, a heat-stable chemical fuel, and luciferase, a heat-labile catalyst that, when added to the fuel, jumpstarts the reaction. Over time it was shown that each different light-emitting organism made its own unique combination of luciferin and luciferase. The reactions require the presence of oxygen that is converted into carbon dioxide.[6]

What is the adaptive significance of a fungus glowing in the dark? There must be some significant advantage conferred to the individual in expending the energy required to create light in order to explain its presence in diverse taxonomic groups and different locations across the world. The unambiguous answers remain elusive and the questions continue to drive research into bioluminescent organisms, but I will present a few published observations along with a bit of educated conjecture. Bioluminescent fungi make sense if the presence of glowing tissue signals to a potential predator that eating this mushroom or beetle will prove deleterious to its health as is the case with fire flies. Certainly some species of mushrooms that glow are known to be nonedible or toxic, at least to humans. The jack o'lantern (*Omphalotus illudens*) contains a number of chemicals called sesquiterpines; some are responsible for the severe gastrointestinal distress in anyone foolish enough to think it is a chanterelle. In the wild, I rarely see evidence that insects or mammals eat this mushroom despite its bright color and tendency to grow in huge, very noticeable, clusters. The smaller and less noticeable luminescent *Panellus, Panellus stipticus*, is hot and acrid to the taste due to astringent compounds throughout its flesh. It also has a reputation as being poisonous to humans though it is unlikely anyone would take more than a small taste of this fiery mushroom. In both of these mushrooms, the adaptive advantage of advertising toxicity through the development of luminescence might prevent them from being eaten. If an animal gets ill after eating a luminescent *Pannellus*, chances are it will learn to avoid them.

It's not unlike the monarch butterfly, which, with its distinct and bright coloration, advertises the presence of the toxic cardiac glycosides concentrated from the milkweed that make up almost all of its larval diet. Predatory birds avoid these butterflies, and other, non-toxic species of butterflies have adopted similar coloring to hide behind. Of course, at first it seems like a duplication of effort for something that is toxic or unpalatable to expend additional energy to make bright coloration. If a predator takes a bite, it tastes bad or triggers unpleasant symptoms, so why bother advertising unless the point is to warn the predator off *before* it attacks? In the case of mushrooms, a predator's initial onslaught might consume or destroy a significant portion of the fruiting body or mycelium and therefore prevent the release of spores. This is certainly the case in fragile butterflies, where any damage is likely to put them out of commission.

A second adaptive advantage of mushroom luminescence might be to attract invertebrates for spore dispersal. Several glowing mushrooms emit light only from their gills, while in some tropical species only the spores are luminous. It has been shown that glowing mushrooms attract more insect activity than non-glowing individuals of the same species. For example, fungal gnats lay their eggs on mushrooms and produce larvae that then eat the mushrooms. This represents a potential trade-off if some of the animals that are attracted might eat the mushroom while others move its spores into the world. Further complicating the potential trade-offs, research has shown that glowing mushrooms also attract predaceous wasps that prey on the mushroom-eating fungus gnats.[7] It is a complex set of relationships indeed.

The question of the adaptive advantage of the glowing mycelium of the honey mushroom remains a mystery. Honey mushrooms contain a heat-labile toxin that causes gastrointestinal problems in people who eat them raw or undercooked. If the same toxin, or one even worse, is found in the mycelium perhaps the glowing light serves as a warning to insect predators. Several scientists, however, have postulated an entirely different explanation. High concentrations of oxygen are toxic for most living organisms in spite of the fact that we would all die without smaller concentrations. In the breakdown of wood lignins by the mycelium, peroxides are created as a byproduct and oxygen concentrations build to high levels. Oxygen-consuming chemical reactions in fungi may act as a cell antioxidant with light as an inadvertent byproduct.[8, 9] If this theory is proven true, subsequent usefulness in spore dispersal or to deter fungus-eating critters would be an additional and fortuitous use of the light.

Perhaps the serendipitous gift of light-emitting mushrooms is simply magic.

What other phenomenon in nature is capable of eliciting such wonder and triggering the imagination to such flights of fantasy as the sudden appearance of light in the darkness of the forest? Just think what stories we would have concocted had the fairy ring mushrooms been found glowing with otherworldly green light defining their rings in the night.

～ 17 ～

WHO'S EATING THE TRUFFLES?

There are two types of people who eat truffles:
those who think truffles are good because they are dear and
those who know they are dear because they are good.

J. L. VAUDOYER

I lived in Maine for seven years before I saw my first flying squirrels, although when I saw them, they were sleeping, not flying. At the time, I was working as a caretaker and handyman on a beautiful piece of property on the shores of Lake Megunticook. It was deep winter, the middle of February 1986, and there were several feet of virgin snow blanketing the woods around the lake. The homeowner and I were in the vintage kitchen, winterized to allow for islands of comfort in an otherwise cold and drafty old summerhouse. One flue of the massive stone chimney had been relegated to a Rube Goldberg kitchen exhaust system with an old fan mounted in the 8-inch flue opening covered by a copper cap that was removed whenever there was a need for venting. The owner had heard scrabbling noises in the flue in recent days and as we removed the cover to check it out, we exposed a veritable pig pile of flying squirrels packed together in a tight furry ball, all fast asleep. There must have been at least twenty, though they were impossible to count in the jumbled mass. The wire mesh cover of the chimney had obviously come loose over time, and the adaptable rodents took advantage of this great "natural" cavity (one that came with a small level of residual heat included) and moved in for the winter. We decided to leave them in place for the remainder of the cold months and quietly replaced the cover. In April, the flue base was empty and we were able to screen off the top without affecting the survival of these shy and cute little nocturnal squirrels.

Ecology of the Northern Flying Squirrel

The northern flying squirrel, *Glaucomys sabrinus*, is a common, though rarely seen resident of the treetops and cavities of mature spruce fir and hemlock forests across much of the northern half of the United States and throughout the forested regions of Canada. In addition, several subspecies can be found in mountain forests in "islands of refugia" left at higher altitudes in the southern Appalachians following the last great ice age. In New England, they frequent mixed conifer and conifer-hardwood forests, preferring spruce fir forests above all others. The main reason we rarely see them is that they are nocturnal. They sleep through the day and are most active for the two hours after sunset and the 90 minutes before dawn. In between, they hole up in nesting cavities in tree hollows, constructed branch and leaf nests, and the occasional chimney flue.

The northern flying squirrel's preferred nesting site is an abandoned tree cavity created by a woodpecker. As is suggested by our chimney flue "crash pad," flying squirrels are social and share their cavity nests with their kin throughout the year except when females are birthing and raising new kits. Most adults travel between several nesting cavities following food supplies, and males especially will cover a wide territory in search of adequate food. The two most logical reasons for communal living seem to be the limited number of nesting cavities and, more likely, the need to share body heat in order to conserve energy through the long winter when food is scarce.

Fifty years ago, zoologists thought the diet of the northern flying squirrel consisted primarily of plants, including nuts and the seed conifers as well as other vegetation and the occasional insects, bird eggs, or fledglings. In his *Revision of the American Flying Squirrels*, Arthur Howell tells of northern flying squirrels taken in the traps baited with meat and designed to take the larger carnivorous fur-bearing animals with a frequency bordering on nuisance level.[1] It seems these gentle seed-eaters actively seek out animal protein including eggs and small birds to supplement their diet. Over time, and through close analysis of the stomach contents and fecal pellets of squirrels, zoologists began adding fungi into the diet mix of the flying squirrels.

By using spore analysis to identify the fungi, researchers learned that the list of fungi in the squirrels' diet included various species of hypogeous fungi (those fruiting below ground) in addition to a number of different epigeous (above ground) fungi including russulas, boletes, *Lactarius*, and other common wood-land species. If you've ever come upon mushrooms tucked into the crooks of trees and wondered how they got there, your answer may lie with the manic collection efforts of these and other foraging squirrels. Several species of squir-rels in addition to the flying squirrel cache mushrooms for future use, and the best way to prepare them for storage is to air dry the mushrooms in a tree. As scientists looked closer into the flying squirrels' diet, they began to note that at certain times of the year and in certain regions of the United States—such as the coastal forests of western Washington and Oregon where mild climates and abundant rainfall make for a mushroom paradise—fungi and lichen showed up as a main component of their diet. Indeed, in those coastal rainforests of the Pacific Northwest, flying squirrels subsist almost entirely on a wide variety of truffles and other mushrooms and lichens to the exclusion of most other foods.[2] But even in regions with more extreme seasonal weather patterns and normally high snow pack, the squirrels find and consume truffles and other fungi year round. In northeastern Alberta, the winter diets of flying squirrels showed significant consumption of epigeous fungi belonging to the *Boletus*, *Russula*, and *Cortinarius* genera and a smaller proportion of hypo-geous fungi.[3] In southern New Brunswick, Canada, fecal analysis revealed fungi as a component in the diet of flying squirrels and red squirrels, ranging from a 40 percent low in winter to nearly 100 percent in summer and fall. The fungi consumed by both species over the two-year period in New Brunswick were largely species of truffles.[4] The Alberta study strongly suggests that flying squirrels dry and store mushrooms for winter use, while in the New Brunswick region, the two squirrel species also were reported to include wintertime forag-ing for mushrooms either buried beneath the snow or in the leaf duff.

In 1990, the northern spotted owl was listed as threatened under the Endangered Species Act.[5] The federal listing has triggered intensive research to determine the causes for the population decline and to identify the actions needed to protect this small owl. The northern spotted owl lives in cavities of large-diameter trees found primarily in old growth forests where their primary prey is the northern flying squirrel. Their short stubby wings are ideal for maneuvering between tree trunks and branches within the confines of a mature forest. Suddenly the survival of the rare owl seemed dependent, not only on the preservation of old growth forest, but also on the fortunes of a shy nocturnal squirrel.

The interrelationship between mycorrhizal fungi, especially various truffle species, small mycophagous forest mammals such as the northern flying squirrel, and dominant tree species in the forest is complex and significant. The symbiotic fungi play a vital role in helping the trees to procure nutrient minerals and water and, in turn, the trees supply the fungi with carbohydrate food produced through photosynthesis. The fruiting bodies of the fungi represent a significant food source for the rodents, one that is available throughout much of the year, though with significant seasonal variation. The squirrels consume the spores from the fungi along with the rest of the mushroom and, in passing them through their digestive tracts, redistribute the fungi broadly through the forest environment. This triangular inter-reliance of trees, fungi, and squirrel is called a keystone complex due to the fundamental importance the complex dynamics represent to the health of the forest and forest species.[6] To forest ecologists, herbivorous and omnivorous animals can be categorized based on their consumption of fungi. There are obligate mycophagists such as the flying squirrel (in coastal forests), the California red-backed vole, and a few other small forest rodents. There are preferential mycophagists such as the northern flying squirrel (in most other forests), a number of other squirrels, and other rodents. And there are a wide variety of occasional or opportunistic mycophagists, an extensive list that includes large mammals such as mountain goats, deer, elk and moose, bears, a variety of birds, and rodents including woodchucks, pika, and many others. Opportunistic mycophagists eat above-ground fungi in the late summer and fall when fruiting tends to peak, whereas preferential and obligate mycophagists eat more truffles in addition to other above-ground mushrooms. Since truffles are slow growing and more protected from drying out than fungi above the ground, they tend to have a longer fruiting season and therefore a more consistent availability. With this increased availability, they show up with more prominence in the diets of some small animals.[7]

Truffles: The Almost Unnoticed Pillar of Forest Health

There are many species of fungi that establish mycorrhizal relationships with trees, shrubs, and herbaceous plants in the forest and field. I present a number of the well-known species under sections on edible, poisonous, and otherwise interesting mushrooms in this book. But even among people whose eyes have been opened to mushrooms, most move through their lives unaware of the preponderance of truffles in our forests. We almost never see and appreciate the underground vegetative growth of the mycelial colony that gives rise to the colorful and showy epigeous mushrooms we bring home for our morning omelets, but in the case of the hypogeous truffles, they are even more "out of sight, out of mind" because both the mycelial network and the fruiting bodies are completely underground. Most people associate truffles with the wildly expensive gourmet fungi that we rarely might have—shaved thin enough to see through each slice—on a plate of expensive pasta or think of them as rich, tasty chocolates. But both definitions barely scratch the surface. The term "truffle" has been popularly applied to the underground fruiting bodies of members in the genus *Tuber*, home to some of the most prized edible species, but also home to many other inedible or less-delectable species. Other hypogeous fungi belonging to a number of other genera have been at times referred to as false truffles or "truffle-like fungi." It is becoming more common to refer to all underground-fruiting fungi as truffles, a practice I follow in this chapter.

At first glance, it is easy to assume that all of the hypogeous fungi share a common ancestry. For the most part, truffles are irregularly spherical, potato-like fruiting bodies with a spore mass maturing inside a toughened rind-like skin. Ranging from the size of a pea to several inches in diameter, they often resemble puffballs fruiting underground. Truffles rely on animals to locate them and, by consuming the spore mass, to spread their spores beyond the close confines of their soil duff bed. Many have spores that are larger than their epigeous fungi cousins and have thickened cell walls capable of surviving passage through an animal's digestive system. The tough spores also are able to survive long periods of exposure in the environment. Most share another trait: Truffles, though essentially odorless when young, develop strong distinctive odors when mature, which attract animals to their locations resulting in their being eaten at just the right time to facilitate spore dispersal. Though all truffles share a common set of characteristics, we now know that the truffle growth habit has evolved many times over and has originated from a number of very different mushroom ancestral lines. *Tuber*, genus to most of the prized edible truffles, is a member of the sac fungi, or ascomycetes, which include that other popular edible, the morels. More than 200 ascomycete truffles have been described in the world to date. In parts of the world where truffles haven't yet been studied extensively, including much of the continental United States, there are a number of yet-to-be described species, as more are found each year. In the process of evolving into a completely underground fruiting body, the ascomycete truffles lose their ability to forcibly eject their spores into the air since it would serve no useful purpose to blast their spores into an enclosed body buried in the soil. Truffles therefore need a flying squirrel or some other mammal or insect to dig up and consume the stinky delectable morsel and later redeposit the spores in a location favorable to future growth.

Members of the basidiomycetes also have evolved fungi that form underground fruiting bodies. These "false truffles" are generally less symmetrically globose and have a very different interior anatomy than do most of the ascomycete truffles. The basidiomycete truffles have arisen from a number of different families including boletes, puffballs, and gilled mushrooms, such as *Russula*, *Cortinarius*, and others. One significant difference between the ascomycete truffles and those evolved from basidiomycetes, beyond the anatomy, is their durability. Like most epigeous *Basidiomycete* mushrooms, these false truffles are generally short lived; they form and mature their spores within a few days and quickly rot.

True truffles can take months to mature after an initial small fruit forms, and it is not unusual for some species to start development in the late fall, overwinter as immature truffles, and ripen in the spring. The strong, distinctive smell does not begin to emerge until the spores are fully mature. In Europe, ripe edible truffles are located by their smell with the aid of dogs or the occasional pig and therefore are never harvested prior to maturity. In the United States, some people rake truffles out of the soil duff layer and collect them without an adequate determination of their maturity. Since the taste and smell of raked truffles is not as predictable, the value of American truffles rarely achieves the level of the best European ones. Though lacking the marketing hype and long history of use, North America's edible truffles are gaining in stature in the eyes of the truffle world.

Undoubtedly, it was by observing pigs and other larger mammals unearth and eat the fine European truffles that rural people began to use pigs as guides to find and expose them. One problem with using pigs as truffle hunters is that the great ravenous rooters love to find truffles for their own dining pleasure, so truffle hunters have to be quick to ensure their prize ends up in the basket and not down the pig's throat. In the past, it was not unusual to see truffle hunters with mangled or missing fingers, the legacy of wresting truffles from the jaws of a hungry mushroom-loving pig. Today, truffle hounds have largely replaced pigs. They tend to be better companions, can ride in the front seat of the truck, and, best of all, are happy to get a dog treat as a reward rather than consume the treasure they locate and unearth. Most important is that a dog's olfactory ability rivals that of the snuffle pig.

It's an understatement to say that edible truffles are highly prized. There is an intense passion and mystique reserved for the best Italian and French truffles that rivals the feeling for any other food. In 2007, a new record price was set at auction for an Italian white truffle from the Piedmont town of Alba. A group of Hong Kong enthusiasts, with very deep pockets, paid 210,000 US dollars for a truffle weighing 750 grams. That was about $127,000.00 per pound! Alba, Italy, and her famous truffles were again in the news in February 2009 when an unnamed businessman and his five guests sat down to a dinner at Cracco's, one of the world's top restaurants, and, without looking at the menu, ordered white truffles. When the waiter presented the businessman with a $5,058.00 bill, he balked and protested, claiming he wasn't told the cost or the weight of the fungi, but finally agreed to pay half. At last report, the matter was headed for a court resolution.

Truffle Evolution

Truffles have evolved in many regions of the world from a diversity of ancestors over geologic time. Karen Hansen, a research associate with Harvard's Farlow Herbarium of Botany, has done extensive molecular and genetic examinations of the *Ascomycete* truffles and estimates that the truffle lifestyle has evolved independently at least fifteen times within six different families in the order *Pezizales* alone.[8] Many epigeous members of the cup fungi form deep urn-like cups at or just below the soil surface. Others have cups almost completely enclosed with only a small opening at the apex. It involves rather small and incremental steps to form fruit remaining underground and spore sacs that no longer forcibly eject their cargo into the air. Examples exist of species in all phases of the evolutionary progression from open cup to enclosed and then to more complex and convoluted structure. Some, like most members of the genus *Tuber*, are compact, spherical, and dense with a network of light colored veins running through the spore-bearing gleba. Others are more simple, folded cups, with hollow spaces between but no opening.

Several morphological steps must occur in order for a fungus to be considered evolved into truffledom:

- The spore-bearing tissue must become enclosed within a skin that will protect the spores while they mature. Many of the non-Ascomycete truffle-like species have evolved from genera that have a well-developed annulus or partial veil that at times persists into maturity, covering the gills.

- The spore-release mechanism loses the ability for explosive or forcible discharge.

- The mature fruiting body develops a distinctive and strong odor, signaling to animal mycophagists that dinner is ready. The animals become the mechanism to get the spores to the surface of the ground for release into the environment.

- This last point is somewhat conjectural on my part. We know that essentially all truffle-like fungi form mycorrhizal associations with woody plants. The nature of the symbiotic relationship generally ensures that the mycelial colony of the fungus is perennial, existing for a number of years associated with the same host tree. It could be that the perennial nature of the vegetative component of the fungi confers a stability that, early in the evolution toward hypogeous status, allows for greater latitude in fruiting failure while still ensuring survival of the individual over time. If, while developing sufficient scent to attract foraging animals, there are years in which no spores make it to the soil surface, the stability of the mycelium helps to ensure survival of the fungus. An organism with a less stable life-course would have less chance of survival. As I said—conjecture.

The evolutionary pathway to a hypogeous lifestyle must be effective since it's happened repeatedly in numerous fungal groups on several continents. Australia, which may represent the nirvana of truffle evolution, has the highest number of hypogeous fungi when measured as a percentage of the overall fungal population. This is the case, even though it is acknowledged that Australian fungi—particularly the truffles—have not been well studied. The evolution toward a hypogeal habit is reported to occur more frequently in warmer and drier climates since fungi have a harder time protecting the fragile spore-making tissue from drying. The protection afforded by underground development is a major boost in likely success.[9]

Truffle Ecology: The Pivotal Role of Mycorrhizal Fungi

Truffles are most abundant in the first few inches of soil beneath trees and other woody plants. That organic layer of soil is the most biologically active; it is where dead leaves, needles, twigs, and other organic matter are broken down and recycled and the nutrients that are bound up in their tissue are released. It is estimated that a single teaspoon of healthy forest soil might contain as much as 100 meters of fungal mycelium and that with each step we take, our feet cover several miles of fungal strands busily invigorating the forest.

We know that the mutualistic fungi-plant associations we call mycorrhizal likely began shortly after plants and fungi emerged from the primordial seas and colonized the land. Though fossil records are somewhat scant due to the delicate nature of plant tissues, we have evidence that indicates club mosses formed primitive fungus-root structures as early as 400 million years ago. Today, essentially all gymnosperms and 80 percent of angiosperm plants form mycorrhizal associations with fungi. A number of plants can live independent of fungal associations and have evolved to be successful colonizers in new territory and a number of the most invasive weeds in the world fit into this group.[10] But most plants are mycorrhizal-dependent, meaning that they readily accept at least one fungal mycobiont into their tissues and that their long-term survival is dependent on the formation of these symbiotic relationships. Often these plants can function without a fungal association for brief periods of time, especially in nutrient-rich soil, but they appear nutrient deprived, stunted, and sickly.

All of the known truffle-producing fungi form mycorrhizal associations with woody plants, mostly trees and shrubs. Mycorrhizal symbionts are essential components of a healthy forest and their perpetuation is necessary for the survival of the forest. Sometimes foresters learn the hard way what an essential role mycorrhizal fungi play in the survival of trees, as happened with an outplanting of Douglas fir seedlings in a nursery field in Oregon in the 1960s.[11] The field, which was converted from potato cultivation, was fumigated with a strong fungicide prior to planting the tree stock because of concern about lingering fungal diseases. Because the fumigation eliminated residual soil mycorrhizal fungi for the seedlings, the firs quickly became stunted and sickly and had a high mortality rate the first year and an elevated rate the second year despite the application of fertilizer and adequate irrigation. There were, however, islands of thriving seedlings where wind-borne or residual soil spores established mycorrhizal associations with the emerging seedlings. These islands of normal vigorous growth spread out as the fungal mycelium expanded.

All fungi are examples of "more than meets the eye," but none more so than truffles and their cornerstone relationships with the trees and animals they nourish. A significant percent of the fungal symbionts of forest trees produce underground fruiting bodies. The perpetuation of these mushroom species is vital for the ongoing health of the forests, and their perpetuation depends on the vitality of the population of animals who locate, unearth, and consume these truffles. The next time you have the opportunity to take a nighttime forest stroll, listen for the sounds of the flying squirrels as you swat the odd mosquito. The squirrels have a characteristic behavior as they collect and store nuts or fungi. They place the food in a shallow cavity or into the V formed by two intersecting branches and then rear back and jam the food item into place by vigorously hammering with their forepaws. It makes a distinct "thwak thwak thwak" sound. Remind yourself that the health of the forest might depend on the success of this seldom-seen nocturnal squirrel and its relationship with the rarely seen forest truffles.

WOODPECKERS, WOOD DECAY FUNGI, AND FOREST HEALTH

On meadows, where were wont to camp
White mushrooms, rosy gilled,
At dawn we gathered, dewy-damp,
Until the basket filled!
ANON, REMINISCENCES OF CHILDHOOD
FROM SONGS OF LUCILLA, 1901

*H*enry has been an avid duck hunter since he was a young teen and, as a man, he married the right woman with all the skills needed to make duck and sauerkraut, his favorite dish. Today, decades later, he walks quietly through prime wood duck nesting habitat with not a bird in sight. The mature hemlocks overhang the still river water on this late spring day. As he seeks his quarry, his favorite shotgun lies cradled in his arms, specially hand-loaded cartridges in both barrels. He has gone light on the powder, but packed in with the wadding is a special ingredient that makes this hunt unique. Carefully inserted into the hollow shotgun slug is a softwood dowel colonized with the cultivated mycelium of the red-belted polypore, *Fomitopsis pinicola*. There across the river is his prey, partially hidden in the gloom of the dense overstory but exposed by the opening over the river. From seventy-five feet he takes careful aim and lets fly. When the smoke clears he can clearly see the gash on the trunk of the large hemlock where his payload has shredded bark, imbedding slugs into the pale softwood cambium some thirty feet above the river surface. His hope and plan is that by forcibly inoculating the tree with the vegetative "seed" of the fungus, sometime in the next five to fifteen years, his small investment in time and shotgun ammo will turn into a decaying mature hemlock sprouting red-belted conks and containing several new woodpecker cavities and their associated tenants. On this particular day he is not shooting to kill a duck, but aiming to create habitat for future generations of woodpeckers, owls, flying squirrels, cavity-nesting ducks, and their kin. But this story starts in another place in time and space.

The Changing Forest Landscape

We have changed the face of this planet through the fruits of our labor, our burgeoning numbers, and our need for homes, food, and stuff: lots of stuff. From almost the first moment Europeans landed on the shores of the Americas, settlers began harvesting the seemingly endless forest that marched inland from every shore. Trees provided fuel for our fires and timber for ships, homes, and towns. They also posed an almost impenetrable obstacle to farming, grazing livestock, and westward expansion in the early days of European colonization. For the next 300 years, as settlers explored, conquered, colonized, and otherwise domesticated much of this great land, the forests became less like a wilderness and more like a renewable resource to be cut, grown, and cut again. Most forested regions of America have been through a number of tree harvesting cycles. The virgin forests are but a dream and the remaining timber is younger—a second, third, or fourth growth following successive clearing operations. Forest management has become a science and a business, designed to maximize marketable timber harvesting and to reduce the time required to mature a generation of trees to marketable size. Over the past century, this timber management strategy led to an increasingly narrow mix of tree species and a movement toward stands of trees all the same age and size. We have actively, even aggressively, managed many forests for the production of softwood conifer species, the most valuable for lumber or pulp production—at the expense of deciduous trees like oaks, beech, and other nut trees. In recent years, foresters and ecologists have found that a decreasing diversity of tree age and species brings with it a decreased diversity and populations of many animals that rely on a mix of tree species and the presence of large snags and mature old trees.

A snag is a dead standing tree, generally defined as at least 8 inches in diameter (though often much larger) and of sufficient height to stand well above the forest floor. Large snags and living trees of large girth now are recognized as a vital part of a healthy forest community because they provide food, shelter, and nesting sites for the birds and mammals that have evolved to live in tree cavities. These include birds that are able to create their own cavities (known as primary cavity nesters or PCNs) such as large woodpeckers and flickers. They also encompass other birds, mammals, and insects that move into abandoned cavities made by woodpeckers and naturally occurring cavities (called secondary cavity nesters, SCNs). One other group of important cavity creators or cavity preparers is the rarely acknowledged wood-degrading, heart-rot fungi.

The Role of Heart-Rot Fungi

Heart-rotters are a group of fungi that specialize in the breakdown of the dead wood fibers that make up the bulk of any tree trunk or sizable branch. The fungi typically are introduced into the living tree through insect activity or an injury that disrupts the bark, exposing the softwood cambium or the heartwood itself. Such an injury can happen when a branch breaks off in high wind or a falling branch or tree strikes the trunk. It also can happen through the action of any number of animal activities, including the foraging of insects, woodpeckers, porcupines, and beavers. Most fungi spread through the dispersal of airborne spores, which, when they land and germinate on the exposed wood, are the beginning of the fungal invasion of the tree. A fungus invades its host by literally eating its way through the wood as its mycelium grows along the wood fibers. The wood colonized by the fungus becomes punky, losing both density and structural integrity. In a standing trunk, the growth occurs more rapidly in a vertical direction than it does horizontally because the mycelial growth faces little obstacle when growing in the same direction as the wood fibers.

In a large living tree, a heart-rot fungus often is able to grow within the trunk for years without any noticeable effect, leaving a sturdy living layer of softwood cambium. The invasion becomes apparent when we see a fruiting body form on the trunk or nearby ground or when the tree is cut or falls in a storm, exposing the rotten or hollow center. A tree often continues growing for years with the fungal mycelium slowly softening and hollowing the center without visible damage or visibly slowing the growth of the tree. Hollow trunks occur only in trees living with a heart-rot fungus where, over time, the softening heartwood collapses. In most cases, this process takes years.

Other wood decay fungi begin their work following the death of a tree and start the process of softening the wood from the bark inward as they extract nutrients by breaking down the wood fibers. A dead tree, without the antifungal defenses present in living tissue, rots much more quickly than a living tree. On a large snag, there typically are several or even many different species of fungi working in concert or in different regions feeding on the tree at any moment in time. Different wood-rotting species grow better in different microhabitats created by variations in sun exposure or shade, near the ground just under the bark, or deeper in the true heartwood. Some of the better-known heart-rot fungi include the red-belted polypore, the artist's conk, turkey tails, the various varnished conks, the tinder conk, and more fleshy fungi such as hen-of-the-woods and the sulfur shelf. A healthy forest contains scores of different species of wood rot fungi.

Deadwoodology, the study of the ecology of deadwood, is a thriving research field in which wood-decaying fungi play a major role as vigorous ecosystem engineers. The action of wood-decaying fungi increases the availability of resources such as nutrients and humus for plants and other fungi, and feeding and nesting sites for other living organisms including insects, birds, and mammals.[1]

Of Woodpeckers and Fungi

Most people know that woodpeckers and their relatives make their nests in cavities in the trunks of trees; fewer are aware that it is an unusually strong woodpecker that is capable of actually excavating a cavity in hard virgin living wood. Most primary cavity nesters seek dead trees or living trees whose wood has already been softened by colonizing fungi. The birds locate and make their nest holes in living trees displaying the fruiting bodies of a heart-rot fungus or ones infected with the fungus but not yet sporting a fruiting body. This is the case with quaking aspen infected with the aspen heart-rot fungus, *Phellinus tremulae*, which is commonly found on larger mature aspen. In a study of two sites in Wyoming, 71 percent of aspen with cavities created by sapsuckers had visible conks of *P. tremulae*, though less than 10 percent of all aspen in the area showed conks.[2] Other studies showed similar though somewhat lower results with other bird species. Cavity-excavating birds choose trees with fungal invasion as a means of finding softer and more easily excavated sites.

One bird famous for the vigor and impact of its ecosystem engineering is the pileated woodpecker, the largest woodpecker in North America. Detritus from the feeding and nest-building activity of these birds litters the ground around the base of the trees, and the noise created by their loud excavations proclaims the presence of the otherwise shy birds. This woodpecker is referred to as a "keystone species," one whose actions modify the forest habitat to such an extent that they single-handedly increase the diversity of species living in the environment. Most large species of woodpeckers and flickers also signifi-cantly affect the forest habitat, but the pileated makes the action of its lesser kin seem puny in comparison. The impacts of the pileated woodpecker that have earned it the keystone species status include:

- The acceleration of the process of wood decay and the associated nutrient recycling through:
- Opening up the bark, sapwood, and even the heartwood in living trees through the activities of feeding and cavity construction, resulting in the wood's infection by decay fungi and insects
- Transfer of wood decay spores and mycelium from tree to tree in its beak and mouth
- Opening up bark and wood surfaces for the exploration and feeding of other species of woodpeckers, birds, and insects
- Creating resting, roosting, and nesting dens for other birds and animals
- Helping to mediate insect outbreaks through feeding on larvae and adults[3]

In some forests, deciduous trees are the preferred choice for feeding and nesting of keystone woodpeckers. Studies of aspen, *Populus tremuloides*, in the western United States have shown that a number of bird species rely on the tree for roosting and nesting sites and at least one, the red-naped sapsucker, is a primary or obligate aspen nester. Across the range of aspen, the aspen heart-rot fungus, *Phellinus tremulae*, infects the heartwood of mature aspen producing distinctive fruiting conks at the site of old branch stumps, and studies have shown that several species of sapsuckers prefer aspens as nest sites and appear to seek out trees where *P. tremulae* is fruiting. The fungus typically attacks older living aspen and rots the heartwood while the sapwood remains alive and intact. In one study plot in Wyoming, the average age of aspen with woodpecker cavities was 115 years. Researchers have hypothesized that the birds locate trees with heart rot either by noting the presence of fruiting bodies or by noting the difference in resonance of hollow versus solid trunks when pecked.[4]

Though the cavities in aspen are made by various species of woodpeckers, sapsuckers, and flickers, they then are used by a number of secondary cavity nesters, including chickadees, bluebirds, and smaller woodpeckers as well as birds that require trees of a larger diameter including barn, barred, and screech owls, and even wood ducks and buffleheads. The mammals that use large cavities include squirrels, opossums, raccoons, martens, and fishers.[5]

Big brown bats and silver-eared bats appear to prefer cavities in aspen to several other available tree species as a choice daytime roost.[6, 7] The living trees offer firm sapwood for roosting and are five degrees cooler than conifers in the heat of summer. Other species of bats have been long associated with tree cavity roosts, as well. All forest-roosting bats are affected by the loss of large-diameter snags and old-growth stands. Some researchers recommend the preservation and restoration of cavity-promoting habitats as a management strategy for ensuring adequate populations of insectivorous bats in forest habitats.[8]

Managing Forests for Cavity Nesters

Decades of forest management practices that recommended the removal of older snags and harvest of wind-downed timber sites, along with other human interventions that remove large, old trees, have severely reduced the optimum habitat for cavity-nesting birds. This habitat loss has reduced populations of primary and secondary cavity nesters and it is thought that these management practices are responsible for dangerously reducing populations of species such as the endangered red-cockaded woodpecker in Texas, the once-assumed extinct ivory-billed woodpecker, and several primary and secondary cavity nesters known from old-growth forests in the Northwest, chief among them the spotted owl. With the disappearance of large-diameter snags and living trees, serious efforts are being made to determine strategies to increase the suitable habitat for cavity nesters.

A number of strategies have been suggested, attempted, and practiced. One challenge, however, is that there is an immediate short-term need for developed snags in many areas where a severe reduction in snags has resulted from decades of past management practices. In the absence of direct manipulation, it will be decades before the maturing forest naturally creates the needed snags sufficient to support optimal cavity users. Suggested short-term strategies include topping live mature trees just below the first main branches using saws or explosives, which is expensive in time, resources, and money; limbing or otherwise wounding trees to create openings for heart-rot fungal invasion (but that's chancy and requires significant time to produce results); girdling mature trees with either chain saws or fire to kill the tree; and artificial inoculation of live or killed trees with selected hear-rot fungi. This last method is the strategy described in the fictional account of my grandfather, the duck hunter, that opened this story.

In a 2004 paper in the *Western Journal of Applied Forestry*, researchers reported on the results of artificial inoculation of conifers with two heart-rot fungi in forests located in the Coast Range of Oregon. They employed a hitherto untried delivery mechanism that was controversial and very cost effective. The vegetative mycelium of pine conk (*Phellinus pini*) and the rose conk (*Fomitopsis cajanderi*) were grown out onto small wood dowels or sawdust. This "spawn" was then delivered into the trunk of the tree using firearms. The dowels were fitted into specially made hollow slugs for a 0.45-70 rifle, and the sawdust spawn was packed behind 12-gauge shotgun slugs. The spawn was fired into carefully selected sites on live trees or recently artificially topped trees. In a five-year follow-up, all of the topped trees were dead and almost all of the trees showed the presence of decay and fruiting bodies of the target fungi and other species. Almost half of the trees showed evidence of use by primary cavity-nesting species of birds and other wildlife. The live inoculated trees showed little evidence of fungal growth and no sign of wildlife use, but samples of wood collected around the injury site showed that in most cases, fungal invasion was under way. The researchers concluded that topping (killing) a tree was a more rapid method for creating a cavity nester habitat, but use of living trees would likely be effective over a longer period of time.[9] One difference in use of living versus topped trees is the cost. Topping involves either the risky use of chain saws high above the forest floor or, in some cases, the use of explosives to sever the tree high above the ground. Either method costs hundreds of dollars per tree versus the much cheaper and easily delivered firearm inoculation. A very realistic and more commonly used alternative to blasting a tree with a large-caliber slug involves the use of larger dowels colonized with a target fungus and tapped into predrilled holes in the trunk of a living tree. This technique has been used to increase nesting sites for the endangered red-cockaded woodpecker in the southeastern United States[10] and as a general habitat restoration technique using the red-belted polypore in the Pacific Northwest.[11]

Certainly the use of explosives to create snags may be needless overkill, but the idea of infecting a living tree with a fungus that will lead to its eventual weakening and death has not been met with open criticism. The intentional use of fungi to perform the role they are naturally suited for is an effective way to undo the damage of narrowly focused forest management practices. Though the opening vignette about my grandfather Henry is fictionalized, the activity described would be a farsighted and effective way for hunters to look out for the overall health of the forest *and* ensure the long term availability of good habitat for their favored prey.

Man's past intervention and management of forest environments has resulted in marked reduction in the habitat and presence of cavity nesters, a group of species of vital necessity to a healthy forest. If we can integrate recent lessons about the desirability of cavity nesters and the role of mature snags and wood-rotting fungi into wise management strategies, our positive manipulation of the forest might significantly increase the population of cavity nesters in the decades to come.

PART VI

TOOLS FOR A NEW WORLD

GROWING MUSHROOMS IN THE GARDEN
A How-to Story

Fungino genere est; capite se totum tegit.

He is of the race of the mushroom;
he covers himself altogether with his head.
Titus Maccius Plautus (254 b.c.–184 b.c.)

The first time I encouraged mushrooms to fruit in a garden, it was an accident. My friend Mark DiGirolomo and I had a small hobbyish business cultivating "exotic" mushrooms in the 1980s. We were part of an early wave of people cultivating wood-decay mushrooms on hardwood sawdust. The technology was coming out of Japan and China and being studied heavily at the University of Pennsylvania for use in the American mushroom industry. We started our business on a frayed shoestring budget by borrowing unused space beneath benches in a commercial greenhouse and using a decrepit 1940s concrete root cellar, located on a friend's property, as a fruiting room. Our inability to finely control the environmental conditions needed to optimize fruiting in the Maine winters resulted in many "mistakes" and lots of painfully learned experience as we moved from the relatively easily cultivated oyster mushrooms to the more exacting shiitake and sulfur shelf varieties. At one juncture, we found ourselves in possession of a number of blocks of oak sawdust colonized with shiitake spawn but stubbornly refusing to fruit. Unfortunately, we needed to remove them from our root cellar to make room for a more promising crop. At the time, I was a caretaker on the property where the root cellar was located, property that also contained a bed of raspberries in need of mulching. We transferred several cartloads of the shiitake blocks onto the raspberries and called it good. Several months later, as spring turned to summer, I was quite startled to find a crop of shiitake mushrooms fruiting out of the thick sawdust layer on the raspberry patch following an extended period of wet weather. The sawdust mulch, acting as both a protective layer and soil amendment for the berry patch, was also playing the role of garden fungus patch as the mushroom mycelium broke down the wood waste, turning it into soil. There we were, in 1984, practicing permaculture gardening before the popular use of the term hit the media. We also enjoyed the collection and consumption of the shiitake from the garden. I have no doubt that their flavor was superior due to the serendipitous nature of their appearance.

In the years following the raspberry shiitake patch, I left the mushroom cultivation field and turned to other, more lucrative pursuits in my quest to cobble together a living wage in rural New England. I never left behind my interest in mushroom cultivation, however, and over the ensuing years, continued to read the scientific literature and popular press about trends in mushroom growing. Occasionally I delved into cultivating mushroom variet-ies on my in-town property. Early in my research into growing mushrooms, I came across a reference to Hungarians growing oyster mushrooms in their home gardens using logs infected with the fungus. The image I conjured was of a utopian setting with a 2-foot-diameter log of maple tucked into a shady corner of the rustic garden and covered with succulent clusters of fruiting oyster mushrooms. I now find there are many enthusiasts seeking to create their own slice of mushroom utopia by growing mushrooms in their gardens. Unlike the 1980s, today there is an industry in place to aid the home cultivator in the pursuit of knowledge, equipment, and mushroom spawn for planting in the appropriate substrate. Mushrooming in the garden is coming of age in the United States as it has in parts of Europe and Asia. Growing exotic varieties in the backyard represents an opportunity for the person too anxious to collect their own "wild" mushrooms in the forest. He or she still can enjoy interesting varieties of fungi picked fresh and cooked up on the day of collection.

Today's home mushroom cultivation in the United States has its roots in the efforts of our grandfathers to grow a crop of button mushrooms (*Agaricus bisporus*) in beds of composted horse manure in the basement. Starting in the 1920s and continuing through the Depression days of the 1930s, mushroom cultivation on trays of composted manure in farmhouse basements became a relatively common rural pastime. Fueled by the growing taste for mushrooms brought to the United States by soldiers returning from the World War I, mushroom cultivation took hold in America. However, the current movement also owes a great deal of credit to those growers with the primary motivation of securing a predictable and trustworthy source of hallucinogenic mushrooms.

Several of the most significant innovators in the field of exotic mushroom cultivation and the sale of cultivation equipment and products began their careers in the 1970s by learning to grow *Psilocybe cubensis* and other magic mushrooms. The subsequent transfer of these skills to edible mushrooms was a natural response to their own growing interest and the questions and needs of their fellow enthusiasts. The same basic techniques and skills are needed for growing edible, medicinal, or hallucinogenic mushrooms; the fungi have no interest in how we plan to use their fruit after we coax them into growth. So don't be surprised when you come across lots of references and information on hallucinogens as you do your homework on edible mushroom cultivation. We stand on the shoulders of these pioneers and are grateful for the paths they have laid for us to follow.

Basic Cultivation Tips

Today many call the integration of mushrooms into the home and garden landscape permaculture gardening and recognize it as one vital component of creating an intentional sustainable ecosystem in a home or commercial setting. The thoughtful use of saprobic fungi assists in the breakdown and recycling of plant mulches to release nutrients for the growing crops. The fruiting mushrooms are another crop to be used as food. There is an increasing interest in growing our own food, and mushrooms are a logical addition to tomatoes, squash, and beans. Some kinds of mushrooms are easily grown on the average suburban house lot. Just as the vegetable gardener helps to ensure success by learning the techniques for how plants grow best, the mushroom gardener is in need of basic knowledge about the life cycle and growing needs of his or her fungal target species before setting forth outdoors. So, before you run out to buy a new sauté pan for cooking your homegrown mushrooms, there are a few basic cultivation tips to consider. These include:

1. Develop a working understanding of the life cycle and growing needs of mushrooms in general and the specific needs of the mushroom you want to grow; this is vital to the success of the enterprise.
2. Explore your property with an eye to evaluating the overall environment where you live and the microclimates created by tree cover,

slopes, and the shading of buildings. Learn what you can modify easily (and cheaply) to make the site more mushroom friendly.

3. Investigate potential organic food sources for your hungry fungi; what is easily available, inexpensive, and in need of being recycled?

4. Ensure access to water.

5. Cultivate a patient attitude and be comfortable with failure in the pursuit of knowledge.

1. Understand the saprobic mushroom life cycle.

A mushroom is the fruiting body of a fungus, one large enough to be seen easily with the naked eye. Mushrooms take on many forms; the round-domed cap, complete with an intricate radiating set of gills attached to a central stalk-growing on the ground is what most people hold as the classic form. The mushroom is analogous to an apple or tomato or any other fruit from a plant. The reason for its existence is to make, display, and distribute the spores of the next generation. And, just like an apple hanging from its tree in the orchard, a mushroom is a very small portion of the whole fungal body. Where the entire apple vegetative body (tree) is composed of the roots, branches, twigs, fruit, and leaves, the fungus also has a vegetative body, the mycelium. It generally is not visible, so it would be easy to believe that the visible mushroom is the entire organism. This is not the case. For this discussion, I am focusing specifically on the saprobic fungi that live by decomposition of organic matter rather than the mycorrhizal species discussed in the previous chapter. Let's look at the oyster mushroom as an example.

The classic oyster mushroom presentation of multiple fleshy caps fruiting in a cluster on that old sugar maple in late October is the end result of a great deal of life work by *Pleurotus ostreatus*, the formal species name. The current generation of mushrooms began when a spore, the microscopic "seed" of *P. ostreatus*, was released from the parent mushroom and landed in a wound on the maple tree trunk, found the proper amount of moisture and warmth, and germinated. The germinating spore developed into a microscopic thread of hyphae that grew and branched to form the vegetative body of the fungus. Most people know hyphae as the cotton-like fuzz they find on bread wrapped in plastic left too long in their breadboxes. These one-cell-wide hyphal threads grow through the substrate, colonizing the heartwood of the sugar maple, and, as they elongate, they produce enzymes that break down the wood of the tree. These very powerful enzymes flow out of the cell and into the surrounding environment where they do the work of breaking down the complex carbohydrates, such as cellulose and lignin, into simple sugars. These carbohydrates are then brought back into the hyphae as food. The fungus can be said to literally eat its way through its host with the heartwood being the main course.

As the hyphae grow through the maple heartwood (in the case of the oyster mushroom), they are colonizing it. The network of hyphae formed in this process is known as mycelium. The mycelium functions to support the growing fungus through storage of nutrients and water, transport of nutrients and, as the conditions are right, to carry out the formation of the mushroom fruiting body. Before this can happen, fungal sex must occur. This fleeting moment happens when the haploid hyphae originating from one spore meets and combines with the hyphae of another compatible strain of the same species. This doubles the genetic material in the cell and, afterward, the fungus is capable of forming a sexual fruiting body, the mushroom. The combined (diploid) mycelium continues to grow as it colonizes its food source and when the fungus has gained enough food energy (biomass) and the environmental conditions of temperature, moisture, and light (yes, some fungi require specific levels of light to fruit) are conducive, the mycelia will begin to form thick hyphal knots, the precursors to the actual mushroom.

The oyster mushroom does require low levels of light to set fruit, as my mushroom farming partner and I found out. When our bags of sawdust and straw were left too long in near darkness while the fungus colonized the substrate, they started to set fruit. In the absence of adequate light, the mushrooms produced were spindly, almost all stalk and very tiny caps. Consider the adaptive reason for this. If the mycelium that colonized the maple heartwood produced a mushroom deep in an enclosed cavity in the log, one that had no access to the outside air, the resulting spores would never be launched into the wind for dispersal to another possible site to grow. Therefore, low levels of light signal the mycelium that it is near the open air, but not in direct sunlight. The expanding mushroom will be out in the open, but not in the direct drying sun.

We live with the mystery of mushrooms appearing fully developed in our lawns and gardens seemingly overnight. How can it be that they come from nowhere so rapidly? Indeed, there are a number of smaller fragile mushrooms, such as the strikingly beautiful *Coprinus plicatilis*, the parasol inky cap, that appear fully formed on our lawns and paths early in the morning only to dry out and wither in the afternoon sun. This rapid growth is due in part to the fact that, in the mushroom button stage, all the cells of the mature mushroom are already present in a tightly compact state. The high-speed growth happens through water uptake rapidly filling out these compacted cells. Within a very few hours, in some species, the button, which has been forming quietly out of sight for several days, expands into maturity and begins to release its crop of spores into the air. In reality, most fleshy mushroom require several days to reach maturity and will continue to mature and release spores for a number of days if the weather conditions remain moist. Others can remain active for weeks, and some woody polypores for several months.

What does the permaculture mushroom gardener need to take from this fungus life cycle primer? The mushroom species available for cultivating in our gardens are saprobes, and require a source of dead plant material as a food source. Fungi are somewhat clumsy in the uptake of the nutrients they absorb from the environment around their hyphae, and some of these nutrients become immediately available to the roots of plants growing nearby. Later, as the fungi die, they release even more nutrients back into the environment. The decomposition of plant tissue and recycling of nutrients happens constantly in the organic layers of healthy soil and forms the basis for the fertility of topsoil. Cultivation or encouraging mushrooms to grow in an integrated garden is a process in which the growing fungus releases the nutrients bound up in dead organic matter and makes them available to your garden plants. This breakdown of organic matter also builds the fertility and structure of the soil. A byproduct of all this soil-building activity is the crop of mushrooms you bought the sauté pan to cook.

2. Evaluate your property for good mushroom cultivation sites.

Mushrooms are made up of 85–90 percent water and their mycelium is equally high in water. They grow best in habitats with consistent moisture, protected from the drying effects of sun and wind. Most suburban and rural yards are a mixture of microhabitats created by variations in sun exposure, soil texture, existing plantings, and moisture content. It is important to choose a site on your property that makes it easy for your mushroom bed or logs to stay damp. Here is a list of considerations:

- The north and east sides of a house are normally the most fungal friendly because they see the least sun.
- An ideal site has partial to full shade and minimal wind exposure.

These conditions are best formed by a mix of trees and shrubs forming an overstory canopy and a windscreen.

- For mushrooms growing in wood mulch, compost, or planted directly into soil, it is important that the soil drains. Though moisture is vital, sitting in standing water for any period of time will smother the fungus. If you have heavy, wet, clay soil, consider a raised bed.
- Though a mushroom planting will benefit from protective shade, a mushroom bed among crowded trees and shrubs might find itself robbed of moisture by thirsty roots. This happened to me when I put a bed of garden *Stropharia* along the edge of a dense old lilac clump with two nearby trees. The crowded roots drank up the moisture, leaving my *Stropharia* too dry to grow.

Most of the above list is derived from my own trial and error as well as suggestions from a number of general sources.

3. Consider available sources of food for hungry fungi.

If you want to grow mushrooms in the garden, you need a "substrate," a usable source of dead plant material to serve as a food source for the growing fungi mycelium. Any experienced gardener knows that applying a thick layer of wood mulch to the garden helps to retain soil moisture by reducing evaporation from the soil surface and also stops weed seeds from germinating. The fresh raw wood also tends to rob nutrients from the soil in the short term as the nutrients are utilized by the fungi and slime molds to begin the process of rotting the wood fibers. Over time, the nutrients will become available as the mulch is reduced to soil. Mulch, properly chosen and used in a garden protected from both direct sun and complete inundation by water, can be used as a food source for a number of fungi. Other fungal food sources useful in outdoor home mushroom cultivation might include:

- Stumps of trees, both hardwood or conifer, left in place
- Recently cut lengths of wood (logs)
- Straw, hay, or other agricultural waste
- Shredded cardboard or paper
- Cotton cloth or old clothing, made of other natural fibers (avoid silk)
- Composted leaf piles or composts of mixed yard waste

234 • TOOLS FOR A NEW WORLD

Look around your yard, neighborhood, and town for any likely source of uncontaminated plant waste and consider its potential to make mushroom mycelium happy and you may have a substrate for home cultivation. Remember, this is an opportunity to reuse or recycle plant waste that, in the past, you may have paid to be carted off to a landfill. Some substrates to avoid include branches or logs that have been dead for more than several months (less time if cut during the warm or dry time of the year). Also avoid composted wood mulch, as it is already colonized by fungi and less likely to be a welcoming home for new species. Also avoid mulch that is made up of only bark. Avoid any paper, cardboard, or plant material that might be contaminated with chemicals or pesticides and definitely avoid any contaminated with fungicides.

4. Ensure that you have access to water.

There will be times when nature will not deliver the moisture needed by your mushroom crop on the schedule the fungus needs. Ask any farmer or gardener; nature cooperates when it pleases *her*. Since the single most crucial environmental need for mushroom cultivation is water in adequate amounts delivered at reasonable intervals, a handy source of water and a garden hose are almost essential. The drier and more unpredictable your growing environment is, the more important it will be to have a back-up water source. A sprinkler or spray is generally ideal, though for log cultivation, especially for shiitake mushrooms, the ability to soak your logs in water to trigger fruiting is important. A thirty-gallon plastic trash receptacle works very well for a small number of logs.

5. Cultivate patience and active observation.

We live in an age that tends to encourage the belief that events unfold magically, without effort and planning. Our media images and sound bites are filled with meals instantly appearing out of microwaves, homes being cleaned with a wave of the hand, and children marching directly to bed with clean faces and homework finished while we complete our graduate programs online in our spare time. Mushrooms do not watch TV, and don't have cable or Internet access; they are fickle, earth-based living creatures with specific living requirements and their own internalized clocks. When we cultivate mushrooms, we seek to carefully set up a living situation that will make them happy enough to give us their offspring for dinner. That takes time and requires that we stay aware of the needs of our wards and respond, as needed, to make their lives easy. Just as growing a backyard vegetable garden requires that we learn the skills and techniques to make the vegetable plants happy, growing mushrooms requires us to build similar skills. The difference is that we have been cultivating plants for many centuries and can peer back on a long line of ancestors whose lives depended on the skills of plant cultivation. We have a complex, established civilization today due, in part, to their success in making plants grow. Man is a beginner at growing mushrooms, and very few of us can rely on the teachings of past generations of relatives to pass on the skills.

The Russians refer to mushroom picking as the quiet hunt. There is no noise of guns, drama of blood, or death throes; it is a time of being at one with the forest. I see growing mushrooms as quiet farming.

Cultivating mushrooms requires that you learn about the growing needs of fungi and how to create a suitable environment. Then it requires that you monitor your crop as it develops in order to continue to supply those needs over time. At the very least, and in ideal conditions, it takes three to four months in a temperate climate for the first crop of mushrooms to appear. Commonly, you will wait six months or even a full year before you see your first mushroom from a log or bed you planted the previous spring. Just as a tomato patch needs soil preparation, seed planting, watering, weeding, thinning, pinching off leaders, staking, weeding, watering, fertilizing, and vigilant watchfulness for pests, so will a mushroom patch benefit from regular care and feeding. As the mycelium of the fungus is colonizing the sawdust, log, or compost as it grows, it is not nearly as visible and encouraging as watching the tomato vines grow larger and bushier, flower, and develop green fruit. Fungi grow out of sight, hidden beneath the bark of the log or under the covering top layer of straw, soil, or wood chips. There is little visible sign or encouragement before, magically, just like TV, the developing mushrooms appear on the surface and almost leap into your basket. The quiet farming is the long interval between bed preparation and planting and the eventual sign of fruit. It is during this interval that active patience is most needed to ensure that the fungi maintain moisture. Look for signs of drying by poking beneath the top layers in a mushroom bed or observing signs of checking on the cut end of a log in which the fungus is growing.

Getting Started with Home Mushroom Cultivation

Want to grow your own mushrooms? Start small and start easy. Just as you wouldn't start your six-year-old out on a unicycle, choosing instead a tricycle or a bike with training wheels, begin growing those mushrooms that are easy and generally give encouraging results. Many mushroom companies offer products that only require you to provide a microclimate to encourage fruiting. They send you a block of sawdust or other suitable substrate mix that is fully colonized with the mycelium of your choice of mushroom and ready to fruit in the appropriately moist setting. The most popular species include varieties of shiitake and oyster mushrooms, though there are other species to choose from that are edible, medicinal, or both. Fungi Perfecti of Olympia, Washington (www.fungiperfecti.com) has been offering such kits for many years and stands behind their products.

Some mushroom companies, such as Field and Forest Products out of Pestigo, Wisconsin (www.fieldforest.net) offer kits that include all the material you need to grow mushrooms on an unused roll of toilet paper or paper towels (a ready source of cellulose). The kits include the spawn (mushroom mycelia grown out on sawdust), special breathable bags to create a microclimate, and complete instructions. Both of the companies above and others offer a wide range of mushrooms for the home or commercial grower and the cultivation products and support needed to increase the likelihood of success. Few companies will guarantee success—that is up to you.

An advantage of indoor cultivation is the ability to control temperature, moisture, and air circulation more easily. Starting indoors also helps fill in the learning curve in a manner that is somewhat independent of seasons. As long as you set it up thoughtfully, you can create the right temperature and humidity needed for your indoor patch in any season of the year.

If you decide to pursue outdoor cultivation, it is vital to plan your mushroom cultivation to match your location and climate; your macrohabitat. The species and varieties of mushrooms that grow well in Georgia and South Carolina will generally struggle in the harsher winters and cool springs of northern New England. Today we benefit from several decades of careful strain selection of the commonly cultivated mushrooms and you can purchase strains suitable for cultivation in a range of temperatures. Shiitake mushroom strains available from a number of companies have been selected for the broadest climate ranges. Whether you grow shiitake in Maine, Georgia, California, or Michigan, you can choose strains to match your climate and choose them to start fruiting in the cool late spring and, with strains that fruit in warmer temperatures, extend the availability of your harvest into the warm days of summer. The same is true with oyster mushrooms, though it is often accomplished with differing species. Some species have evolved in tropical climates and others, like the almost ubiquitous *Pleurotus ostreatus*, will fruit in a variety of conditions and climates and thrive in the northern United States. Most reputable companies will provide the information needed to choose appropriate varieties; a small list accompanies this text along with additional sources of information (see the Appendix).

Depending on the vagaries of your particular climate, outdoor cultivation is best begun in the non-winter months. For much of the United States, with our temperate climate, most mushrooms are best started outdoors in the spring to early summer or in late summer to fall. The climates of the Deep South, Southwest, and West Coast will each require manipulation of the timing of planting to optimize success in those regions. For log cultivation, the ideal is to cut the trees in the end of winter and to plant the spawn into the logs in the first warm days of late spring. A live tree has some built-in defenses against fungal invasion, and waiting a short time after cutting allows for easier invasion by your chosen mushroom. There is a balance, though; if you leave the cut logs around very long, you allow other species of fungi to attack the new tasty wood and these invaders will compete with your crop.

The Easiest Mushrooms to Grow at Home

Wine Cap *Stropharia*

The wine cap *Stropharia* or garden giant, *Stropharia rugosoannulata*, has not been a well-known edible in the United States until recently. This is a wild species that has become increasingly common due to our use of wood mulch as a landscape element. It is an aggressive and voracious wood rotter in a moist bed of wood chips and soil, and fruits prolifically, if not predictably. Grow these in a bed of mixed hardwood chips and sawdust, or on the mulch for your raspberries. If you use wood chips to make paths through your garden or woods, inoculate your path with *Stropharia* and enjoy collecting your dinner from the edge of the path. This mushroom is best planted in late spring or early fall with crops in spring and late summer to fall beginning the following season. I also have grown these in my potato beds by hilling up the spuds with a mixture of soil and wood mulch inoculated with wine caps. The base of each mushroom usually has thick threads of mycelium attached. Use the cut bases of wild mushrooms as a means to plant this species into your garden mulch bed. This beautiful mushroom with burgundy cap and deep gray gills is best picked and eaten before the cap fully expands. Commercial spawn is available from several sources to get wine caps started in your mulch bed.

Oyster Mushrooms

Oyster mushrooms (genus *Pleurotus*) come in a number of different species and a bewildering array of varieties and cutivars suitable for a wide range of growing conditions. Depending on your climactic needs and personal proclivities, there are oysters that will grow from Puerto Rico to Alaska and all stops between. You can find oysters that produce white, gray, blue, yellow, or pink mushrooms, and species that fruit in the summer's swelter or only after the first frost of autumn. They are assertive, forgiving growers and can consume and fruit on a bewildering array of organic food sources, from logs and wood chips to straw, paper waste, coffee grounds, newspaper, banana leaves, cotton waste. . . . The list of substrates used successfully worldwide would fill this page and overflow your imagination. For the beginner urban, suburban, or rural American, start out using logs of soft hardwoods (poplar, alder, soft maple, and such), straw, wood chips, or sawdust.

Shiitake

Shiitakes are the button mushroom of Japan and China. For the past century, this species was the dominant cultivated mushroom in Asia and remains a stalwart in those regions of Asia where mushroom cultivation innovation has reigned supreme for many years. Historically grown on logs of the shi tree in Japan, log cultivation remains the easiest method for the home cultivator in the United States. The shi tree is a member of the oak family and shiitake grow best on oak logs, though success has been high on several other tree species. A cut section of a recently dead tree with bark intact is an excellent incubation chamber, protecting the growing mycelium from the drying effect of sun and wind and the attack of bacteria, molds, and insects. Shiitake mycelium is sold as spawn colonizing small wooden dowels. These are "planted" into the log via a series of spaced holes bored into the fresh log, filled with the wood dowels and then sealed over with wax to protect the new site from drying. The inoculated logs are stacked in the shade and monitored for adequate moisture for at least six months to give the mycelium the time needed to colonize the log. The home cultivator can choose from a number of shiitake varieties suited to grow in a wide range of climates. Some trigger mushroom fruiting at low temperatures and others will fruit in warmer weather. This allows the grower to have several strains of mushrooms that will extend the time of fruiting for a longer supply of fresh shiitake. The colonized logs can be "shocked" into fruiting by soaking them in water overnight or jarring them with a rubber mallet. The inoculated logs will continue to produce crops of mushrooms seasonally for several years with the longest productivity coming from logs with the greatest diameter.

A number of other mushrooms are readily available for home cultivation. Again, I recommend cutting your teeth with the easy ones and progressing to more challenging mushrooms as your skill level matches the challenge. Mushroom cultivation requires learning, time, and some attention to details. Beyond that, any twelve-year-old can do the work. Then you can motivate the pre-adolescent to learn cooking skills to use with his or her first crop!

APPENDIX OF RECOMMENDED AND SUPPLEMENTAL READING

Helpful Books for Mushroom Identification

Field Guides for the Beginning Mushroomer

Barron, George. 1999. *Mushrooms of Northeast North America; Midwest to New England.* Edmonton, Alberta, Canada: Lone Pine Publishing.

Kuo, M. 2007. *100 Edible Mushrooms.* Ann Arbor: University of Michigan Press.

Spahr, David. 2009. *Edible and Medicinal Mushrooms of New England and Eastern Canada.* Berkeley, Calif.: North Atlantic Books, Berkeley.

More Comprehensive Field Guides

Arora, David. 1986. *Mushrooms Demystified: A Comprehensive Guide to the Fleshy Fungi.* Berkeley, Calif.: Ten Speed Press.

Bessette, Allan E., William C. Roody, and Arlene R. Bessette. 2000. *North American Boletes.* Syracuse, N.Y.: Syracuse University Press.

Lincoff, Gary. 1981. *The Audubon Society Field Guide to North American Mushrooms.* New York: Alfred Knopf.

Phillips, Roger. 2005. *Mushrooms and Other Fungi of North America.* Richmond Hill, Ontario, Canada: Firefly Books.

Trappe, Matt, Frank Evans, and James Trappe. 2007. *Field Guide to North American Truffles.* Berkeley, Calif.: Ten Speed Press.

Regional Field Guides

Bessette, Alan E., Arleen R. Bessette, and David W. Fischer. 1997. *Mushrooms of Northeastern North America.* Syracuse, N.Y.: Syracuse University Press. Covering 600 species with keys leading to photographs of the more common mushrooms.

Evenson, Vera Stucky. 1997. *Mushrooms of Colorado and the Southern Rocky Mountains.* Denver, Colo.: Denver Botanic Gardens.

Horn, Bruce, Richard Kay, and Dean Abel. 1993. *A Guide to Kansas Mushrooms.* Lawrence: University of Kansas Press. An older guide, but one that addresses midwestern mushrooms with good photos as well as many pages of additional information about mushrooms and mushrooming in the prairie states.

Roody, William C. 2003. *Mushrooms of West Virginia and the Central Appalachians.* Lexington: The University Press of Kentucky. Covers about 400 species in the Appalachian Mountains region. Well written and easy to use.

Russell, Bill. 2006. *Field Guide to the Mushrooms of Pennsylvania and the Mid-Atlantic.* University Park: Keystone Books, Penn State University Press.

Trudell, Steve, and Joe Ammirati. 2009. *Mushrooms of the Pacific Northwest.* Portland, Ore.: Timber Press.

Great Books about Mushrooms, Mycology, and Related Stuff

Boa, Eric. 2004. *Wild Edible Fungi, A Global Overview of Their Use and Importance to People.* Non-Wood Forest Products Report #17. *Online at* http://www.fao.org/docrep/007/Y5489E/y5489e00.htm

Czarnecki, Jack. 1998. *Joe's Book of Mushroom Cookery.* New York: Macmillan.

Kuo, M. 2005. *Morels.* Ann Arbor: University of Michigan Press.

Masser, Chris, A. W. Claridge, and J. M. Trappe. 2008. *Trees, Truffles, and Beasts: How Forests Function.* New Brunswick, N.J.: Rutgers University Press.

Persson, Ollie. 1997. *The Chanterelle Book.* Berkeley, Calif.: Ten Speed Press

Pieribone, V., and D. Gruber. 2005. *Aglow in the Dark.* Cambridge, Mass.: Harvard University Press. As the title suggests, this book is dedicated to bioluminescence in all its forms, not just fungi.

Stamets, Paul. 1996. *Psilocybin Mushrooms of the World.* Berkeley, Calif.: Ten Speed Press.

Stamets, Paul. 2005. *Mycelium Running: How Mushrooms Can Save the World.* Berkeley, Calif.: Ten Speed Press.

Wasson, R. G. 1968. *Soma: Divine Mushroom of Immortality.* New York: Harcourt Brace Jovanovich. Not in print, but available through some libraries.

Medicinal Mushroom Resources

Hobbs, Christopher. 1995. *Medicinal Mushrooms: An Exploration of Tradition, Healing and Culture.* Botanica Press (through various distributors). Great store of information coming from the focus of an herbalist.

Marley, Greg A. 2009. *Mushrooms for Health: Medicinal Secrets of Northeast Fungi.* Camden, Me.: Down East Books. A field guide and comprehensive look at the most researched and promising of the medicinal mushrooms, the research supporting use, and preparation tips.

Mushroom Poisoning Books and Resources

Benjamin, D. R. 1995. *Mushrooms: Poisons and Panaceas — A Handbook for Naturalists, Mycologists, and Physicians.* New York: W.H. Freeman.

Hallen, H., and G. Adams. 2002. *Don't Pick Poison When Gathering Mushrooms for Food in Michigan.* Mich. State University Extension Service Bulletin E-2777. Available online at: https://www.msu.edu/user/hallenhe/E-2777.pdf. This is a very well-written and informative bulletin of the common and problematic mushrooms. At forty-three bi-fold pages, it is quite comprehensive without being overwhelming.

Internet Resources

www.mushroomexpert.com A well-organized and developed site for mushroom identification and general information with good links to other resources. Has a great section devoted to morels. Includes keys to many mushroom genera and related groups.

www.mykoweb.com An award-winning California site filled with a wide range of mushroom-related resources, identification supports, articles, and good links. Broadly comprehensive and a little overwhelming initially. Also home to the online Fungi of California.

www.rogersmushrooms.com Rogers Mushrooms is the work of mushrooming author Roger Phillips. This site contains the information published in the above book by the author. It also contains a good section on mushroom toxins and a better visual key to help identify mushrooms to genus.

http://hymfiles.biosci.ohio-state.edu/projects/FFiles/ The Firefly Files by Marc Branham, 1998. A great source of information for kids and adults about the world of fireflies.

www.tomvolkfungi.net Tom Volk's Fungi. Tom is a professor of mycology at the University of Wisconsin and has made an incredible impact on mycologists of all levels of interest and accomplishments over the past fifteen years. His Web site is a treasure trove of information, mostly easily laid out, fun, and informative. Since 1997 he has added monthly mushrooms to a growing list sure to form the basis of an undergraduate degree in mycology.

Journals and Magazines for the Amateur Mushroomer

Fungi Magazine. The newer kid on the block and a very welcome addition, this journal is presented in a friendly, colorful style, and is packed with information helpful for amateur and quasi-professional alike. Mail: Fungi Magazine, P.O. Box 8,1925 Hwy. 175, Richfield, Wisconsin 53076-0008. Phone 262-227-1243, email bbunyard@wi.rr.com, or online at http://www.fungimag.com/ $38.00 for 5 issues.

Mushroom: The Journal of Wild Mushrooming. For twenty years this has been the bedrock for amateur mushroomers and a source of great information, inspiration, and a connection to other American mushroomers. Mail: Leon Shernoff, 1511 E. 54th St. Chicago, IL 60615, or email: leon@mushroomthejournal.com $25.00 for four issues. http://www.mushroomthejournal.com/index.html

Resources for Learning about Mushroom Cultivation

Web Sites for Information, Spawn, and Equipment

www.fieldforest.net Field and Forest Products has been in the business of mushroom cultivation for twenty-five years and has all the ups and downs to prove it. A great source of cold-weather growing strains.

www.fungi.com A leader in the field of mushroom cultivation and mushrooming eco-philosophy, Paul Stamets offers a very full range of products and support for mushroom growing.

www.themushroompatch.com The Mushroom Patch is a Canadian company with a wide range of information and products for the home grower. The company specializes in low-cost and low-tech growing.

Books on Mushroom Cultivation

The Mushroom Cultivator by Paul Stamets and J. S. Chilton. 1983. Agarikon Press. One of the first comprehensive books on mushroom cultivation and a great primer that addresses basic techniques and laboratory skills. A good treatment of the specific growing parameters for a number of common edible and a few hallucinogenic mushrooms.

Growing Gourmet and Medicinal Mushrooms by Paul Stamets. 1993. Ten Speed Press. This book adds to the knowledge base built in *The Mushroom Cultivator* and includes the background information and growing needs for some medicinal species in addition to edibles and magic mushrooms. A rich source for cultural and historical information as well.

Mushrooms in the Garden by Hellmut Steineck. 1981. Mad River Press. A translation from the original German text, Steineck wrote this guide following many years of practicing his passion for integrating mushrooms into his home landscape. More of a guide to the possibilities than a stepwise recipe for cultivation, it will open your eyes to a new world.

Regional Mycological Organizations to Join

North American Mycological Association (NAMA)
Bruce Eberle, Executive Secretary, North American Mycological Association 6586 Guilford Road, Clarksville, MD 21029-1520
Phone: 301-854-3142
Email: Bruce_Eberle@msn.com

Northeast—The Mycological Association of Washington (DC)
7400 Clifton Road, Clifton, VA 20124-2106
Web: mawdc.org
Email: bruceaboyer@cox.net

Northeast Mycological Federation
Web: www.nemf.org
Email: ursula.hoffmann@lehman.cuny.edu

Gulf States Mycological Society- FL, LA, MS, TX
262 CR 3062, Newton, TX 75966-7003
Web: www.gsmyco.org
Email: plewis@jas.net

Southwest-Four Corners Mushroom Club-AZ, UT, CO, NM
Email: 4cmc@mycowest.org
Web: www.mycowest.org/4cmc

For a state-by-state listing of clubs affiliated with the North American Mycological Association, go to: http://www.namyco.org/clubs/index.html

North American Truffling Society (NATS)
P.O. Box 296
Corvallis, OR 97339
Phone: 503-451-5987 or 503-752-2243
Web: www.natruffling.org

Canada

Alberta Mycological Society
P.O. Box 1921 10405 Jasper Avenue, Edmonton, AB, T5J 3S2
Web: www.wildmushrooms.ws

South Vancouver Island Mycological Society
2552 Beaufort Road, Sidney, BC V8L 2J9
Web: www.svims.ca
Email: jeanwade@islandnet.com

Southern Interior Mycological Society
16152 Schaad Road, Lake Country, BC V4V
 1C2
Web: www.mycowest.org/sims.htm
Email: rodpooley@uniserve.com

Vancouver Mycological Society
101-1001 W Broadway, Box 181, Vancouver,
 BC V6H 4E4
Web: www.vanmyco.com
Email: info@vanmyco.com

Mycological Society of Toronto
2106-812 Birnhamthorpe Road,Toronto, ON
 M9C 4W1
Web: www.myctor.org
Email: stella.tracy@sympatico.ca

Le Cercle des Mycologues de Montreal
4101 Rue Sherbrooke Est, Montreal, QC
 H1X 2B2
Web: www.mycomontreal.qc.ca/
Email: mycomtl@mycomontreal.qc.ca

Mexico
Myco Aficionados of Mexico
Apdo.73, Tlaxcala, Tlax 9000 Mexico
Web: www.mexmush.com/
Email: gundi_jeffrey@yahoo.com

ENDNOTES

Introduction
1. Paul Stamets, *Mycelium Running: How Mushrooms Can Save the World* (Berkeley, Calif.: Ten Speed Press, 2005).
2. R. Gordon Wasson, *Soma: The Divine Mushroom of Immortality* (New York: Harcourt Brace Jovanovich, 1968).
3. Ibid.
4. Ibid.
5. William Delisle Hay, *An Elementary Textbook of British Fungi* (London: S. Sonnenschein, Lowrey, 1887).

Chapter 1
1. Alexander Viazmensky, "Picking Mushrooms in Russia," *Mushroom: The Journal of Wild Mushrooming*, Winter 1990–91, pp. 5–7.
2. Ibid.
3. Jane from Ohio, "Slovak Christmas Eve Mushroom Soup, Recipezaar, November 19, 2006, at http://www.recipezaar.com/196554, accessed April 2, 2008.
4. Valentina Pavlovna and R. Gordon Wasson, *Mushrooms, Russia and History* (New York: Pantheon Books, 1957).
5. Ernest Small, *Baba Yaga* (Boston: Houghton Mifflin, 1966).
6. Larissa Vilenskaya, "From Slavic Mysteries to Contempory PSI Research and Back, Part 3," at http://www.resonateview.org/places/writings/larissa/myth.htm, accessed April 1, 2008.
7. Vladimir Nabokov, *Speak, Memory: An Autobiography Revisited* (New York: G. P. Putman's Sons, 1966.
8. Sergei T. Aksakov, *Remarks and Observations of a Mushroom Hunter*, 1856.
9. Steve Rosenberg, "Russian Mushroom Pickers Threaten Aircraft," BBC News, September 25, 2000, at http://news.bbc.co.uk/2/hi/europes/941634.stm, accessed July 4, 2009.
10. Craig Stephen Cravens, *Culture and Customs of the Czech Republic and Slovakia* (London: Greenwood Press, 2006).
11. Snejana Tempest, *Mushroomlore, Mushrooms in Russian Culture*. Web site accessed on November 2, 2008 at https://www.lsa.umich.edu/slavic/mushroomlore
12. Milka Parkkonen, "Death Cap Mushroom Claims Hundreds of Victims in Southern Russia," *Helsingin Sanomat*, July 31, 2000.
13. Ibid.
14. "Wild Mushrooms Kill 10 and Poison Hundreds in Russia," *PRAVDA*, July 18, 2005, at http://english.pravda.ru/hotspots/disasters/8585-mushrooms-0, accessed March 28, 2008.
15. V. N. Padalka, I. P. Shlapak, S. M. Nedashkovsky, O. V. Kurashov, A. V. Alexeenko, A. G. Bogomol, and Y. O. Polenstov, "Can Mushroom Poisoning Be Considered as a Disaster?" *Prehospital and Disaster Medicine* 15, no. 3 (2000), s76.

Chapter 2
1. Katherine Mansfield, "Love and Mushrooms," 1917 journal entry, More Extracts from a Journal, ed. J. Middleton Murry, in *The Adelphi* (1923), p. 1068.
2. William D. Hay, *An Elementary Textbook on British Fungi* (London: S. Sonnenschein, 1887).
3. Louis C. C. Krieger, *The Mushroom Handbook* (New York: Dover, 1967).
4. Antoin Kiely, advertisement for walk dated October 16, 2005, *The Ballyhoura Country News*, www.ballyhouracountry.com/view.asp?ID-153, accessed October 8, 2008.
5. Michael W. Beug, Marilyn Shaw, Kenneth W. Cochran, "Thirty Plus Years of Mushroom Poisoning: Summary of Approximately 2,000 Reports in the NAMA Case Registry," *McIlvainea* 16, no. 2 (2006), pp. 47–68.
6. C. L. Fergus, *Common Edible and Poisonous Mushrooms of the Northeast* (Mechanicsburg, Pa.: Stackpole Books, 2003).
7. Francis De Sales, *Introduction to the Devout Life*, 1609.

8. Eric Boa, "Wild Edible Fungi, A Global Overview of Their Use and Importance to People," FAO Non-Wood Forest Products Report #14, from http://www.fao.org/docrep/007/y5489e/y5489e00.htm#TopOfPage, accessed March 2, 2004.

Part II Introduction
1. Eric Boa, "Wild Edible Fungi, A Global Overview of Their Use and Importance to People," FAO Non-Wood Forest Products Report #14, from http://www.fao.org/docrep/007/y5489e/y5489e00.htm#TopOfPage, accessed March 2, 2004.

Chapter 3
1. Clyde M. Christensen, *Common Edible Mushrooms* (Minneapolis: Univ. of Minnesota Press, 1943).
2. Gary Alan Fine, *Morel Tales: The Culture of Mushrooming* (Cambridge, Mass.: Harvard University Press, 2003).
3. Michael Kuo, *Morels* (Ann Arbor: University of Michigan Press, 2005).
4. Michael Kuo, mushroomexpert.com Web site: http://www.mushroomexpert.com.html, accessed 2002?
5. D. R. Benjamin, Mushrooms: *Poisons and Panaceas—A Handbook for Naturalists, Mycologists, and Physicians* (New York: W. H. Freeman and Company, 1995).
6. E. Shavit, "Arsenic in Morels Collected in New Jersey Apple Orchards Blamed for Arsenic Poisoning," *Fungi* 1, no. 4 (2008), pp. 2–10.
7. Eleanor Shavit and Efrat Shavit, "Lead and Arsenic in Morchella esculenta Fruitbodies Collected in Lead Arsenate Contaminated Apple Orchards in the Northeast United States: A Preliminary Study," *Fungi* 3, no. 2 (2010), pp. 11–18. Published online at http://www.fungimag.com/winter-2010-articles/shavit-morels.pdf
8. David Pilz et al., "Ecology and Management of Morels Harvested from the Forests of Western North America," USDA General Technical Report, PNW-GTR-710 (2007).
9. Ibid.
10. David Arora, *Mushrooms Demystified, A Comprehensive Guide to the Fleshy Fungi* (Berkeley, Calif.: Ten Speed Press, 1986).
11. Gary Lincoff, *The Audubon Society Field Guide to North American Mushrooms* (New York: Knopf, 1981).
12. M. Kuo, "Calvatia gigantea," September 2005. Retrieved from the mushroomexpert.com Web site: http://www.mushroomexpert.com/calvatia_gigantea.html
13. T. J. Volk, "Laetiporus cincinnatus, the White-Pored Chicken of the Woods," 2001. Retrieved from www.tomvolkfungi.net
14. Harold Burdsall and Mark Bank, "The Genus Laetiporus in North America." *Harvard Papers in Botany* 6, no. 1 (2001), pp. 43–55.
15. Scott Redhead, "Bully for Coprinus—A Story of Manure, Minutiae, and Molecules," *McIlvainea* 14, no. 2 (2001) pp. 5–14.
16. T. J. Volk, "Coprinus comatus, the Shaggy Mane," 2004. Retrieved from http://botit.botany.wisc.edu/toms_fungi/may2004.html

Chapter 4
1. Lorelei Norvell and Judy Roger, "The Oregon Cantharellus Study Project: Pacific Golden Chanterelle Preliminary Observations and Productivity Data (1986–1997), *Inoculum* 49, no. 2 (1998), p. 40.
2. D. Pilz, L. Norvell, E. Danell, and R. Molina, "Ecology and Management of Commercially Harvested Chanterelle Mushrooms." Gen. Tech. Rep. PNW-GTR-576, U.S. Department of Agriculture, Forest Service, Pacific Northwest Research Station, Portland, Oregon (2003), 83 pp.
3. Ollie Persson, *The Chanterelle Book* (Berkeley, Calif.: Ten Speed Press, 1997).
4. D. Pilz, L. Norvell, E. Danell, and R. Molina, "Ecology and Management of Commercially Harvested Chanterelle Mushrooms." Gen. Tech. Rep. PNW-GTR-576, U.S. Department of Agriculture, Forest Service, Pacific Northwest Research Station, Portland, Oregon (2003), 83 pp.

5. Lorelei Norvell and Judy Roger, "The Oregon Cantharellus Study Project: Pacific Golden Chanterelle Preliminary Observations and Productivity Data (1986–1997)," *Inoculum* 49, no. 2 (1998), p. 40.

6. D. Pilz, L. Norvell, E. Danell, and R. Molina, "Ecology and Management of Commercially Harvested Chanterelle Mushrooms." Gen. Tech. Rep. PNW-GTR-576, U.S. Department of Agriculture, Forest Service, Pacific Northwest Research Station, Portland, Oregon (2003), 83 pp.

7. Eric Boa, *Wild Edible Fungi: Global Overview of Their Use and Importance to People*, FAO Non-Wood Forest Products Report #17 (2004).

8. Sinclair Tedder and Darcy Mitchel, "The Commercial Harvest of Edible Wild Mushrooms in British Columbia, Canada," text of paper presented to the XII World Forestry Congress (2003), accessed at: www.fao.org/DOCREP/ARTICLE/WFC/XII/0379-B1.HTM

9. D. Pilz, L. Norvell, E. Danell, and R. Molina, "Ecology and Management of Commercially Harvested Chanterelle Mushrooms," Gen. Tech. Rep. PNW-GTR-576, U.S. Department of Agriculture, Forest Service, Pacific Northwest Research Station, Portland, Oregon (2003), 83 pp.

Chapter 5

1. Allan E. Bessette, William C. Roody, and Arlene R. Bessette, *North American Boletes* (Syracuse, N.Y.: Syracuse University Press, 2000).

2. Ernst Both, *Boletes of North America: A Compendium* (Buffalo, N.Y.: Buffalo Society of Natural History, 1993).

3. Michael W. Beug, Marilyn Shaw, and Kenneth Cochran, "Thirty-Plus Years of Mushrooming Poisoning: Summary of the Approximately 2000 Reports in the NAMA Case Registry," *McIlvainea* 16, no. 2 (2006), pp. 47–68.

4. Jack Czarnecki, *Joe's Book of Mushroom Cookery* (New York: Macmillan, 1998).

Chapter 6

1. M. Kuo, "The Genus Agaricus," August 2007, retrieved from the mushroomexpert.com Web site: http://www.mushroomexpert.com/agaricus.html

2. *Agaricus bisporus*. In Wikipedia, The Free Encyclopedia, retrieved June 22, 2009, from http://en.wikipedia.org/w/index.php?title=Agaricus_bisporus&oldid=297932208

3. L. R. Chariton, "Trial Field Key to the Species of Agaricus in the Pacific Northwest," 1997, retrieved from the Pacific Northwest Key Council Web site on April 1, 2009: http://www.svims.ca/council/Agari2.htm

4. David Arora, *Mushrooms Demystified, A Comprehensive Guide to the Fleshy Fungi* (Berkeley, Calif.: Ten Speed Press, 1986).

5. Louis Krieger, *The Mushroom Handbook* (New York: Dover, 1936, reprinted 1967).

Part III Introduction

1. Denis R. Benjamin, *Mushrooms: Poisons and Panaceas* (New York: W. H. Freeman, 1995).

2. Michael W. Beug, M. Shaw, and K.W. Cochran, "Thirty Plus Years of Mushroom Poisoning: Summary of the Approximately 2,000 Reports in the NAMA Case Registry," *McIlvania* 16, no. 2 (2006), pp. 47–68.

3. Michael W. Beug, "NAMA Toxicology Committee Report for 2009; North American Mushroom Poisonings," *McIlvania* 20 (unpublished manuscript).

4. Michael W. Beug, M. Shaw, and K.W. Cochran, "Thirty Plus Years of Mushroom Poisoning: Summary of the Approximately 2,000 Reports in the NAMA Case Registry," *McIlvania* 16, no. 2 (2006), pp. 47–68.

Chapter 7

1. Michael W. Beug, M. Shaw, and K.W. Cochran, "Thirty Plus Years of Mushroom Poisoning: Summary of the Approximately 2,000 Reports in the NAMA Case Registry," *McIlvania* 16, no. 2 (2006), pp. 47–68.

2. Michael W. Beug, "NAMA Toxicology Committee Report for 2006: Recent Mushroom Poisonings in North America," *McIlvainea* 17, no. 1 (2007) pp. 63–72.

3. Eric Boa, "Wild Edible Fungi: A Global Overview of Their Use and Importance to People,"

FAO Non-Wood Forest Products Report #14, 2004, at http://www.fao.org/docrep/007/y5489e/y5489e00.htm#TopOfPage, accessed March 2, 2008.

4. David Arora, *Mushrooms Demystified*, 2nd edition (Berkeley, Calif.: Ten Speed Press, 1986). Denis R. Benjamin, *Mushrooms: Poisons and Panaceas* (New York: W. H. Freeman, 1995). Gary Lincoff, *The Audubon Field Guide to North American Mushrooms*, (New York: Knopf, 1981). "Mushroom poisoning," Wikipedia, The Free Encyclopedia, accessed February 26, 2008, at http://en.wikipedia.org/w/index.php?title=Mushroom_poisoning&oldid=193723564.

5. Denis R. Benjamin, *Mushrooms: Poisons and Panaceas* (New York: W. H. Freeman, 1995).

6. Louis C. C. Krieger, *The Mushroom Handbook* (New York: Dover, 1967).

7. Charles McIlvaine and Robert K. MacAdam, *One Thousand American Fungi* (New York: Dover, 1973).

8. Denis R. Benjamin, *Mushrooms: Poisons and Panaceas* (New York: W. H. Freeman, 1995), p. 348.

9. Denis R. Benjamin, *Mushrooms: Poisons and Panaceas* (New York: WH Freeman, 1995).

10 R. R. Griffiths, W. A. Richards, and R. Jesse McCann, "Psilocybin Can Occasion Mystical-type Experiences Having Substantial and Sustained Personal Meaning and Spiritual Significance," *Psychopharmacology* 187 (2006), pp. 268–283.

11. Paul Stamets, *Psilocybin Mushrooms of the World* (Berkeley, Calif.: Ten Speed Press, 1996).

Chapter 8

1. Denis R. Benjamin, *Mushrooms: Poisons and Panaceas* (New York: W.H. Freeman, 1995). V. Grimm-Samuel, "On the Mushroom which Deified the Emperor Claudius," *Classical Quarterly* 41 (1991), pp. 178–82.

2. Denis R. Benjamin, *Mushrooms: Poisons and Panaceas* (New York: W. H. Freeman, 1995), p. 200.

3. Anne Pringle et al., "The Ectomycorrhizal Fungi Amanita phalloides Was Introduced and Is Expanding Its Range on the West Coast of North America," *Molecular Ecology* (2009).

4. Michael Kuo, "*Amanita bisporegera*" at mushroomexpert.com, http://www.mushroomexpert.com/amanita_bisporigera.html. (October 2003).

5. Denis R. Benjamin, *Mushrooms: Poisons and Panaceas* (New York: W. H. Freeman, 1995).

6. Ibid.

7. H. Faulstich and T. Zilker, "Amatoxins," in *Handbook of Mushroom Poisoning, Diagnosis and Treatment*, D. G. Spoerke and B. A. Rumack, eds. (Boca Raton, Fla.: CRC Press, 1994).

8. Denis R. Benjamin, *Mushrooms: Poisons and Panaceas* (New York: W. H. Freeman, 1995).

9. Michael W. Beug, "Toxicology: Reflections on Mushroom Poisoning in North America," *Fungi* 1, no. 2 (2008), pp. 42–44.

10. P. Hydzik et al., "Liver Albumin Dialysis (MARS) Treatment of Choice in *Amanita phalloides* Poisoning," *Przegl Lek.* 62, no. 6 (2005), pp. 475–9.

11. Michael W. Beug, "Toxicology: Reflections on Mushroom Poisoning in North America," *Fungi* 1, no. 2 (2008), pp. 42–44.

12. C. Lionte, L. Sorodoc, and V. Simionescu, "Successful Treatment of an Adult with Amanita phalloides-Induced Fulminant Liver Failure with Molecular Adsorbent Recirculating System (MARS)," *Romanian Journal of Gastroenterology* 14, no. 3 (1995), pp. 267–71.

13. Michael W. Beug, "Toxicology: Reflections on Mushroom Poisoning in North America," *Fungi* 1, no. 2 (2008), pp. 42–44.

14. Ibid.

15. Michael Kuo, *100 Edible Mushrooms* (Ann Arbor: University of Michigan Press, 2007).

Chapter 9

1. Michael Kuo, "Gyromitra: The False Morels," at mushroomexpert.com, http://www.mushroomexpert.com/gyromitra.ht, accessed December 2006.

2. Ibid.

3. Denis R. Benjamin, *Mushrooms: Poisons and Panaceas* (New York: W. H. Freeman, 1995).

4. John H. Trestrail, III, "Monomethlyhydrazine-Containing Mushrooms—A Form of Gastronomic Roulette," *McIlvainea* 11 (1993), pp. 45–50.

5. Denis R. Benjamin, *Mushrooms: Poisons and Panaceas* (New York: W. H. Freeman, 1995).
6. John H. Trestrail, III, "Monomethlyhydrazine-Containing Mushrooms," in *Handbook of Mushroom Poisoning, Diagnosis and Treatment*, D. G. Spoerke and B. A. Rumack, eds. (Boca Raton, Fla.: CRC Press, 1994).
7. Denis R. Benjamin, *Mushrooms: Poisons and Panaceas* (New York: W. H. Freeman, 1995).
8. John H. Trestrail, III, "Monomethlyhydrazine-Containing Mushrooms," in *Handbook of Mushroom Poisoning, Diagnosis and Treatment*, D. G. Spoerke and B. A. Rumack, eds. (Boca Raton, Fla.: CRC Press, 1994).
9. Michael W. Beug, M. Shaw, and K.W. Cochran, "Thirty Plus Years of Mushroom Poisoning: Summary of the Approximately 2,000 Reports in the NAMA Case Registry," *McIlvania* 16, no. 2 (2006), pp. 47–68.
10. John H. Trestrail, III, "Monomethlyhydrazine-Containing Mushrooms," in *Handbook of Mushroom Poisoning, Diagnosis and Treatment*, D. G. Spoerke and B. A. Rumack, eds. (Boca Raton, Fla.: CRC Press, 1994).
11. Charles McIlvaine and Robert K. MacAdam, *One Thousand American Fungi* (New York: Dover, 1973).
12. Louis C. C. Krieger, *The Mushroom Handbook* (New York: Dover, 1967).
13. Clyde M. Christensen, *Common Edible Mushrooms* (Minneapolis: University of Minnesota Press, 1943).
14. Rene Pomerleau, *Mushrooms of Eastern Canada and the United States* (Montreal: Chantecler, 1951).
15. Orson K. Miller, *Mushrooms of North America* (New York: E. P. Dutton, 1977).
16. Gary Lincoff, *The Audubon Field Guide to North American Mushrooms* (New York: Knopf, 1981). David Arora, *Mushrooms Demystified*, 2nd edition (Berkeley, Calif.: Ten Speed Press, 1986).
17. John H. Trestrail, III, "Monomethlyhydrazine-Containing Mushrooms," in *Handbook of Mushroom Poisoning, Diagnosis and Treatment*, D. G. Spoerke and B. A. Rumack, eds. (Boca Raton, Fla.: CRC Press, 1994).
18. Denis R. Benjamin, *Mushrooms: Poisons and Panaceas* (New York: W. H. Freeman, 1995).
19. Marianna Paavankallio, "False Morels" at Marianna's Nordic Territory, http://www.dlc.fi/~marian1/gourmet/morel.htm , accessed on March 19, 2010.
20. Finnish Food Safety Authority, Evira, "False Morel Fungi" (2003).

Chapter 10

1. T. Kato, "An Outbreak of Encephalopathy after Eating Autumn Mushroom (Sugihiratake; Pleurocybella porrigens) in Patients with Renal Failure: A Clinical Analysis of Ten Cases in Yamagata, Japan," *No To Shinkei* 56, no. 12 (2004), pp. 999–1007.
2. David Arora, *Mushrooms Demystified*, 2nd edition (Berkeley, Calif.: Ten Speed Press, 1986).
3. Hiroshi Akiyama et al., "Determination of Cyanide and Thiocyanate in Sugihiratake Mushroom Using HPLC Method with Fluorometric Detection," *Journal of Health Science* 52, no. 1 (2006), pp. 73–77.
4. H. Sasaki, H. Akiyama, Y. Yoshida, K. Kondo, Y. Amakura, Y. Kasahara, and T. Maitani, "Sugihiratake Mushroom (Angel's Wing Mushroom)-Induced Cryptogenic Encephalopathy May Involve Vitamin D Analogues," *Biological and Pharmaceutical Bulletin* 29, no. 12 (December 2006), pp. 2514–8.
5. Tatsuya Nomoto et al., "A Case of Reversible Encephalopathy Accompanied by Demyelination Occurring after Ingestion of Sugihiratake Mushrooms," *Journal of Nippon Medical School* 74 (2007), pp. 261–274.

Chapter 11

1. Larry Beuchat, *Food and Beverage Mycology* (New York: Springer, 1987), pp. 393–396.
2. M. Winklemenn, W. Stangel, I. Schedl, and B. Grabensee, "Severe Hemolysis Caused by Antibodies against Mushroom *Paxillus involutus* and Its Therapy by Plasma Exchange," *Klin Wochenschr* 64 (1986), pp. 935–38.

3. Denis R. Benjamin, *Mushrooms, Poisons and Panaceas* (New York: W. H. Freeman, 1995).
4. R. Flammer, "Paxillus Syndrome: Immunohemolysis Following Repeated Mushroom Ingestion," *Schweiz. Rundsch. Med. Prax.* 74, no. 37 (1985), pp. 997–99.
5. M. Winklemenn, W. Stangel, I. Schedl, and B. Grabensee, "Severe Hemolysis Caused by Antibodies against Mushroom *Paxillus involutus* and Its Therapy by Plasma Exchange," Klin Wochenschr 64 (1986), pp. 935–38. Denis R. Benjamin, *Mushrooms, Poisons and Panaceas* (New York: W. H. Freeman, 1995).
6. Ibid.
7. Michael W. Beug, M. Shaw, and K.W. Cochran, "Thirty Plus Years of Mushroom Poisoning: Summary of the Approximately 2,000 Reports in the NAMA Case Registry," *McIlvania* 16, no. 2 (2006), pp. 47–68.
8. Charles McIlvaine and Robert K. MacAdam, *One Thousand American Fungi* (New York: Dover, 1973).
9. Morten Lange and F. B. Hora, *Mushrooms and Toadstools* (New York: E. P. Dutton, 1963).
10. Orson Miller, *Mushrooms of North America* (New York: E. P. Dutton, 1972).
11. A. Marchand, *Champignons du Nord et du Midi*, vol. 2 (Perpignan: Hachette, 1973).
12. A. H. Smith, *The Mushroom Hunter's Field Guide Revised and Enlarged*. (Ann Arbor, University of Michigan Press, 1974).
13. R. Haard and K. Haard, *Poisonous and Hallucinogenic Mushrooms*, 2nd edition (Seattle: Homestead Book, 1977).
14. Gary Lincoff, *The Audubon Society Field Guide to North American Mushrooms* (New York: Knopf, 1981).
15. A. M. Young, *Common Australian Fungi* (Sydney: UNSW University Press, 1982).
16. D. Arora, *Mushrooms Demystified* (Berkeley, Calif.: Ten Speed Press, 1986).
17. A. Bessette and W. J. Sundberg, *Mushrooms: A Quick Reference Guide to Mushrooms of North America* (New York: Collier Macmillan, 1987)
18. Luigi Fenaroli, *Funghi* (Firenze: Giunti, 1998).

Part IV Introduction

1. Paul Stamets, *Psilocybin Mushrooms of the World* (Berkeley, Calif.: Ten Speed Press, 1996).
2. Lester Grinspoon and James B. Bakalar, "The Psychedelic Drug Therapies," *Current Psychiatric Therapies* 20 (1981), pp. 275–83.
3. Peter T. Furst, *Hallucinogens and Culture* (Novato, Calif.: Chandler and Sharp, 1976).
4. C. A. P. Ruck, J. Bigwood, D. Staples, J. Ott, and G. Wasson, "Entheogens," *The Journal of Psychedelic Drugs* 2, nos. 1-2 (1979).
5. Ibid.
6. Stanislav Grof, "The Potential of Entheogens as Catalysts of Spiritual Development," in *Psychoactive Sacramentals: Essays on Entheogens and Religion*, Thomas B. Roberts, ed. (San Francisco: Council on Spiritual Practices, 2001).

Chapter 12

1. U. Hoffman and M. Hoffman, "Der Fliegenpilz: An Oral History and Intergenerational Dialog," Entheo 1 (2001), accessed online www.entheomedia.org on May 15, 2009.
2. Rangifer.net, "Human Role in Reindeer/Caribou Systems," accessed at http://www.rangifer. net/rangifer/resresources/biblio.cfm on February 18, 2010.
3. Sveta Yamin-Pasternak, "From Disgust to Desire: Changing Attitudes toward Beringian Mushrooms," *Economic Botany* 62, no. 3 (2008), pp. 214–22.
4. Brian Inglis, *The Forbidden Game: A Social History of Drugs* (New York: Charles Scribner, 1975).
5. Robert C. Hoffman, *Postcards from Santa Claus: Sights and Sentiments from the Last Century* (Garden City, N.Y.: Square One, 2002).
6. Gordon Wasson, *Soma: Divine Mushroom of Immortality* (New York: Harcourt Brace Jovanovich, 1968).
7. Sveta Yamin-Pasternak, "From Disgust to Desire: Changing Attitudes toward Beringian Mushrooms," *Economic Botany* 62, no. 3 (2008), pp. 214–22.

8. Sveta Yamin-Pasternak, *How the Devils Went Deaf: Ethnomycology, Cuisine, and Perception of Landscape in the Russian North*, doctoral thesis, University of Alaska, May 2007.
9. Gary Lincoff, "Is the Fly-Agaric (Amanita muscaria) an Effective Medicinal Mushroom?" Talk given at the 3rd International Medicinal Mushroom Conference (2005). Accessed online at: http://www.nemf.org/files/various/muscaria/fly_agaric_text.html
10. Gordon Wasson, *Soma: Divine Mushroom of Immortality* (New York: Harcourt Brace Jovanovich, 1968).
11. Dead Sea scrolls. In Wikipedia, The Free Encyclopedia. Retrieved May 9, 2009, from http://en.wikipedia.org/w/index.php?title=Dead_Sea_scrolls&oldid=288603346
12. Tom Robbins, "Superfly: The Toadstool That Conquered the Universe," *High Times*, December 1976.
13. Gordon Wasson, *Soma: Divine Mushroom of Immortality* (New York: Harcourt Brace Jovanovich, 1968).
14. Fritz Staal, "How a Psychoactive Substance Becomes Ritual: The Case of SOMA, *Social Research* (Fall 2001).
15. Dennis R. Benjamin, *Mushrooms, Poisons and Panaceas* (New York: W. H. Freeman, 1995).
16. Alexander H. Smith, *The Mushroom Hunter's Field Guide* (Ann Arbor, University of Michigan Press, 1963).
17. William Rubel and David Arora, "A Study of Cultural Bias in Field Guide Determinations of Mushroom Edibility Using the Iconic Mushroom, Amanita muscaria as an Example," *Journal of Economic Botany* 62, no. 3 (2008), pp. 223–43.
18. David W. Rose, "The Poisoning of Count Achilles de Vecchj and the Origins of American Amateur Mycology," *McIlvainea* 16, no. 1 (2006), pp. 37–55.
19. Dennis R. Benjamin, *Mushrooms, Poisons and Panaceas* (New York: W. H. Freeman, 1995).
20. Michael W. Beug, M. Shaw, and K.W. Cochran, "Thirty Plus Years of Mushroom Poisoning: Summary of the Approximately 2,000 Reports in the NAMA Case Registry," *McIlvania* 16, no. 2 (2006), pp. 47–68.
21. G. Geml, A. Laursen, K. O'Neill, H. Nusbaum, and D. L. Taylor, "Beringian Origins and Cryptib Speciation Events in the Fly Agaric (Amanita muscaria)," *Molecular Ecology* 15 (2006), pp. 225–39.
22. I. A. Dickie and P. Johnston, "Invasive Fungi Research Priorities with a Focus on Amanita muscaria," *Landcare Research Contract Report* LC0809/027 (2008).
23. Rodham Tulloss and Zhu-Liang Yang, "Studies in the Genus Amanita Pers. (Agaricales, Fungi)" (2009). Accessed at: www.pluto.njcc.com/~ret/amanita/mainaman.html
24. Dennis R. Benjamin, *Mushrooms, Poisons and Panaceas* (New York: W. H. Freeman, 1995).
25. D. Michelot and L. M. Melendez-Howell, "Amanita muscaria: Chemistry, Biology, Toxicology, and Ethnomycology," *Mycological Research* 107, no. 2 (2003), pp. 131–146.
26. Dennis R. Benjamin, *Mushrooms, Poisons and Panaceas* (New York: W. H. Freeman, 1995).

Chapter 13
1. R. Gordon Wasson, "Seeking the Magic Mushroom," *Life*, May 5, 1957.
2. R. Gordon Wasson and Valentina P. Wasson, *Mushrooms, Russia and History* (New York: Pantheon Books, 1957). R. Gordon Wasson, "Seeking the Magic Mushroom," *Life*, May 5, 1957.
3. Ibid.
4. Albert Hofmann, *LSD—My Problem Child.* (New York: McGraw-Hill, 1980).
5. Ibid.
6. Albert Hofman, 1996, " LSD; Completely Personal." *MAPS Newsletter* 6 no. 3 (Summer,1996).
7. Ibid.
8. Walter N. Pahnke, "Drugs and Mysticism," *International Journal of Parapsychology* 3, no. 2 (1966), pp. 295–313.
9. Ibid.
10. Rick Doblin, "Pahnke's Good Friday Experiment: A Long-Term Follow-up and Methodological Critique," in *Psychoactive Sacramentals: Essays on Entheogens and Religion* (San Francisco: Council on Spiritual Practices, 2001).

11. Walter N. Pahnke, "Drugs and Mysticism," *International Journal of Parapsychology* 3, no. 2 (1966), pp. 295–313.
12. M. W. Johnson, W. A. Richards, and R. R. Griffiths, "Human Hallucinogen Research: Guidelines for Safety." *Journal of Psychopharmacology* 22, no. 6 (2008), pp. 603–20.
13. Ibid.
14. John Marks, *The Search for the Manchurian Candidate: The CIA and Mind Control.* Times Books, 1978.
15. Gaston Guzmán, J. W. Allen, and J. Garrtz, "A Worldwide Geographical Distribution of the Neurotropic Fungi, An Analysis and Discussion" (2000), *Annali dei Museo Civico*, Rovereto, Italy, vol. 14:1890280.
16. Paul Stamets, *Psilocybin Mushrooms of the World* (Berkeley, Calif.: Ten Speed Press, 1996).
17. Ibid.
18. Dennis R. Benjamin, *Mushrooms, Poisons and Panaceas* (New York: W. H. Freeman, 1995).
19. Paul Stamets, *Psilocybin Mushrooms of the World* (Berkeley, Calif.: Ten Speed Press, 1996).
20. Dennis R. Benjamin, *Mushrooms, Poisons and Panaceas* (New York: W. H. Freeman, 1995).
21. R. A. Griffiths, W. A. Richards, U. McCann, and R. Jesse, "Psilocybin Can Occasion Mystical-Type Experiences Having Substantial and Sustained Personal Meaning and Spiritual Significance," *Psychopharmacology* 187 (2006), pp. 268–83.
22. Dennis R. Benjamin, *Mushrooms, Poisons and Panaceas* (New York: W. H. Freeman, 1995).
23. Paul Stamets, *Psilocybin Mushrooms of the World.* (Berkeley, Calif.: Ten Speed Press, 1996).
24. Ibid.
25. M. D. Abraham, "Places of Drug Purchase in the Netherlands," Proceedings of the 10th Annual Conference on Drug Use and Drug Policy, September 1999.
26. R. A. Griffiths, W. A. Richards, U. McCann, and R. Jesse, "Psilocybin Can Occasion Mystical-Type Experiences Having Substantial and Sustained Personal Meaning and Spiritual Significance," *Psychopharmacology* 187 (2006), pp. 268–83.
27. Ibid.
28. Ibid.
29. M. W. Johnson, W. A. Richards, and R. R. Griffiths, "Human Hallucinogen Research: Guidelines for Safety," *Journal of Psychopharmacology* 22, no. 6 (2008), pp. 603–20.
30. F. A. Moreno, C. B. Weigand, E. K. Taitano, and P. L. Delgado, "Safety, Tolerability, and Efficacy of Psilocybin in Nine Patients with Obsessive-Compulsive Disorder," *Journal of Clinical Psychiatry* 67, no. 11 (November 2006), pp. 1735–40.
31. Benjamin St John Sessa, "Are Psychedelic Drug Treatments Seeing a Comeback in Psychiatry?" *Progress in Neurology and Psychiatry* (2008), accessed at www.progressnp.com
32. Ralph Metzner, "Hallucinogenic Drugs and Plants in Psychotherapy and Shamanism," *Journal of Psychoactive Drugs* 30, no. 4 (1998), pp. 1–10.
33. T. Leary, G. H. Litwin, and R. Metzner, "Reactions to Psilocybin Administered in a Supportive Environment," *Journal of Nervous and Mental Disease* 137 (1963), pp. 561–73.

Chapter 14
1. Natalie Angier, "Twin Crowns for 30-Acre Fungus: World's Biggest, Oldest Organism," *New York Times*, April 2, 1992.
2. Myron L. Smith, Johann N. Bruhn, and James B. Anderson, "The fungus *Armillaria bulbosa* Is among the Largest and Oldest Living Organisms," *Nature* 356 (April 2, 1992), pp. 428–431.
3. Tom Volk, "The Humongous Fungus—Ten Years Later," *Inoculum* 53, no. 2 (2002), pp. 4–8.
4. Ibid.
5. C. L. Schmidt and M. L. Tatum, "The Malheur National Forest; Location of the World's Largest Living Organism," *MAL* 08-04.
6. Tom Volk, "Key to North American *Armillaria* Species Using Macroscopic, Microscopic and Distributional Characteristics" (2008). Accessed at http://tomvolkfungi.net/ on April 3, 2008.
7. Susan Hagle, "*Armillaria* Root Disease: Ecology and Management." Forest Health Protection and State Forestry Organizations 11-1, February 2006.

Chapter 15

1. F. M. Dugan, "Fungi, Folkways, and Fairy Tales: Mushrooms and Mildews in Stories, Remedies and Rituals, from Oberon to the Internet." *North American Fungi* 3, no. 27 (2008), pp. 23–72.
2. J. Ramsbottom, "Mushrooms and Toadstools," *New Naturalist* 7 (London: Collins, 1953).
3. W. P. K. Findlay, *Fungi: Fiction, Folklore and Fact* (Surrey, England: Richmond, 1982).
4. R. T. Rolfe and F. W. Rolfe, *The Romance of the Fungus World* (London: Chapman & Hall, 1925).
5. Erasmus Darwin, *The Botanic Garden, Part I, The Economy of Vegetation* (London: J. Johnson, 1791).
6. Stephen G. Saupe, "The Biology of Ressurection; Life after Death in Fungi" (2004). Accessed at: www.employees.csbsju.edu/SSAUPE/essays/anhydriobiosis.htm

Chapter 16

1. D. E. Desjardin, M. Capelari, and C. Stevani, "Bioluminescent *Mycena* Species from São Paulo, Brazil," *Mycologia*, 99, no. 2 (2007), pp. 317–31.
2. David Rose, "Bioluminescence and Fungi," *Spores Illustrated*, Connecticut-Westchester Mycological Association, Summer 1999.
3. J. R. Potts, "Bushnell Turtle (1775)." Accessed February 18, 2010 online at http://www.military-factory.com/ships/detail.asp?ship_id=Bushnell-Turtle-1775
4. Central Intelligence Agency. "Intelligence Techniques" (2007). Accessed February 18, 2010 online at https://www.cia.gov/library/center-for-the-study-of-intelligence/csi-publications/books-and-monographs/intelligence/intelltech.html
5. V. Pieribone and D. Gruber, *Aglow in the Dark: The Revolutionary Science of Biofluorescence* (Cambridge, Mass.: Harvard University Press, 2005).
6. Ibid.
7. J. Sivinski, "Arthropods Attracted to Luminous Fungi," *Psyche* 88, nos. 3-4 (1981), pp. 383–90.
8. O. Shimomura, "The Role of Superoxide Dismutase in Regulating the Light Emission of Luminescent Fungi," *Journal of Experimental Botany* 43 (1992), pp. 1519–25.
9. D. E. Desjardin, M. Capelari, and C. Stevani, "Bioluminescent Mycena species from São Paulo, Brazil," *Mycologia*, 99, no. 2 (2007), pp. 317–31.

Chapter 17

1. Arthur H. Howell, *U.S. Biological Survey: North American Fauna*, no. 44, Revision of the American Flying Squirrels, June 13, 1918.
2. Daniel K. Rosenberg and Robert G. Anthony, "Characteristics of Northern Flying Squirrel Populations in Young Second- and Old Growth Forests in Western Oregon," *Canadian Journal of Botany* 70 (1991), pp. 161–66.
3. R. S. Currah, E. A. Smreciu, T. Lehesvirta, M. Neimi, and K. W. Larsen, "Fungi in the Winter Diets of Northern Flying Squirrels and Red Squirrels in the Boreal Forest of Northeastern Alberta," *Canadian Journal of Botany* 78 (2000), pp. 1514–20.
4. K. Vernes, S. Blois, and F. Barlocher, "Seasonal and Yearly Changes in Consumption of Hypogeous Fungi by Northern Flying Squirrels and Red Squirrels in Old-Growth Forest, New Brunswick," *Canadian Journal of Zoology* 82 (2004), pp. 110–17.
5. Daniel K. Rosenberg and Robert G. Anthony, "Characteristics of Northern Flying Squirrel Populations in Young Second- and Old Growth Forests in Western Oregon," *Canadian Journal of Botany* 70 (1991), pp. 161–66.
6. Andrew Carey, W. Colgan, J. M. Trappe, and R. Molina, "Effects of Forest Management on Truffle Abundance and Squirrel Diet," *Northwest Science* 76, no. 2 (2002), pp. 148–57.
7. Chris Masser, A. W. Claridge, and J. M. Trappe, *Trees, Truffles, and Beasts: How Forests Function* (New Brunswick, N.J.: Rutgers University Press, 2008).
8. Karen Hansen, "Ascomycota Truffles: Cup Fungi Go Underground," *Newsletter of the Friends of the Farlow*, no. 47 (2006).
9. Chris Masser, A. W. Claridge, and J. M. Trappe, *Trees, Truffles, and Beasts: How Forests Function* (New Brunswick, N.J.: Rutgers University Press, 2008).

10. J. M. Trappe and D. L. Luomo, "The Ties that Bind: Fungi in the Ecosystem," in *The Fungal Community: Its Organization and Role in the Ecosystem*, G. C. Carrol and D. T. Wicklow, eds. (New York: Marcel Decker, 1992).
11. Chris Masser, A. W. Claridge, and J. M. Trappe, *Trees, Truffles, and Beasts: How Forests Function* (New Brunswick, N.J.: Rutgers University Press, 2008).

Chapter 18
1. David Lonsdale, M. Pautasso, and O. Holdenrieder, "Wood-Decaying Fungi in the Forest: Conservation Needs and Management Options," *European Journal of Forest Research* 127 (2008), pp. 1–22.
2. J. H. Hart and D. L. Hart, "Heartrot Fungi's Role in Creating Picid Nesting Sites in Living Aspen," USDA Forest Service Proceedings, RMRS-P-18 (2001).
3. K. B. Aubry and C. M. Raley, "The Pileated Woodpecker as a Keystone Habitat Modifier in the Pacific Northwest," USDA Forest Service Gen. Tech. Rep. PSW-GTR-181 (2002).
4. J. H. Hart and D. L. Hart, "Heartrot Fungi's Role in Creating Picid Nesting Sites in Living Aspen," USDA Forest Service Proceedings, RMRS-P-18 (2001).
5. David Lonsdale, M. Pautasso, and O. Holdenrieder, "Wood-Decaying Fungi in the Forest: Conservation Needs and Management Options," *European Journal of Forest Research* 127 (2008), pp. 1–22.
6. M. C. Kalcounis and R. M. Brigham, "Secondary Use of Aspen Cavities by Tree-Roosting Big Brown Bats," *The Journal of Wildlife Management* (1998).
7. M. J. Vonhof and J. C. Gwilliam, "A Summary of Bat Research in the Pend D'Oreille Valley in Southern British Colombia" (2000), Columbia Basin Fish and Wildlife Compensation Program. Accessed online at www.cbfishwildlife.org
8. Ibid.
9. G. M. Filip, C. G. Parks, F. A. Baker, and S. E. Daniels, "Artificial Inoculation of Decay Fungi into Douglas-Fir with Rifle or Shotgun to Produce Wildlife Trees in Western Oregon," *Western Journal of Applied Forestry* 19 (2004), pp. 211–15.
10. S. B. Jack, C. G. Parks, J. M. Stober, and R. T. Engstrom, "Inoculating Red Heart Fungus (*Phellinus pini*) to Create Nesting Habitat for the Red-Cockaded Woodpecker," in Proceedings of the Red-Cockaded Woodpecker Symposium (2003), pp. 1–18.
11. J. Huss, J. Martin, J. C. Bednarz, D. M. Juliano, and D. E. Varland 2002. "The Efficacy of Inoculating Fungi into Conifer Trees to Promote Cavity Excavation by Woodpeckers in Managed Forests in Western Washington," USDA Forest Service Gen. Tech. Rep. PSW-GTR-181 (2002).

INDEX

Agaricus
  caveats, 83–84
  common species, 82–83
  description, 82
  ecology, habitat, and occurrence, 84–85
  recipes, 85–88
  taxonomy, 80–81
Agaricus abruptibulbus, 82–83
Agaricus arvensis, 50, 80, 82, 84, 195
Agaricus bisporus, 80–81, 82, 228
Agaricus campestris, 15, 80, 82, 84, 194, 195
Agaricus meleagris, 83
Agaricus placomyces, 83, 96
Agaricus silvicola, 80, 82–83
Agaricus xanthodermus, 83, 96
Aksakov, Sergei T., 7
alcohol inky, 95, 97, 98
alcohol use, 95, 97, 98
Alice in Wonderland (Carroll), 156
Allegro, John Marco, 154
Amanita bisporigera, xvi, 94, 96, 113, 115–16
Amanita brunescens, 96
Amanita caesarea, 112, 159
Amanita crenulata, 97, 157
Amanita flavoconia, 96
Amanita flavorubescens, 96, 105
Amanita frostiana, 96, 157
Amanita muscaria
  active components, 161–62
  description and taxonomy, 159–61
  ecology, habitat, and occurrence, 161
  in fairy rings, 195
  in literature, 156
  overview, 148–51
  Russian term for, 12
  toxicity, 97, 156–59
  use of, in 1960s America, 154–56
  use of, in various cultures, 151–54, 163
Amanita ocreata, 94
Amanita pantherina, 97, 157, 161
Amanita phalloides, 10–12, 94, 96, 108,
  112–13, 115, 159
Amanita rubescens, 120
Amanita sp., 49, 83, 107–08, 112–21
Amanita verna, 114
Amanita virosa, 94, 96, 113, 114
amatoxins, 115–121
Anderson, James, 185
angel wings, 96, 132–135
Armillaria bulbosa, 185. *See also* honey
  mushrooms

Armillaria gallica, 187
Armillaria mellea, 12, 97, 98, 187
Armillaria ostoyae, 187
Armillaria root rot, 189–90
Arora, David, 46, 83, 100, 129, 133
arsenic poisoning, 37
ascomycetes, 35, 211, 213
aspen mushrooms, 12
Audubon Guide to North American Mushrooms
  (Lincoff), 49, 100, 108, 129, 151
A Visit from St. Nickolas (Moore), 151

Baba Yaga (folk tale), 5, 7
basidiomycetes, 212
beliy grib, 3, 8, 12
Benjamin, Dennis, 36, 103, 130, 162
Bessette, Alan, 72
Bessette, Arlene, 72
Beug, Michael, 75, 92, 119, 127, 138, 158
big laughing gym, 97, 111, 173, 189
bioluminescence, 200–06
black morels, 35, 40, 124
black-staining Hygrocybes, 96
blond morels. *See* yellow morels
blusher mushrooms, 120
Boa, Eric, 19, 20
Boletus chippewaensis, 73
Boletus clavipes, 73
Boletus edulis
  caveats, 75–76
  common names, 72–73
  description, 74–75
  ecology, habitat, and occurrence, 76–77
  false truffle and, xvi
  Italian cooking and, 27
  recipes, 77–79
  Russian culture and, 3, 8, 12
  taxonomy, 73–74
Boletus huronensis, 75–76
Boletus nobilis, 73
Boletus pinophilus, 12, 73
Boletus sensibilis, 96
Boletus subvelutipes, 96
Borovik (mushroom king), 6
The Botanic Garden (Darwin), 194
Both, Ernst, 72
Boyle, Robert, 203
British Fungi (Hay), xii
brown rolled-rim mushrooms, 136
Bruhn, Johann, 185

Bushnell, 202
buttery mushrooms, 12
button mushrooms, 80, 82, 85, 228

Caesar's mushroom, 159
Calvatia cyathiformis, 47
Calvatia gigantea, 45, 47, 49, 195
Calvatia spp., 15, 32–33, 46
Cantharellus cibarius, 8, 12, 27, 61–62
Cantharellus formosus, 62
Cantharellus lateritius, 63
Carroll, Lewis, 156
cavity nesters, 218–24
chanterelles
    caveats, 64
    description, 63–64
    ecology, habitat, and occurrence, 64–66
    economic value, 70–71
    false, 97
    of Oregon, 42
    popularity of, 60–61
    preservation of, 27
    recipes, 66–70
    in Russian culture, 8, 12
    taxonomy, 61–62
chicken mushrooms, 51–55
chicken with chanterelles and fettuccini,
    69–70
Chlorophyllum molybdites, 92, 96, 195
Christensen, Clyde M., 31–33, 51, 53, 128–29
Clitocybe claviceps, 97
Clitocybe dealbata, 84, 96, 195, 198
Clitocybe geotropa, 193
clubfoot *Clitocybe*, 97
Common Edible Mushrooms (Christensen),
    32–33, 128–29
Conocybe, 177
Conocybe filaris, 96
Controlled Substances Act, 177
Coprinus, 56
Coprinus atramentarius, 95, 97
Coprinus comatus, 15, 32–33, 64–65
Coprinus plicatilis, 231
coral mushrooms, 96
Cordyceps ophioglossoides, xvi
Cortinarius, 209
couscous, 87–88
crapaudin, 149
Craterellus, 61–64
Craterellus ignicolor, 64
Craterellus lutescens, 64
Craterellus tubaeformis, 63–64
Cravens, Craig, 8

Crepidotus, 135
crimini mushrooms, 80
cultivation
    basics, 229–35
    getting started, 236–37
    overview, 227–29
    oyster mushrooms, 238
    shiitake, 238–39
    wine cap *Stropharia*, 237–38
cultural attitudes, x–xvi. *See also* specific
    cultures, such as Russian
Czarnecki, Jack, 78

Darwin, Erasmus, 194
deadly conocybes, 96
deadly galerina, 96
Dead Sea Scrolls, 154
deadwoodology, 220
death caps, 94, 96, 112–21, 159. See also
    Amanita phalloides
deliquescing, 56
destroying angels, 96
De Vecchj, Achilles, 158
The Dictionary of Edible Mushrooms, 19
DiGirolomo, Mark, 227
Doblin, Rick, 168–69
Dodgson, Charles L., 156
The Doors of Perception (Huxley), 144
Dubois, Raphael, 204
Duran, Diego, 164
duxelles sauce, 86

early morels, 36
earth ball mushrooms, 96
economic value, 70–71
egg and chanterelle omelet, 68–69
Elaphomyces, xvi
entheogens, 145–46
Entoloma lividum, 96
epigeous fungi, 208, 213
ethnic differences, x–xvi. *See also* specific
    cultures, such as Russian

fairy rings, 49, 84, 192–99
false chanterelles, 97
false morels, 36, 95, 96, 122–31
false truffles, xvi, 212
famines, 9, 164
Fantasia, 156
Farlow Herbarium of Botany, 213
fear of mushrooms, x–xi, 17–19. *See also*
    poisonings

Fenaroli, Luigi, 140
Fergus, Charles, 18
festivals, 41–42
fiber caps, 96
Field and Forest Products, 236
field guides, 10, 16, 32, 108, 139
Fine, Gary, 33
Finnish fugu, 130–31
fireflies, 203
Flammer, R., 137
fliegenpilz, 149
fly agarics, 12, 148–49, 195. See also *Amanita muscaria*
flying squirrels, xvi, 207–10, 216
fly killer mushrooms, 12, 149
fly mushrooms, 12, 97
Fomitopsis cajanderi, 223
Fomitopsis pinicola, 217
forest ecology, ix, 40–41, 160, 210–13, 218–24
forest fires, 40
foxfire, 201
Francis de Sales, Saint, 19
Franklin, Benjamin, 202
Funghi (Fenaroli), 140
Fungi Perfecti, 236

Galerina, 177, 188
Galerina autumnalis, 96, 177, 188
gastrointestinal distress. See poisonings
gastromycetes, 46
gem-studded puffballs, 47–48
giant puffball, 47
Gibbons, Euell, xv, 15
Glaucomys sabrinus, 208
gleba, 46, 48–49
glückspilz, 149
goldenthread cordyceps, xvi
Gomphus, 61
Gomphus clavatus, 61
Gomphus floccosus, 61, 63, 96
Good Friday experiments, 167–69
green-gilled *Lepiota*, 195
green-spotted *Lepiota*, 92, 96
Griffiths, Roland, 180
Grifola frondosa, 50, 99
Grof, Stanislav, 145
growing. See cultivation
gruzd, 3, 12
guide books, 10, 16, 32, 108, 139
Guzman, Gaston, 171
Gymnopilus, 173
Gymnopilus spectabilis, 111, 173, 189
Gynnopilus spectabilis, 97

Gynnopilus validipes, 97
Gyromitra esculenta, 36, 95, 96, 123, 127–30
Gyromitra gigas, 124
gyromitrin poisoning, 125–31

half-free morels, 36
hallucinogenic mushrooms. See also *Amanita muscaria*; psilocybin
    culture and, xi
    historical overview, 143–47, 228–29
    toxicity and, 97, 110–11
Hansen, Karen, 213
happiness mushrooms, 149
harvesting techniques, 65
Hay, Willliam Delisle, xii
health effects. See poisonings
heart-rot fungi, 219–24
Hebeloma crustuliniforme, 96
Heim, Roger, 165
Helms, Richard, 170
hemlocks, xvi
hemolytic anemia, 137
hen-of-the-woods, 50, 99
Historia General de tas Cosas de Nueva Espana, 164
Hofmann, Albert, 166, 170
Homola, Richard, 190
honey mushrooms. See also *Armillaria bulbosa*; *Armillaria mellea*
    bioluminescence, 201
    caveats, 191
    description, 188–89
    ecology, 189–90
    edibility, 190
    Russian term for, 12
    size and age, 185–87
    toxicity of, 97, 98
horse mushrooms, 50, 80, 82–83, 85, 195
Howell, Arthur, 208
hunting mushrooms, 3–5, 7–9, 19–20, 40–41
Huxley, Aldous, 144
Hydnum repandum, 67
Hygrocybe conica, 96
Hygrophoropsis aurantiaca, 97
hyphae, ix, 39, 46, 194
hypogeous fungi, 208–09, 211, 213–15

ibotenic acid, 161–62
illness. See poisonings
inky caps, 33, 56–57
Inocybe spp., 96, 177
insects and pests, 66

jack o-lantern mushrooms, 92, 96, 106–07, 188, 201, 204
Jacobs, Edward, 81
Japan, 132–33
Jefferson Airplane, 156
Joe's Book of Mushroom Cookery (Czarnecki), 78
Johns Hopkins Psilocybin Research Studies Group, 181
Johns Hopkins University School of Medicine, 179

king bolete mushrooms, 72, 74
korvasieni, 130–31
Krieger, Louis, 15, 85, 100, 128
Kuo, Michael, 35, 50, 120

Lactarius, 152, 209
Lactarius chrysorrheus, 96
Lactarius deliciosus, 12
Lactarius rufus, 96
Lactarius torminosus, 96
Laetiporus, 33, 51
Laetiporus cincinnatus, 51, 53
Laetiporus conifericola, 51, 52
Laetiporus gilbertsonii, 51
Laetiporus huroniensis, 51, 52
Laetiporus sulphureus, 8, 12, 21, 51, 97, 98
lawn mower's mushrooms, 97, 172–73
lawyer's wig mushrooms, 55–59
lead poisoning, 37
Leary, Timothy, 168–69, 181
Leccinum, 12, 74, 152
Leccinum aurantiacum, 12
leek and shaggy mane potato soup, 58–59
Lepiota, 108, 195
Lepiota castanae, 96
Lepiota cristata, 96
Lepiota josserandi, 96
liberty cap mushrooms, 97, 174
lilac-brown boletes, 100–01, 109
Lincoff, Gary, 49, 100, 129, 151, 153
little brown mushrooms, 110, 177
little fox mushrooms, 12
LSD (lysergic acid diethylamide), 143–44, 146, 166–67. *See also* hallucinogenic mushrooms
Lycoperdon, 12, 32–33, 46
Lycoperdon marginatum, 49
Lycoperdon perlatum, 47–48
Lycoperdon pyriforme, 48

Macrolepiota, 108
Macrolepiota procera, 195
Macrolepiota rhacodes, 195
magic mushrooms, xi, 164–71. *See also* hallucinogenic mushrooms
Marasmius oreades, 84, 194, 195, 198–99
Marks, John, 170
McIlvaine, Charles, 101, 128, 139, 157
meadow mushrooms, 15, 80, 82–83, 84–85, 195
milk-caps, 3, 8, 12, 21
milky caps, 96
Miller, Hope, 50
Miller, Orson, 129
MKULTRA project, 170–71
Molecular Absorbent Recirculating System (MARS), 117–18
monomethylhydrazine (MMH), 125–27
Moore, Clement, 151
Moore, James, 170–71
Morchella, 12, 32, 35
Morchella elata, 35, 124
Morchella esculenta, 34, 35–36, 124
Morchella semilibera, 36
Morchella spp., 97
morels
  acceptance of, xv
  caveats, 36–38, 97
  description, 35–36
  ecology, habitat, and occurrence, 38–42
  false, 36, 95, 96, 122–31
  overview, 33–34
  recipes and preservation, 42–45
  Russian term for, 12
  taxonomy, 34–35
Morels (Kuo), 35
Morel Tales (Fine), 33
mukhomor, 149, 151
Mulvey, Michaeline, 40
muscarine, 110, 157, 162, 198
muscimol, 161–62
The Mushroom Handbook (Krieger), 15, 85, 100, 128
Mushroom Hunter's Field Guide (Smith), 157
mushroom rain, 3
Mushrooms and Other Fungi of Great Britain and Europe (Phillips), 133
Mushrooms and Other Fungi of North America (Phillips), 20, 101, 133
Mushrooms Demystified (Arora), 46, 100, 129, 133
Mushrooms of North America (Miller), 129
Mushrooms: Poisons and Panaceas (Benjamin), 36, 103, 130

Mycelium Running (Stamets), ix
Mycena, 201
mycophobia *vs.* mycophilia, x–xi, 17–19
mycorrhizal associations
    amanitas, 160
    chanterelles, 64
    false morels, 124
    poison pax, 138–39
    porcini, 76
    symbiotic host trees, 21, 38
    truffles, 210–13, 215–16

Nabakov, V.I., 7
Naematoloma (Hypholoma) fasciculare, 96
NAMA (North American Mycological
    Association), 75, 101, 125
National Morel Mushroom Festival, 41
National Mushroom Poisoning Case Registry,
    101
North American Boletes (Bessette, Roody and
    Bessette), 72
North American Mycological Association
    (NAMA), 75, 101, 125
Northern New England Poison Control
    Center, 104, 173
northern spotted owl, 209, 222
nutritional content, 26–27, 85

Omphalotus illudens, 64, 96, 106–07, 204
One Thousand American Fungi (McIlvaine),
    128
orange milk mushrooms, 12
Osmond, Humphry, 144
oyster mushrooms, 12, 134, 230–31, 237,
    238

Paavankallio, Marianna, 130
Pacific golden chanterelle, 42, 62. *See also*
    chanterelles
paddy straw mushrooms, 108, 114
pagan mushrooms, 12
Pahnke, Walter, 167–69
Panaeolus, 106, 172, 198
Panaeolus foenisecii, 97, 172–73
Panellus, 201, 204
parasitic mushrooms, xvi, 53
parasol inky caps, 231
parasol mushrooms, 195
Pavlovna, Valentina, x, 163–64
Paxillus involutus, 96, 136–40
pear-shaped puffballs, 48
peckerheads, 36

permaculture, 229, 232
pesticides, 37, 84
pests and insects, 66
Pezizales, 213
Phellinus pini, 223
Phellinus tremulae, 220–22
Phillips, Roger, 20, 101, 133
Pholiota squarrosa, 96
pigskin puffball, 48, 96
Pilz, David, 62
pine conk, 223–24
pine mushrooms, 12
pink bottom mushrooms, 80, 82
Pleurocybella porrigens, 96, 133
Pleurotus, 238
Pleurotus ostreatus, 12, 134, 230, 237
Pleurotus populinus, 135
poisonings
    Agaricus, 83–84
    Amanita sp., 97, 112–21, 156–59
    angel wings, 132–35
    bolete family, 75–76
    case studies, 100–01, 104–11
    chanterelles, 64
    deaths, 91–93
    false morels, 124–31
    hallucinogenic mushrooms, 97, 110–11
    honey mushrooms, 97, 98
    lawn mower's mushrooms, 173
    morels, 36–38
    poison pax, 136–40
    psilocybin mushrooms, 102, 105–06, 173,
        174–76
    risks of, 94–95, 98–99
    in Russia and Slavic countries, 10–11
    symptoms, 102–03
    toxic mushrooms, 96–97
    in U.S., 18–19
    wood rotting mushrooms, 188–89
poison pax mushrooms, 96, 136–40
poison pie mushrooms, 96
Polyporaceae, 51
Polyporus, 51
Polyporus sulphureus, 32–33
Pomerleau, Rene, 129, 139
porcini mushrooms, xvi, 27, 72–73. See also
    Boletus edulis
portabellas, 80
potato and shaggy mane leek soup, 58–59
preservation techniques, 27, 43, 67–68, 78, 85,
    198–99
protein content, 26–27
psilocin, 102, 105–06
Psilocybe, 198

Psilocybe cubensis, 172, 229
Psilocybe mexicana, 165–66
Psilocybe quebecensis, 174
Psilocybe semilanceata, 97, 174
psilocybin mushrooms
    big laughing gym, 173
    description, 171–72
    history, 164–71
    lawn mower's mushroom, 172–73
    legal status, 177–78
    recreational use of, 176–77
    research, 179–81
    therapeutic and ceremonial use, 144, 146,
        167–71
    toxicity, 102, 105–06, 173, 174–76
Psilocybin Mushrooms of the World (Stamets),
    110, 171
psychedelics, 144–45, 167–71, 181
psycholytic therapy, 144
psychotominetics, 144
puffballs, 12, 15, 32–33, 45–50, 96
purple-spored puffballs, 47
Pushkin, Alexander, 7

Ramaria formosa, 96
recipes
    Agaricus, 85–88
    chanterelles, 66–70
    morels, 42–45
    porcini mushrooms, 77–79
    puffballs, 50
    shaggy manes, 58–59
    sulphur shelf mushrooms, 54–55
Redhead, Scott, 56
regional differences, 108–09
rehydration resurrection, 197–98
reindeer, 149–51
Revision of the American Flying Squirrels
    (Howell), 208
Richardson, Allan, 163
risotto, 78–79
Ristich, Sam, 101
Robbins, Tom, 154
Roody, Bill, 72
rose conk, 223–24
rough boletes, 12
Rubel, William, 157
Russell, Kenelm, 186
Russian culture, xi, 3–13, 21
Russula densifolia, 96
Russula emetica, 96
Russula nigricans, 96
Russulas, 3, 8, 12, 20–21, 73, 209

Sabina, Maria, 163–64, 165, 170
sac fungi, 35, 123, 211
The Sacred Mushroom and the Cross (Allegro),
    154
Safford, W.E., 165
Sahagun, Bernardino de, 164
Sandoz Company, 166, 170
Santa Claus, 149–51
saprobes
    Agaricus mushrooms, 84
    chanterelles, 64
    cultivation, 232
    fairy rings, 194
    honey mushrooms, 189
    morels, 38–39
    psilocybin, 171–72
    shaggy manes, 56
    sulphur shelf, 53
Sarychev, Gavril, 150
scaly vase chanterelles, 96
Schaffer, Julius, 137
Scleroderma puffballs, 48–49
Scleroderma spp., 96
Scotch bonnets, 196–99
*The Search for the Manchurian Candidate: The
    CIA and Mind Control* (Marks), 170
seasonality, 41
Serna, Jacinto de la, 164
shaggy manes, 15, 32–33, 55–59, 64–65
shaggy parasols, 195
Shavit, Efrat, 37
Shavit, Eleanor, 37
Shaw, Terry, 186
shiitake mushrooms, 227–28, 236–39
Siberian culture, 151–53
Slavic culture, 3–13, 21, 73
Slick, Grace, 156
Slow Food movement, xv
Smith, Alexander, 157
Smith, Myron, 185
snowbank false morels, 124
Soma: Divine Mushroom of Immortality
    (Wasson), 150, 153
soups
    creamy mushroom, 86–87
    shaggy mane potato, 58–59
Soviet Union, 9. *See also* Russian culture
sponge mushrooms. *See* morels
spore prints, 29, 36, 83, 159
spotted owls. *See* northern spotted owl
Staal, Frits, 155
Stalking the Wild Asparagus (Gibbons), 15
Stamets, Paul, ix, 110, 171
stir fry with chicken mushrooms, 54–55

Strahlberg, Filip Johann von, 151
Stropharia, 174
Stropharia rugosoannulata, 237–38
sugihiratake, 133
Suillus, 74, 76
Suillus luteus, 12, 97
sulfur tuft mushrooms, 96
sulphur shelf mushrooms, 32, 50, 51–55, 97,
    98
Super Mario Brothers, 156
sweating mushrooms, 84, 96, 195, 198
sweet tooth mushrooms, 67
syroezhkas (Russula), 3

Tanglewood 4-H Camp and Learning Center,
    200
therapeutic and ceremonial uses, 144, 146,
    167–71
timber management, 218–24
tippler's bane, 95, 97
toadstools, 19
Tolstoy, Leo, 7
tomatoes and porcini mushrooms, 77–78
torchwood, 201
toxicity. *See* poisonings
toxic mushrooms, 96–97
tree species. *See* forests
Trestrail, John, 125
Tricholoma pardinum, 97
truffles
    ecology, 215–16
    evolution of, 213–15

false, xvi, 212
flying squirrels and, 207–10, 216
forest health and, 210–13
Tuber genus, 211, 213
tue-mouche, 149
Tulloss, Rod, 113, 115, 161
turkey, deep-fried, with morels, 42
Tylopilus, 100
Tylopilus eximius, 75, 97, 100–01, 109

Verpa bohemica, 36
Viazmensky, Alexander (Sasha), 4
Volk, Tom, 56, 186, 190
Volvariella speciosa, 108, 114
Volvariella volvacea, 114

Wasson, R. Gordon, x–xi, 32, 150, 153, 155,
    163–66, 170
Wasson, Valentina Pavlovna, 163–164
white mushrooms, 3, 12, 74. See also *Boletus
    edulis*
wild mushrooms, xiv–xv, 16–17, 21–22, 28–29,
    70–71. *See also* hunting mushrooms
wine cap *Stropharia*, 237–38
woodland agaricus, 80, 82
woodpeckers, 218–24

Yamin-Pasternak, Sveta, 152
yellow boletes, 12
yellow morels, 35–36, 40, 124

"This logo identifies paper that meets the standards of the Forest Stewardship Council. FSC is widely regarded as the best practice in forest management, ensuring the highest protections for forests and indigenous peoples."

Chelsea Green Publishing is committed to preserving ancient forests and natural resources. We elected to print this title on 30-percent postconsumer recycled paper, processed chlorine-free. As a result, for this printing, we have saved:

12 Trees (40' tall and 6-8" diameter)
4 Million BTUs of Total Energy
1,154 Pounds of Greenhouse Gases
5,559 Gallons of Wastewater
337 Pounds of Solid Waste

Chelsea Green Publishing made this paper choice because we and our printer, Thomson-Shore, Inc., are members of the Green Press Initiative, a nonprofit program dedicated to supporting authors, publishers, and suppliers in their efforts to reduce their use of fiber obtained from endangered forests. For more information, visit: www.greenpressinitiative.org.

Environmental impact estimates were made using the Environmental Defense Paper Calculator. For more information visit: www.papercalculator.org.

the politics and practice of sustainable living

CHELSEA GREEN PUBLISHING

Chelsea Green Publishing sees books as tools for effecting cultural change and seeks to empower citizens to participate in reclaiming our global commons and become its impassioned stewards. If you enjoyed *Chanterelle Dreams, Amanita Nightmares*, please consider these other great books related to food.

WILD FERMENTATION
SANDOR ELLIX KATZ
ISBN 9781931498234
Paperback • $25.00

CHEESEMONGER
A Life on the Wedge
GORDON EDGAR
ISBN 9781603582377
Paperback • $17.95

THE EARTH'S BEST STORY
*A Bittersweet Tale of Twin Brothers
Who Sparked an Organic Revolution*
RON and ARNIE KOSS
ISBN 9781603582391
Paperback • $19.95

GROWING, OLDER
*A Chronicle of Death,
Life, and Vegetables*
JOAN DYE GUSSOW
ISBN 9781603582926
Paperback • $17.95

the politics and practice of sustainable living

For more information or to
request a catalog, visit **www.chelseagreen.com**
or call toll-free **(800) 639-4099**.